So You Want To Get To Heaven

BOOK SHARE

After you have found out how to bring peace to the world, truly enjoy life and heal your infirmities, pass this book on. Visit our web site at www.ProbePress.com

Probe Press, Carlsbad, California

So You Want To Get To Heaven

By Warren Luce

Published by:
Probe Press
Post Office Box 919
Carlsbad, CA 92018-0919

All rights are reserved, however, credited excerpts from this text may be used for the purpose of promoting love, peace, harmony, self-esteem and good health.

Copyright © 1998 by Warren W. Luce

Printed in the United States of America

ISBN 0-9663987-1-8

Library of Congress Catalog Card Number: 98-91452

TABLE OF CONTENTS

A Note From The Author i
Chapter One: **The Dawning** 1
Chapter Two: **Excommunication** 19
Chapter Three: **Change** 43
Chapter Four: **Armageddon or a Golden Age?** 53
Chapter Five: **Materialism and Spiritualism** 63
Chapter Six: **Winds of Change?** 67
Chapter Seven: **As We Think, So Are We** 75
Chapter Eight: **The Nature of Man** 87
    The Physical Body and the Conscious Mind 89
    The Soul or the Sub-Conscious 101
Chapter Nine: **Does God Really Exist?** 109
    Is There a Record? 115
    The Near-Death Experience 118
Chapter Ten: **The Nature of God** 125
Chapter Eleven: **The Nature of Our World** 137
    Blessing and Prayer 147
Chapter Twelve: **Religion the Great Barrier** 155
    The Scriptures - The Bible 159
    The Scriptures - The Koran 166
    Islamic Doctrine 173
Chapter Thirteen: **Christianity Gone Astray** 177
Chapter Fourteen: **The Experiencers** 191
Chapter Fifteen: **The Joy of Death** 211
    Heaven, Hell and the Devil 222
Chapter Sixteen: **Health, Healing and Medicine** 235
    The Mind Connection 264
Chapter Seventeen: **Conclusion** 275
Reference Index 287
Order Form 297

A NOTE TO THE READER
FROM THE AUTHOR

Different religious denominations hold varied beliefs as to the way to heaven. For example, most of the almost one billion Christians living today believe the *only* way to heaven is through Jesus Christ. Almost all of the billion Muslims believe paradise can be achieved *only* by following Muhammad. There has to be a logical, inescapable conclusion that both cannot be right. If one is right--it doesn't matter which one--then billions upon billions of humans are going to end up in hell. There they will suffer eternally, according to both Christian and Islamic doctrine.

Our intellect and especially our hearts should tell us something is terribly wrong with that religious dogma. Both Islam and Christianity teach that God is loving, compassionate and perfect in justice. How then is it possible for God to send, to eternal hellfire, a child or any other who has never come to know a Christ or Muhammad? That would surely be cruel and unjust. It should give any thinking person cause to wonder about any religion that proclaims that God condemns to hell all who do not believe as that religion does. Could it be that both Christianity and Islam are wrong and that there is another way to heaven? I believe that there is and finding that way has very little to do with one's religious persuasion. I'll be providing you with a great deal of logic, reference material and scriptural evidence to support that idea. The concept that we must follow certain theological beliefs in order to be saved is a tenet of religion that needs to be questioned.

We would do well to evaluate the consequences that sectarian religion has brought to the human race through its man-made, thus potentially flawed doctrine. Religion is considered as something desirable to have. Most parents express a desire to raise their children in some religious faith; yet if we honestly analyze the effects that religion has had on humanity, we would have to conclude that it has caused humankind a great deal of grief. It has divided the human race like no other issue, causing discord, enmity and violence when it should be uniting people in harmony with one another and with God. The religious denominations of the world must be held to account for that.

Religion often teaches the wrong message. Every Sunday, in thousands of churches throughout the world, hundreds of millions of people are conditioned to think that they are by nature sinful and unclean. Their minds are programmed with, and their memories have stored, the concepts that it is human to err and that they will continue to sin for the rest of their mortal lives. *As they think, so are they!* We know how the implanting of thoughts and concepts in our minds, especially with repetition and emphasis, brings those things to fruition in our lives. I have little doubt that the continuous programming of millions of church-goers, with the idea that they are poor sinners who will remain so until they die, has become the greatest, and most unfortunate, self-fulfilling prophecy in the history of humankind. In that manner, religion has unwittingly kept us in bondage to sin thus stifling spiritual growth.

But that is *not* our true nature at all. It is an image of humankind that must be *totally* rejected. We are better, and much more than that. We must perceive ourselves as magnificent, sentient beings who are masters of our own destiny, who can control circumstances along the road that leads to it. We must accept what God tells us about ourselves: that we are made in his likeness, that we are wonderfully and respectfully made, that we are the salt of the earth and the light of the world, that we can bring forth good things from the goodness of our hearts, that we can turn from our wrongdoing and *choose* to do what is right and good. We need to understand that the human body is a self-healing organism which, with the cooperation of our powerful mind, can eliminate disease and suffering.

In addition to those matters, this book discusses the purpose of life and death, spirituality and miraculous healing. It is about prayer--God does not answer prayer in the way we think; the nature of God, and the true nature of humankind. It suggests the likely truth about hell and the devil--that there is no such place or being. You will see how love that is caring, compassionate and forgiving can make this world the paradise that it was intended to be. New insights into all of the above subjects will be presented.

I'll tell you how my excommunication from the church, for questioning religious doctrine, has set me free to live in peace and harmony with all of my fellow human beings, thus to truly enjoy life. Although I have provided reasonable evidence to support the perceptions set forth, I am not asking you to blindly accept them. I don't claim to have the truth but believe that what I am saying is reasonable and closer to the truth than what is commonly taught. Obviously, my opinion is involved and, of course, we can't know the absolute truth in some of these matters--at least not yet. I am only asking you to examine them with an open mind, seek further knowledge and decide for yourself. I wish you well.

Love and Regards,
Warren

Chapter One

THE DAWNING

"Blessed is the man who destroys you. Blessed is the man who takes your babies and smashes them against the rocks." Those words can be found in Psalm 137 of the Christian Bible. They were written by King David about the Babylonians who had destroyed Jerusalem. Did God really inspire David to write those words? "Kill all the Midianite men, male children and women who have lain with a man, but you can keep the young virgins for yourself." Those are supposedly the instructions, recorded in Numbers 31:17, that God gave to Moses as the Israelites moved into the promised land. Would God really bless the soldier who smashed his enemy's babies against the rocks in vengeance against the father? Does God value virgin females more than he does baby boys? According to Christian Church dogma, God would and does, for that doctrine declares that the Bible, including those words of David and those instructions to Moses, was inspired by God and therefore is infallible and without error.

For over forty years I had blindly accepted church teaching about the Bible. That all of the Bible is the inspired, unfailing and inerrant word of God is part of Christian belief. Inspired in that God in some way guided the writings, and infallible in that they are completely trustworthy and free from error.

Certainly all Christian denominations do not embrace such dogma, but in my former church, the Bible was not to be questioned. I had read the Old Testament, and all the violence therein many times, but never questioned it. In bible class, the minister or lay teachers seemed to have an acceptable explanation. Those people against whom the violence was directed were generally evil or opposed God and God's chosen people and so deserved to die.

However, the last time I came across those words of David about smashing babies against the wall, something happened to me. I stopped cold and couldn't continue. I would read a little further, then stop and return to that passage about the babies. How could a loving God possibly condone, let alone bless, a soldier who bashed an innocent baby's head against a rock wall? I studied it in context, looking for a possible answer. It wasn't forthcoming.

The next Sunday, I asked the pastor about it. His answer was rather vague to the effect that we cannot always understand, yet there is a reason for all scripture. Needless to say, I was not satisfied. That was the beginning of my journey to excommunication. When it came, I have to say that, although I was frustrated at not finding the solutions that I was seeking and saddened by the intolerance and closed-mindedness of my religious leaders, I actually felt happy about the excommunication. It was a feeling of being set free; freedom from what I knew, in my heart and in my mind, was wrong. It liberated me from the enslavement to man-made dogmas that kept me apart from the real God and kept me from unconditional love for all my fellow human beings. It led me to a better understanding of the nature of God, myself and this world that we live in. It freed me to master life and enjoy it fully.

It certainly strengthened my resolve to seek further knowledge of religious and spiritual matters. I truly became a seeker of knowledge and remain so to this day, even though I have found most of the answers that I sought. I know why I am here and the purpose of life. I understand the true nature of my being. I know that I am immortal as well as mortal and divine as well as human.

I have discovered the secret of good health. For me, the norm used to be a couple of visits to the doctor, two or three colds, and usually the flu each year. I haven't seen a doctor, had a cold or the flu in over five years. I've cured myself of a number of ills. All of us in the totality of our being--our body, mind and soul--have the ability to heal ourselves and maintain good health. I'll discuss that and miracle healing, at length, in the chapter entitled Health, Healing and Medicine.

I believe I now understand what and who God is and what the Deity expects of humanity. God is a Being, yet not a person with humanoid countenance. We need to think of God in spiritual terms rather than anthropomorphically. When we better understand the nature of that spirit, then we can comprehend how the universe was created and the true nature of our world. God has no gender, being neither masculine, feminine nor neuter, but simply spirit. The pronoun *he*, in referring to God in this text, is only for literary convenience. The Deity is not a God of vengeance, anger and wrath as some religions often teach. God does not judge, condemn or punish. We need not bend the knee and hang the head in worship of God. True worship of God is much more meaningful than that. We'll examine all those ideas in the chapter entitled The Nature of God.

I am beginning to understand what it means to be one with God. Since I have embraced and live by the scriptural message that love is the way of atonement, that is, being at one with God, strange and wonderful things have happened to me. Events that I like to think of as spiritual happenings. Not a near-death experience, nor visions; not out-of-body experiences, nor psychic phenomenon, but simple yet extraordinary and exhilarating occurrences. To me they were true and profound spiritual experiences that involved the reality of everyday living.

Part of my health-perfection routine is a moderate yet regular exercise regimen. I walk most every day and swim two or three times a week, weather permitting. And it permits most of the time here in southern California. It has been during these daily outings that I have found myself near to God in an unusual way. About half of my walking takes place on the beach, not only for exercise but as a form of meditation. Feeding the pigeons and seagulls, on occasion, also became a part of the routine.

The pigeons would gather by the dozens about my feet and even walk over my shoes. One morning about two hundred of them had gathered in a circle around my feet like a round gray blanket completely covering the sand. Suddenly one of them flew up and sat on my arm, then ate out of my hand. Then another and another. It is not uncommon for pigeons to sit on people. Most of us have seen pigeons do that to people who feed them, usually in the parks. But what happened next was quite remarkable.

After the food was gone the three of them seemed content to remain there on my arm. As I began to talk to them, telling them that they were beautiful, they were my friends whom I would never harm but always protect, they would cock their heads to the side and nod, looking up at me, as if to say, "we know." Then one of them walked up my arm, sat on my shoulder and started to rub his beak against my ear.

It was a fascinating time with my feathered friends. It is difficult to describe the feelings that I experienced. Enchanting, thrilling and magical might be appropriate, but it was more than that. I felt a wave of emotion at being one with those little creatures, of being one with all of creation, of being one with God.

When I turned to go back to the parking lot, I noticed a woman standing there who had apparently been watching me. She came running over to me and exclaimed, "That was wonderful to see! How did you do that?" I was sort of hesitant to speak out about my feeling of oneness with the birds, especially to a stranger. But I decided to do so anyway telling her also of my love for all of creation and that I believed the pigeons sensed all of those things in me. She nodded and said that she understood; that sometimes she felt much the same way. She asked if I thought she could experience such an encounter with the birds. I told her most certainly and be sure to send them thoughts of love and kindness when you feed them.

When I would go swimming, prior to entering the pool, I would walk around it to see if any little critters needed rescuing. When I first started doing that I was somewhat self-conscious, and I noticed a few people look askance at me. But soon it was routine for me as well as the others at the pool who had either accepted or were ignoring my unusual behavior. Although one person did give me a genuine smile of, what I believe, was understanding.

One day I noticed a hornet floundering in the pool. I have seen them land on water and take off again, but somehow this little guy had gotten into trouble for he was over on his side feebly struggling to right himself. I scooped him out, let the water drain out of my hands and watched him as he lay motionless in my hand. I placed him on the side of the pool and started my laps. Each time I came back I would check on him. Soon he was on his feet but not moving, apparently drying out. After five minutes or so, he was still there and starting to flutter his wings. All the time I had been sending him kind thoughts about surviving and flying away. The last time I checked on him I said to him in thought, "you should be able to fly by now." As I was watching him, he took off, started to fly directly away from me, turned in a large arc, swooped right in front of me and off he went.

Simply a coincidence? Perhaps. But I like to think not. I believe that he sensed no fear of him in me, but rather the compassion and love I felt for that little creature and all of God's creation. It was his way of acknowledging that and thanking me.

There was another incident with a honey bee. A small restaurant named Mariah's is near the beach where I walk. One early morning I decided to stop in for a toasted English muffin and tea. It was summer, the door was wide open and, and as they had just opened, no other customers were present, just the waitress, the cashier--who I think was Mariah, the proprietress-- and myself.

As I seated myself at a table against the window, I noticed the honey bee buzzing about the pane. While I was watching it, the waitress came over to take my order, at the same time raising the menu to swat it and saying she would get rid of it. I said, "Oh, don't kill him, he won't harm anyone." So she took my order and left.

As I continued to watch the little critter I said to him in thought, "You just want to be outside and free, don't you?" Right away he landed on the edge of the window sill right next to the edge of the table. I placed my finger on the sill in front of him and watched him climb onto my finger and just sit there. He stayed there as I got up from the table, walked across the restaurant and out through the open door. But he didn't fly away, even when I made upward motions in the air with my hand.

He seemed as content in his contact with me as I was in my contact with him. But as I knew my order was coming soon, I said, "Off you go little friend," and away he flew toward a honeysuckle-covered wall. As I walked back across the restaurant feeling exhilarated and with a little more spring in my step, Mariah, who had been taking all this in, smiled and said, "That was a nice thing to do." I simply smiled back. I enjoyed my tea and muffin immensely.

It is my belief that little children, animals and even insects are particularly able to sense the feelings and emotions of other creatures, unless they are hardened and conditioned otherwise. It is unfortunate that almost all humans assume the hardened condition that separates us from the rest of creation, especially one another. Animals and insects are also conditioned to be wary because of human aggressiveness toward them. Have you ever noticed how wildlife in pristine areas, where it has not been exposed to human hostility, shows no fear of human beings? But that feeling of oneness with all of creation is not lost forever. We can get it back when we come to understand the nature of the universe, God and our own being. They are inextricably connected. We will explore that concept in the chapter entitled The Nature of Our World.

I have had some extraordinary experiences with people in my work as a hospice volunteer. I seem to be able to form a special bond with those who are terminally ill. The hospice volunteer supervisor considers me her "trouble shooter." Sometimes when a difficult situation with a terminally ill patient arises, she calls on me.

One lady expressed astonishment and delight that I had established a bond with her husband on the first visit, a bond that she thought quite unusual, given her husband's shy temperament and usual aloofness with strangers especially in the latter stage of his illness when he wanted little to do with anyone. After I had been helping Jerry's wife take care of him for about a week, he would become restless after I left and would ask his wife, "When is Warren coming?" When I would arrive, sit by his bed and hold his hand, he would settle into a relaxed and seemingly content mood. Another patient, John, was nearing the end. I was visiting almost every day to provide support and help him and his wife through the final days. Early one day his wife called saying John was near death and was asking for me. I was there in minutes, as he lived near by. He smiled at me when I came in and shortly thereafter he died with that smile on his face as his wife and I sat on either side of his bed holding his hands.

It was not that I am "silver tongued" in my verbal communication with terminally ill people; sometimes very little verbal communication takes place. Nor could I be considered as having a "magnetic personality," that might be responsible for the warm and close bond that is established.

I firmly and deeply believe that no one should have any fear of death and that we should look forward to the death of this physical body with great anticipation and joy. Accordingly, my demeanor around the terminally ill is not sad, morose or unhappy, but rather happy and cheerful, which is conveyed to the dying patient and caregiver. But I believe it goes much deeper than that.

It is known that people near death often seem to be psychic and able to sense feelings and even thoughts of others. It may be that those dying people sensed in me my closeness to the God that they, in physical death, were about to confront, and received comfort and perhaps even contentment from that understanding.

We have been conditioned for too long to fear death, placing too much value on this temporary, physical existence we call "life." False teachings about life and death have complicated our understanding. The meaning of life and death is not complex. It is my belief that the purpose of life, our reason for being, is very simple. *God wants our spiritual being, which he creates, to experience and enjoy **physical** existence.* So he made the earth and created man--body *and* spirit--to live in that paradise and ***enjoy*** *it.* He saw that *"**all** he had made was very good."* Death is simply a return, from this physical existence, to the spiritual presence of God. Throughout the text you will read more about life and how we are to live it. Hopefully you will agree, after you read the chapter on the Joy of Death, that the prevailing concepts of death are wrong and need to be discarded.

But we do indeed make everything complicated. We try to establish beginning, intermediate and advanced lessons for understanding life, death, religion and spirituality. When the "advanced" concepts of those subjects begin to emerge from the mind of humankind, then confusion reigns; we lose sight of the truth and trouble begins. That is especially true among organized, denominational religions.

Another unusual experience occasionally happened to me over the years of interaction with the theologians and during the period in which I was writing this book. Whenever a difficult situation arose in my exchange with the ministers--usually a question they would pose to me--I would find the answer in an astonishing way. For example, one minister asked me how, if I did not accept Christ as the only way to be saved, did I then explain the scriptural passage where Christ says, "No man comes to the Father but by me?"[1] That evening I reflected on the question before going to sleep. About three o'clock in the morning I awoke, which was unusual for me as I most often sleep very well. The question came to mind and as I pondered it, the answer came to me. That explanation is covered in detail in Chapter Thirteen, Christianity Gone Astray.

This happened to me on a number of occasions. In that manner, I found the answer to why God seems to answer some prayers and not others and why "bad things *really* happen to good people." Those answers also are covered at length in later chapters.

It might be tempting to think that some spiritual entity was providing me with those explanations. Although I don't completely discount that possibility, I do not believe that is what was happening. It is my belief that the answers are within us. Kahlil Gibran, beloved poet and philosopher, has said in his great work THE PROPHET, "No one can teach us aught, than that lies half slumbering in our consciousness." Our consciousness is not only our mind but the soul, that field of energy given from God who gives us life and is the source of all knowledge. We all have the ability to access that knowledge and I believe that is the meaning of the scriptural passage that says, "Ask and it shall be given you; seek, and you shall find; knock, and it shall be opened to you."[2]

We can do amazing things with the mind. We have consistently underestimated the power of our minds. Through thought we are capable of extraordinary things. We create ideas, like space travel, and transform them into reality. Consider the taken-for-granted function of speech. A small child, through the power of the mind, listens to the language of the adult and then, by thought, sends signals to the muscles in the diaphragm, larynx, vocal cords, tongue, mouth and lips so as to duplicate words. It's a truly amazing achievement when you stop to really analyze what is happening when a child is learning to speak.

Think of the beauty that man can construct, not only architecturally, but in less tangible areas such as music and the written word. We create music out of nothingness and then bring it to reality through the voice in the form of song or through instruments that we construct. Consider the incredibly intricate plots in literature and the beautiful prose and poetry that man can create through imagination. In our creative abilities we are God-like, to a limited degree.

We are indeed God-like. After all, scripture declares we are made in his image. Also Christ said, "Is it not written in your law, I said, 'Ye are Gods'?"[3] We have great power but generally don't recognize it. We often belittle ourselves by portraying the human being as weak, error prone and inferior, a condition that is fostered by the teaching of the Church. We are capable of marvels in the physical realm, from sports to space ships; from sky scrapers to ocean liners; our capacities are endless.

Even more importantly, we possess tremendous mental power in the energy of our minds. God has endowed us with an incredibly powerful mind. But that latent power of the mind is not understood nor used by most of us. We refuse to accept

God's statement to us that we are "wonderfully and fearfully made" with amazing abilities; even the ability to do miracles. Instead, we accept and believe the word of men that we are innately sinful, basically corrupt, inclined to err, and subsequently those characteristics are brought to fruition in our lives. But when we understand and accept that we are made in God's likeness, we can do wonderful things with our minds such as heal ourselves of disease.

But with that power of the mind and the free will that we possess we also can create ugliness and misfortune for ourselves and others. It is the wrong thoughts of our minds that bring about violence, discord and disunity in the world. Through iniquitous and distorted thought we make ourselves capable of heinous behavior, sometimes even conditioning ourselves to believe that it's okay. It is likely that complex thoughts that have gone awry are responsible for some mental illnesses. By thought we are capable of weaving intricate patterns of bizarre and delusional behavior. For example, one is capable of thinking of himself as having more than one personality, creating characteristics of each in the mind. Then in continually holding and believing those thoughts, so one becomes.

Although foreign substances introduced into brain cells, or the lack of necessary chemicals in the brain may adversely affect the brain and, hence, thought, the primary culprit is the wrongful use of the mind. The secular and spiritual truth of "as we think, so are we" is a major factor when it comes to mental health. Yet no matter how distorted the mind may become, we have the power within us to change it. God has given us the ability to do that. God is for us and wants the best for us. Caring, giving, goodness, kindness, patience, compassion, forgiveness and *free will* define the nature of God and they are the qualities that we share, being created in his likeness.

Manifesting those attributes in a relationship with our fellow beings is the way of life that God intends for us. Who can deny the benefit of caring over indifference, of love rather than hatred, of being kind rather than cruel and of forgiving rather than exacting vengeance, fixing blame and holding a grudge? We all know in our hearts that it is right and good to live in an atmosphere of brotherly love. Even the religions of the world embrace love of humanity as a cornerstone of their beliefs. Islam declares, "No one of you is a believer until he loves for his brother what he loves for himself."[4] Judaism proclaims, "No Jew can love God unless he is in a loving relationship with his neighbor."[5] Christianity says we are to "Love our neighbor as our self."[6]

Despite that acknowledgment of the wonderful qualities of love, we only give it lip service. We neither teach it nor live it. Caring, compassionate and forgiving love is not taught in the home, the schools or the churches. We don't learn it ourselves and, most unfortunately, do not teach it to our children! In the Mideast, Arab children are taught to hate Jews, and vice versa. In the United States our children are taught materialism and violence. Even in our Christian Sunday schools, the children are often taught theology and denominational church doctrine rather than love for one another; caring for and forgiving others. We do not bring them up in the nurture and admonition of the Lord as he has told us to do. The children do not learn self-esteem and self love, which they must do if they are to love others. They are taught that they are sinners who can do nothing by themselves to change that condition. They are often programmed with the idea that "Jesus loves them" even if they are a *bad person*.

It has rightly been said that if we would raise one generation of children with unconditional love, we could change the world and empty the prisons. Love *is* the true panacea. It is powerful. Wrongdoing cannot exist in the presence of love. Love is the greatest commandment of all. Under a total outpouring of love and goodness, *which we human beings are capable of*, even the Hitlers and Stalins of the world would capitulate and reform. Even more basically, in an atmosphere of love, caring, mercy and forgiveness, those types of people whose character is bred by hatred, anger, greed and vengeance, would never come to be.

But we not only don't teach love, we don't understand *how* to teach love. We don't understand the power of our minds. We don't seem to understand that the continual programming and conditioning of our minds with hatred and violence manifests those things in our actions, often creating a hell on Earth. We haven't grasped the concept that implanting values such as love, goodness, caring and mercy in our minds causes those values to become manifest in our behavior, changing our lives and the world for the better.

In my search for knowledge, I have come to understand a law that most have heard of, but the incredible significance of which few understand. That law is: "As a man thinketh, in his heart, so is he."[7] It is a universal law of the mind and heart established by God. It is not only God's word found in the scriptures, but a widely accepted maxim in the secular sense that how and what we think forms the kind of person we are. Whatever we think or believe with our minds, and hold with deep conviction in our hearts, is what we will be.

James Allen, a nineteenth century English author, wrote a book by that title, AS A MAN THINKETH. He put it well when he said, "A man is literally what he thinks, his character being the sum of his own thoughts. As a being of power, intelligence and love and the lord of his own thoughts, man holds the key to every situation, and contains within himself that transforming and regenerative ability by which he may make himself what he wills."[8] Whatever we implant in our minds, by thought, controls our behavior. The power of the mind is beyond our comprehension. We know that we can literally make ourselves ill, even cause death, through the power of negative thoughts that we program into our minds. By the same token, we actually can think ourselves well. Thousands of cases have been documented in confirmation.

Scriptures tell us that we are "wonderfully and fearfully made."[9] God created a magnificent human being when he made man. We take ourselves too much for granted in not accepting how remarkable we really are. He gave us an immensely powerful mind with which we can accomplish things beyond our wildest imagination.

When we use our minds properly, we can promote healing, good health, well-being, happiness and success in our lives. We can change *every* aspect of our behavior by thought and the power of the mind. Through the use of that incredible computer we call the mind, we can learn unconditional love and change the world. We can make war, crime, homelessness and hunger obsolete. We *do* have a choice. We can make this world a paradise or we can destroy it. We are well on our way to doing the latter. By continuing our present course of hatred, anger, violence and disobedience to God's instructions, this world is destined to die. Through the simple expedient of love we can save it and make it a veritable paradise.

What if, from cradle to grave, at home, in school and at church, we were taught to think that it is our nature to be good and kind? What if we were taught to think that we are indeed "created in God's image,"[10] with the ability to manifest his qualities in our lives? What if we were conditioned to think that we can obey God's instructions? What if we continually implanted in our minds the thought that we can live in peace and harmony with our fellow human beings? *As We Think, So Are We!*

I ***know*** this principle works. Since I have come to understand and accept this universal law of God, since I have come to believe in love as the true panacea, and since I have begun to daily implant in my mind God's truth of love, kindness, caring, mercy and forgiveness as the way to live in peace and harmony with others and achieve true happiness and success, my life has changed dramatically. Anger, hatred, impatience and worry are gone from my life. Never before have I experienced such a sense of peace and well-being.

My philosophy on life, my attitude and my relationship with my fellow human beings have undergone great change. I have to say that I have done things in the past that were something less than good and kind. And although I may still slip along the way, it is now very clear to me that doing what is good and right, and being kind to and considerate of others, is the only way to live and results in true joy of living.

I have found that it is very important to have compassion and forgive. Where I was once a hard-nosed "hang em high" proponent of the death penalty, I am now adamantly opposed to the killing of any human being for any reason. Never would I go to war again; and I would do everything in my power to discourage my children and grandchildren from doing so. I have absolutely no fear of death for myself or others. Actually I look forward with great anticipation to my "death," yet I am perfectly content to wait until that wonderful event occurs, knowing that I have a purpose in this life and that purpose is to enjoy it, loving my neighbor as myself and living in harmony not only with humans but with *all of creation*, thereby helping to promote peace and well-being throughout all the Earth.

At about the same time that I was having trouble with biblical infallibility and "smashing babies against the rocks," I was consuming volumes of literature about the near-death experience. The people who have undergone that experience brought back from their "brief journey to the next life" the message that pursuit of knowledge for the betterment of this life is one of the two most important things one can do in this lifetime. And so I continued my pursuit of knowledge.

I joined IANDS, the International Association for Near-Death Studies. I attended seminars about the "NDE" and talked to "experiencers" in an effort to understand what that phenomenon was all about. Although I was a skeptic at first, I became convinced that their experiences were real and that they had a message with incredible implications. It was readily apparent to me that there was a direct conflict between the message of the experiencers and much of the religious teaching of the world, especially that of the Christian Church.

The message of the experiencers seems to be that God is not interested in organized religion, church dogma or theology. Raymond Moody, medical doctor and NDE researcher, in his book, THE LIGHT BEYOND, relates the account of a man who had studied at a religious seminary before his NDE: "My doctor told me I had 'died' during the surgery. But I told him that I 'came to life.' I saw in that vision what a stuck-up ass I was with all that theory, looking down on everyone who wasn't a member of my denomination or didn't subscribe to the theological beliefs that I did.

"A lot of people I know are going to be surprised when they find out that the Lord isn't interested in theology. He seems to find some of it amusing, as a matter of fact, because he wasn't interested at all in anything about my denomination. He wanted to know what was in my heart, not my head."[11]

The dominant message is that God is concerned with man's relationship with his fellow human beings. Spirituality is more important than religiosity. To seek knowledge of God and spiritual matters is very important. And of greatest importance is love of our fellow humans. It appears that love is **all** important and the **only** requirement for a right relationship with God in the final reckoning.

When I tried to reconcile that message with what the Christian Church teaches, I could not. Love is important in the teaching of Christianity, but the only thing that really counts, according to the Church, is faith. The bottom line is that we are saved by faith alone, without any merit on our part. We must have faith in Christ as the sacrificial lamb on the cross. By believing that he paid for all the sins that we have ever committed or ever will commit, we are then acceptable to God. What we do for others; how we love others is important, but is not the essential factor.

My next step was to go to the Bible to see what it had to say about that apparent contradiction. Lo and behold, I discovered that the message of the experiencers is completely compatible with Christ's message, but the teachings of the Christian Church are not.

I could hardly believe what I was beginning to understand. For years, I blindly accepted the teachings of the Church and its interpretation of the Bible without question. But now, reading scripture with an open mind and the new insight of the message of the experiencers, it was as if the proverbial light bulb had been switched on. It wasn't long before I came to the unbelievable conclusion that the Christian Church, through faulty interpretation of the scriptures, is teaching us the wrong message and, as a result, is hampering mankind's spiritual growth. The error results from zeroing in on St. Paul's writings rather than the words of Christ, and the forging of man-made religious doctrine that has no sound basis in the scriptures.

We are taught from cradle to grave that sin is innate in our character; it is our nature to do wrong. How often I stood in church and recited the liturgy: "God be merciful to me a poor sinful being." That philosophy is even carried over into the secular reasoning that it is human to err. I have no doubt that that kind of conditioning becomes a self-fulfilling prophecy.

As my search for spiritual knowledge progressed and my mind began to open, it became very apparent to me that the sinful characterization of humankind was flawed. I only had to open my eyes and look around me. I knew of people, even had friends, non-Christians, Muslims and even an atheist who lived good decent lives. I also came to know, from personal experience, that the Church's characterization of all human beings as basically poor miserable sinners, wasn't my nature at all. I learned that I can choose to do either right or wrong regardless of temptation or circumstances. Now I choose to do what is good and right and it has nothing to do with my religious persuasion, for I have none.

Thus came a dawning awareness that Christian dogma about many things, especially the nature of humankind, was wrong, and in teaching that flawed doctrine, the Church was literally, albeit unknowingly, keeping much of humanity in bondage to sin. How could it have happened? And so I began to question!

Chapter Two

EXCOMMUNICATION

When I first started my earnest quest for answers to my doubts about Christian Church doctrine, I went to the authorities: the ministers and theologians. I was rather meek and hesitant about it. One can't imagine how difficult it was for me. To just think about those doubts is one thing, but to voice them or communicate them literally is another. After such a long time, to openly question my deepest-held religious beliefs was almost traumatic. I was also concerned about the reaction of those from whom I was seeking the answers. What would they think of me? Would there be ridicule, ostracism or worse? And what of my family and close friends? How would it affect those relationships?

So I went to those I didn't know. I picked ministers out of the Yellow Pages. I wrote to others I read about in publications. I sent queries to editors and publishers of religious works. And I was met with either silence or derision, castigation, amusement and a general unwillingness to answer my questions or address my concerns. I have been called a fool and condemned to hell. I've been branded as a heretic, wolf-in-sheep's-clothing, self-righteous Pharisee, false shepherd and a deceiver who is not sincere about his questions and concerns. All of these unpleasant epithets came from men who are called ministers of God.

I communicated my questions and concerns to eight ministers of varied denominations in the local area. Only one replied. It is interesting to note that it was a woman, a minister of a Christian Science church. She expressed interest in my questions and beliefs, stating that some were not dissimilar to those of their religion. She invited me to attend a service and said she would be happy to discuss these matters with me.

I accepted her invitation and at first liked what I was hearing. They believed in a commitment to spiritual newness, a oneness or kinship with God, to love and serve your neighbor and to follow the example and teachings of Jesus Christ. But it wasn't long before reality set in when I learned more of their religious doctrine based on the teachings of Mary Baker Eddy. In my opinion, it has serious flaws. Eddy contends that we are "wholly spiritual" beings. She believed that matter is nothingness, only a form of *human* belief, an illusion. By saying that, she is contradicting her claim that matter is nothingness, for "human" is matter.

A great deal of her writing is contradictory and illogical. In her work SCIENCE AND HEALTH, she further proclaims, "Material existence is a ghastly farce," and "only the spirit is real." Yet she speaks of such things as, "Christ reappeared with a physical body," "God created all things that exist," "human existence" and "mortal beings." If the physical body does not exist, but is only an illusion, then what is it that is born, is subject to illness and dies? Illusions cannot experience those properties of matter. I suppose we could say that birth, illness and death are illusions of the "wholly spiritual" beings. However, to accept that the spiritual beings all have the exact same illusions is completely unrealistic. Further, they would have to be badly flawed spiritual beings to experience illusions of sickness and death.

Eddy has declared that, "Instead of possessing a sentient material form, man has a sensationless body." If that is so, if we are truly without senses, then there is no such thing as the loving touch of a mother to a child, no such thing as the beauty of flowers. There is no song of the robin, the fragrance of jasmine or the taste of honey. What a terrible fate to contemplate. Christian Scientists practice good values, however, some dogma as espoused by their founder leaves a great deal to be desired--causing confusion, especially about the true nature of humankind. And so I began to look elsewhere for answers.

I finally worked up enough courage to go to a relative who is a Protestant minister of thirty years. We carried on a written dialogue for about two years, yet I was still not getting answers to my questions and concerns over what I perceived as false religious doctrine. It was quite clear from the beginning that his mind was completely closed to any possibility that Christian Church dogma could be in error. Of course, that was understandable, for to consider such a prospect would be, to him, unthinkable. To admit that he had been teaching the wrong message of salvation would be anathema to both him and the Church.

But I had hoped that a meaningful exchange might take place, which might somehow result in a change in the Church's teaching, which then would make the world a better place. My concern from the start was the terrible things that are happening in our world, especially to the children. As a retired air force colonel who has traveled throughout the world, served during three wars and observed first-hand the incredible indifference, unkindness, hatred and terrible violence to which we subject each other, I had often thought that humanity was doing something terribly wrong; that a problem exists which we can't simply lay at the door of man's innately sinful nature as the Church generally teaches. Surely, mankind isn't supposed to live as we do! Surely, God doesn't intend it to be this way. After all, "His will is to be done on *Earth* as in Heaven."[1]

Surely God's will in heaven is goodness, peace and joy. Why isn't it happening on Earth rather than the continued deterioration that is taking place? It seemed to me that a major reason was the failure of religion, especially the Christian Church, to teach the true message of Christ: that loving one another as he loved us is essential to salvation. Had that been taught for two thousand years, there can be little doubt that mankind would be much better off, perhaps even living in total peace and harmony in a paradisiacal world. After all, according to the scriptures, that is what God intended for us.

It seemed to me that the Church was teaching a message that is counterproductive to achieving that status for mankind. Christian dogma declares that man is not responsible for his own faults and wrongdoing; we are innately sinful, it is human to err, and man will always continue to sin. I considered the possibility that that characterization of humankind has become a self-fulfilling prophecy. Accordingly the world will wax worse and worse until we destroy ourselves in some Armageddon-like catastrophe.

According to Christian Church doctrine, all the sins of the world that have ever been committed and will ever be committed are paid for, in full, by Christ's sacrifice. If we believe that, go to church and confess our sins, the minister will forgive us in the name of God. Don't you see that, under that plan, we can go on sinning all we want and it won't matter. As long as we acknowledge Christ as the sacrificial lamb and confess that we are by nature sinful and unclean, we are off the hook. ***We don't have to be responsible.*** And obviously, that lack of responsibility is a major factor in the terrible state of the world.

But Christ doesn't teach that at all. He said we *are* responsible and "you will be judged according to your deeds."[2] He said that calling him Lord won't get us to heaven, but rather the decisive factor is to obey God and do good works.[3] He said "those who listen to me and do good shall rise to eternal life."[4] That's what the Christian Church should be teaching. There is a great deal more to this controversy concerning the teachings of Christ versus the teaching of the Christian Church. It is covered in more detail in later chapters. This is just a brief synopsis of the trouble that I was experiencing with Christian dogma and the basis of my questioning.

At the start, I deferred to the wisdom of those I was questioning. I asked them to show me where I was wrong. But no real attempt to discuss what I was questioning was made. The major thrust was to convince me that I was wrong in doubting Christian doctrine, even to the point of attacking me personally. I found the personal attacks rather disturbing coming from Christian ministers. They even brought my family into the matter, expressing strong pity for my wife, children and grandsons because of the terrible example I was setting. In return I expressed my disquiet with their assault on my character, pointing out that I was not questioning them personally, but rather the doctrine of their religion.

However, it was to no avail. I was told in no uncertain terms that I was out of bounds in expressing doubts about Christian Church doctrine and was subject to judgment unless I came to my senses, ceased what I was doing and repented. Their reaction only tweaked my curiosity and strengthened my resolve to find answers. I have to say that it also made me more strident in my communication and aggressive in my questioning. As I told one pastor, the saying that "we have to fight fire with fire" is often true.

And so I "fired" away. Generally my questions were either ignored or often answered with other questions. Quite often my correspondent would simply reiterate Church doctrine as the answer, usually giving me a big dose of St. Paul rather than what Christ had to say about the issue.

In regard to the accuracy of the Bible, I would keep asking if they thought those words in Psalm 137 about the babies being smashed against the rocks were the inspired and infallible word of God. They simply refused to answer. I questioned them about St. Paul's words in Romans 13 where he said that God put all governments in power and that they are to be obeyed without question, that those who disobey a government ordinance are disobeying God and shall be damned. He says rulers are ministers of God, not a terror to the good, but to evil. I asked them if God put the governments of Hitler and Stalin in power; were they not a terror to the good and were they really ministers of God?

Not one would answer me, although I asked several times to please respond to that question. The more I thought about their refusal to answer, I began to realize that they could not. If they said they did not accept and believe those things about government and rulers, they would be denying their doctrine of God-inspired scriptures. If they said they *did* accept and believe in those words of Paul, then their credibility would be suspect, for anyone who is intellectually honest with himself, knows those words are not, and never have been, true and therefore cannot be the inspired, infallible word of God.

There was only one minister out of perhaps ten, with whom I had interaction, who attempted to give me direct answers to my questions. However, he was very selective in which questions he wanted to answer and, it seemed to me, that some of his explanations were a bit disingenuous and irrational.

His explanation of the passages that directed the Israelites to smash babies against the rocks, and Moses to kill all Midianites except the virgins, was not very credible, in my opinion. He said, "Those things were recorded for our learning to show that God's judgment and justice are perfect; that God is loving and merciful, but he is also a jealous God who punishes severely; that we have to respect God's love and kindness, but also quake in fear of his judgments; that Christ reiterated all this when he threatened the hypocrites, scribes and Pharisees with worse judgment than befell the people of Sodom and Gomorrah; that God's justice is perfectly just."

One *might* say that the inhabitants of Sodom and Gomorrah deserved God's judgment and death as punishment. But to accept the brutal smashing of an innocent new-born baby against the rocks as a right judgment of God seems unconscionable. To kill all the Midianites except the female virgins is not *just* by any standards in heaven or on earth.

Surely God does not value virgin females more than he does baby boys. How can that be God's perfect judgement and justice? How can anyone make our loving God in that image?

In a Bible class with that same minister we were studying the Augsburg Confession concerning the nature of man. In the 16th Century, Emperor Charles V had summoned the Christian secular and religious authorities of Europe to Augsburg, Germany, instructing them to come up with a unified confession of religious faith. As a result, the Augsburg Confession of June 25, 1530, came into being, establishing the basis of much of Christian Church doctrine.

In regard to the nature of humankind, the Confession states, "It is also taught among us that since the fall of Adam all men who are born according to the course of nature are conceived and born in sin. That is, all men are full of evil lust and inclinations from their mothers' wombs and are unable by nature to have true fear of God and true faith in God. Moreover, this inborn sickness and hereditary sin is truly sin and condemns to the eternal wrath of God all those who are not born again through Baptism and the Holy Spirit."[5]

The minister explained that it is certainly true. He quoted Martin Luther who said, "There is not one iota of goodness in man, but only evil and darkness exists in the heart of man."[6] He cited biblical scripture to support that creed and even spoke of all the evil and lust that exists today as verification of the tenet.

I had already come to the conclusion that such characterization of humankind was faulty and decided to speak out, so I said, "But, pastor, how do you account for the good that certain people do, such as non-Christians, who are not baptized and do not believe in the Holy Spirit? And what about Christ's words that we are the 'salt of the earth and light of the world'?"

He thought for a minute and said, "Christ was talking to the disciples. They had accepted Christ and, therefore, were empowered by the Holy Spirit to do good. Consequently Christ was right in calling them the salt of the earth and light of the world." I was quite sure that wasn't right, for although Christ was talking to the disciples, he also was talking to the multitudes who knew little of Christ or the Holy Spirit, and most of whom were not baptized. But, as a good and obedient church member, I didn't want to disrupt the Bible class by starting an argument with the pastor who was the leader and "expert" on biblical matters. I was already getting looks of disapproval from others in the class and knew that if I challenged the pastor there would be some kind of consequences and I wasn't ready for that. It would be sometime before I had the courage to outright challenge the authorities in my own church.

Later in his written response to my questions the same minister attempted to further justify the "total depravity of man," as he called it. He started from Genesis covering many of the references to the wickedness of man. He cited how God destroyed mankind by means of the flood because they were all wicked. He noted that Noah escaped, "not because he was a smidgen better than others, but because he found grace in the eyes of God."

He spoke of the word in Job: "How much more abominable and filthy is man, which drinketh iniquity like water?" In Psalms: "Who can bring a clean thing out of an unclean? Not one." And from Isaiah: "The whole head is sick, and the whole heart faint. From the sole of the foot even unto the head there is no soundness in it, but wounds, bruises and putrefying sores."

He quoted Jesus' words as a "fine reference to the total depravity": "For from within, out of the heart of man, proceed evil thoughts, adulteries, fornication, murders, thefts, covetousness, wickedness, deceit, lasciviousness and evil eye, blasphemy, pride and foolishness." And "an evil man out of the evil of his heart bringeth forth evil things."

He chided me for ignoring all those statements that prove the totally corrupt nature of man in my attempt to formulate my "un-scriptural doctrine of man" being not innately sinful, but rather with the ability to choose either evil or good. He further censured me for picking and choosing from the scripture to support my beliefs.

I was also taken to task by this minister, as well as another, for using my human reason to arrive at some of the conclusions that I have reached. They said, "When you use human reason to interpret scripture, criticize it and reject it as written, you are judging God."

I thought that was somewhat hypocritical and said to them, "Isn't that exactly what the Church does, what all ministers do, what you do and what the theologians did to arrive at the Augsburg Confession? You and they use human reason to interpret scripture to form conclusions that result in religious doctrine. In fact, the theologians have reasoned so much they have totally confused the world about God's truths.

Concerning the nature of man, it was obvious that the minister went through the Bible and picked out only the references to man's ability to do evil, choosing to ignore all the many references about man's ability to do good. When he said that Noah was no better than the others, he completely ignored the passages in Genesis 6 that say, "Noah had no faults and was the only good man of his time. He lived in fellowship with God." In Genesis 7 God goes on to tell Noah, "I have found that you are the only one in all the world who does what is right."

In my reply to the minister I said, "The truth regarding Noah's goodness is so apparent that one could reasonably conclude that you have deliberately omitted scripture so as to deceive, in order to justify your claim that man is totally corrupt. But I know you are not a deceitful man, and therefore, the only other conclusion is that you are so blinded by your beliefs that you literally cannot see the truth."

I asked him why he overlooked Christ's references to the good in mankind: there are good men with goodness in their hearts who do good things; blessed are the pure in heart, we are the salt of the earth and light of the world, and that we are to let our good works shine before men. But a reply was not forthcoming.

I asked him to explain Ezekiel 18 which says, "The righteous person will be rewarded for his own goodness and the wicked for his wickedness. But if a wicked person turns away from all his sins and begins to obey my laws and do what is just and right, he shall surely live and not die. All his past sins will be forgotten and he shall live because of his own goodness." I received only silence.

The same minister called me a wolf-in-sheep's-clothing who was deceiving innocent people with my false teachings. It was a pretty nasty thing to say and absolutely untrue. In the beginning, I had not expressed my questions, doubts or beliefs to anyone, not even my wife of over forty years. I went directly to the religious authorities whom I believe have the responsibility to answer and explain questions that a parishioner might have about religious doctrine. But, for the most part, they refused. I was rebuked, condemned and excommunicated.

I suggested in my response that if he wanted to accept Christ's characterization of a false teacher then we could decide who the deceptive teacher really is. Christ said, "You shall know them by their fruits."[7] Or in another version, "You can know them by what they do." The bottom line is: what are the results of their teachings and examples. I further suggested that if we examined the fruits of what the Christian Church teaches, we could make a pretty good case that Christian ministers are the wolves in sheep's clothing. When we look at the condition of the world after nearly 2000 years of teaching the brand of

Christianity that the Church teaches, we would have to say the fruits are quite spoiled.

Closer to home, in the United States, a nation that counts itself eighty-four percent Christian, where we see a great deal of immorality, wickedness and violence, we would have to conclude that the results are rather disastrous. When we look at what the Serbian Christians in Bosnia-Herzegovina did there, especially to the children, and what some of the Irish Protestants and Catholics do to each other in a country that counts itself as almost 100% Christian, we would have to say that the fruits of Christian Church teaching are pretty rotten.

I told him that, of course, we shouldn't be surprised at that, for Christian doctrine teaches that man is totally corrupt with only evil and darkness in his heart. It teaches that a man is innately sinful and unclean, must sin every day and will continue to sin for the rest of his mortal life. It teaches that we cannot obey God, in effect teaching disobedience to God's instructions as to how we are to live. I expect that one might say, "The fruits of Christian teaching are salvation and eternal life." But that would not be a valid premise because Christ says we have to be able to observe the results. The results of belief alone are not observable. You may be absolutely confident that you are going to get to heaven by your beliefs, but you cannot absolutely know for sure until you get there.

I said to the pastor, "So you see that, by the standards that Christ set, it would have to be you who is the false teacher because the observable fruits of the Christianity you teach leave a great deal to be desired. Yet, I don't think for a moment that you are a wolf-in-sheep's-clothing, even though the empirical evidence does point to you rather than me. I believe you are completely sincere in what you believe, just as I am. The difference is that, although I believe what you teach is wrong, I don't judge or condemn you as you have me."

I found it quite amazing to see the character transformation that seemed to take place in some ministers. Out from under the mantle of their office they are good, kind and decent people. The minister who called me a "wolf-in-sheep's-clothing" and "not sincere about my doubts and questions," is a wonderfully warm and likable person, much beloved by his parishioners. Yet, in their ministerial mode some often become intolerant, harsh, unkind and sometimes even dishonest. Even among themselves there is sometimes bitter dispute about theological matters. Ministers who express differences in opinion about established religious dogma have found themselves and their families literally out in the street--decidedly un-Christian behavior.

I went on to say to the pastor, "It is also very puzzling to me how you can sincerely believe some of the doctrine that you profess. Why do you think of yourself and others as such rotten and corrupt beings? Why are you so ashamed to think that you have the good qualities of God and that he is within you in some manner? Why do you have so much trouble with obedience to God and the doing of what is right and good as the way of being acceptable to God and being saved?

"That is what God tells us from one end of the Bible to the other. Clearly we have the capability to follow his dictates. Why do you refuse to believe the undeniable evidence you see with your own eyes, that there are those who do not believe in Christ or the Holy Spirit, yet are able to do good, living decent, honorable lives?"

Then I spoke to the minister about my beliefs and actions: "I do not go around broadcasting what I do, even to my family. However, under the circumstances, I feel it necessary to tell you something of myself, what I do and the fruits thereof. Jesus said we are to show love to one another, to be of service to others, to care for those in need, to feed the hungry, to help the homeless, to visit the sick and to be kind, merciful and forgiving to all people. He said to 'love your neighbor as yourself,' 'do unto others as you would have them do unto you,' and even to 'love your enemies and do good to them returning evil with goodness.'[8]

"I subscribe wholeheartedly to that philosophy and, indeed, obey Christ when he says to be sure to put those things into practice, not just listen to them. Although I do not always accept what people do, I accept them unconditionally as fellow human beings, always trying to be kind and understanding. I do my best to help those in need. I am a Hospice worker, a hospital volunteer and regularly visit the sick and forgotten in nursing homes. I try to seek out someone every day who is in need. When I buy food for myself, I buy food for others in need of it. I give a great deal to charity.

"I don't pass by the homeless on the street. Whenever possible I stop and greet them with a smile and a handshake. I inquire as to their well-being. I try to give them a kind word and encouragement. I always give them monetary assistance. I have been criticized for doing the latter by people who say it will be used unwisely for booze, etc.; even that it is contributing to their 'fallen' condition. I would rather err in giving to someone who doesn't need it or might misuse it than err in not giving to one who is truly in need.

"Of course, they are all in need of kindness, caring and the human touch, and perhaps the tendering of these things, including financial aid, will bring about a change in them. The best form of teaching is by example. Then when one does all these things that Christ commanded us to do, one truly understands what he meant by a 'little leaven leavening the whole loaf.'[9] The results are quite remarkable. The results are harmony, happiness, good will, a little joy, an improvement in self-esteem, and in a small way, the betterment of mankind.

"I find also that I can truly love my 'enemies' because I do not look at them as totally corrupt human beings. When I look at them I see another of God's creatures, created in his likeness with his characteristic of free will; someone who has probably made a wrong choice, as all of us have at one time or another. I also see God's characteristic of goodness in them and although they may have gone astray, they have the capability to manifest that goodness that is within them. I know that goodness is there, and with love, kindness, compassion and forgiveness, it can be brought out. Even more importantly, I understand that if we would all put into practice what Christ told us to do, and go and teach others to observe those commands as the way to achieve peace and harmony in the world, as well as the way to heaven, there would be no enemies.

"I have to say that I am not comfortable telling you all these things about myself, but feel, under the circumstances, it was necessary, in order to show you what Christ means about fruits and detecting false teachers. I'm sure you want to say, of course, that doing all those things is well and good, but they won't get you to heaven; you must have faith and believe in someone else having paid for your sins. But that would not be a valid observation, for Christ said that we are able to tell who it is that teaches the right way only by what they *do*, not what they say or believe. It has to be something tangible that can be observed.

"And secondly, Christ never said we can gain heaven by believing in him as the sacrificial lamb. *Never* did he equate his suffering and death on the cross with salvation. That simply cannot be found in his gospel. But he did unequivocally say, 'Because you feed the hungry and take care of the needy you shall inherit the kingdom.'[10] He did, unquestionably, say that, in obeying his commands to love others, doing good to them and forgiving others we shall never die but gain eternal life. He clearly said that it is not calling him Lord that will get us to heaven but obeying God and doing good works.[11] But you reject all those words of his by what you teach.

"Who can dispute the good fruits that would be produced if my beliefs were taught to everyone from cradle to grave? Who can deny that the world would be a much better place if my beliefs were put into practice by everyone? God has told us in the scripture that 'as you think, in your hearts, so are you.'" We know from practical experience that this is so. Why not then teach people to think that they are the salt of the earth and the light of the world and are to let their good works shine so as to make the world good? Why not teach people to think that they are required to love one another and do what is good and right so as to be acceptable to God and get to heaven?" But there was only silence.

I finally made the decision to formally challenge Christian Church doctrine through my own local church. There had been a few informal meetings in the pastor's office when the two of us discussed my misgivings about Christian dogma. But I wasn't satisfied with the answers I was getting, so I compiled a thirty-nine page document covering my questions, concerns and doubts about doctrine and my own beliefs. In it I requested a formal reply. At a meeting of the Church Council, of which I was a member, I handed it to the pastor. I informed him what it was about and jokingly told him I was considering nailing it to the front door of the church, but decided it was better this way. He smiled as he accepted it.

A few months went by with no reply forthcoming. I later learned that he had gone to the regional synod with the matter, but they passed the buck back to him for resolution. Not having heard from him, I pressed the matter, asking him in writing when I might expect an answer. He responded saying that he had circulated my document to key members of the congregation asking for their thoughts and input and that a reply would be forthcoming.

Still without a reply, I was summoned to a meeting with the two pastors and elders of the congregation. I was pleased about the meeting knowing that some action had finally been precipitated. Although knowing that I was to be questioned, I was also pleased that I finally would be able to confront them with my questions, and demand answers. The latter was an assumption that turned out to be unfounded.

It was obvious from the entire conduct and tone of the meeting that they were not interested in listening to me to see if my beliefs might possibly have some validity. It was clear that the purpose was to determine whether or not my beliefs were in conflict with the doctrine of the Church, and if so, what disciplinary action was to be carried out.

I was asked by the pastor to briefly state my beliefs. I could see what was coming and replied that I could not adequately do so and discuss this matter in the short time that was allotted for the meeting. However, he insisted that we proceed. In the ensuing discussion, I answered their questions about my beliefs and gave supporting scriptural references. Their answers to my questions were generally not supported by scripture, but rather by quoting Church dogma. I was cut off in the middle of discussions, not being allowed to pursue an issue.

I asked them if they believed that Christ's suffering and death on the cross for all the sins of mankind was the work he was supposed to do? After they replied in the affirmative, I asked them how they accounted for Christ's words in John 17:4 when he said, in praying to God, *before* he went to the cross, "I have glorified you on earth: I have finished the work, which you gave me to do." There was silence for a moment until the pastor commented that it was one of those matters of timing in which we sometimes say things out of sequence with what we actually do. I said to him, "What I hear you saying is that Christ was careless with his words and was telling God a little white lie."

I also queried them about God's nature. Did they believe he was perfect. They agreed that he was. I specifically asked them if they believed he had perfect justice. The answer was the same. I asked how then was it possible for God, with that perfect justice, to punish an innocent person, Jesus Christ, for the sins of someone else? They thought for a long moment and then one elder said, "Well, God can do anything he wants."

It was an unsatisfactory answer, to say the least. Especially in light of other Christian doctrine that recognizes God as immutable. He does not change. He could not have set aside his perfection while he carried out the unjust punishment of Jesus Christ. The certainty of logic, taking into consideration *all* of Christian doctrine, has to question the concept of Christ being punished for our sins as a way of atonement with God. I had started to explain that logic when the pastor cut me off, excusing me from the meeting.

Despite what I considered unfair treatment at the meeting in not allowing me to follow up on my questioning, and their complete unwillingness to consider and examine my views, I felt no anger or animosity toward any of them. I understood that they were doing what they *thought* was right. A few years ago I would have done the same, had someone confronted me with beliefs that contradicted the religious dogma I had completely embraced.

Further, my new philosophy of life, to show love to all regardless of the circumstances, was holding fast. I actually felt a bit of exhilaration, as a result of the meeting. Their lack of scriptural and reasonable response to my questions, as well as their unwillingness to discuss in depth the doubts and concerns that I raised, served to strengthen my beliefs and resolve.

In just a matter of days I received the letter of excommunication. I was barred from communion. I was told that I could not participate in any official function of the congregation, lest I wrongly influence others with my false teachings. I was not to lead other members astray or deceive them concerning doctrine. There were no restrictions on my attending church services, which I continued to do. I recall that I received more than one unfriendly look from other members during those times.

But I had decided to remain, for reasons I explained in an exchange of correspondence with the assistant pastor when he asked me why I wanted to remain among them when I didn't share their beliefs. It had to do with another family who had left the congregation and the comments about that situation by the president of the congregation's board of directors. He had said that if one doesn't agree with everything the church teaches, they shouldn't leave, but make their disagreements known and perhaps bring about a change. He might not have meant that to include doctrinal matters, yet knowing him as a fair and strong-minded person, I'm not so sure he wouldn't allow that dissension.

I said to the assistant pastor, "I think that is a great philosophy, no matter what organization one belongs to. Organized religion has been created by man and nothing of man is sacrosanct. So I am going to stay and pursue my disagreements until I am either removed from church membership or leave of my own accord. I will also continue my pursuit of change until I am proven wrong. So far, that proof is not forthcoming. The discrepancies in your answers to my questions demonstrate to me that your beliefs and Christian Church doctrine are flawed."

I went on to say that I believe change must come to any religion that teaches the damnation to eternal hellfire of little children, or anyone, who has never heard of Jesus Christ; that teaches God blesses those who smash little babies against the rocks; that teaches it is okay to kill women and children who oppose God's "chosen people" yet spare female virgins for sexual use; and teaches that we cannot obey the commands that Christ has given us.

Change must come or that religion will surely fall. As Christ said, "Those who hear his words and do not obey them are like a man who has built his house upon sand and when the storms comes, it will fall with a mighty crash."[12] I concluded,

"Pastor, I believe that the house of Christianity that exists today is in danger of a coming storm." I received no response.

So I continued my search for the truth. The pastor still had not replied to my formal written queries about doctrine, so I spoke to him in person about it. He replied that he was preparing his answer and would like to deliver it personally. I told him he was welcome to come, but that I would prefer he not get into a discussion of doctrinal matters and my beliefs with my wife being present.

She knew generally what was going on with me and the Church, but not in detail and she didn't want to know. She had her beliefs and I had mine. She didn't try to dissuade me from my new beliefs, nor did I try to influence her toward them. She knew of my doubts about Christian doctrine. She even had some of her own. She is a "PK" (preacher's kid) and had been brought up with strict religious convictions, one of which was the doctrine of a God-inspired and infallible Bible. But she couldn't accept that passage in Psalms about God blessing the soldier who would smash his enemies' babies against the rocks, as the word of God.

Nor could she accept Christian teaching that only those who believe in Jesus Christ are saved and will get to heaven. We lived in Turkey for two and one half years in the 1960's and made some very good Muslim friends, some of whom we still see and count as longtime friends. She could not embrace a teaching that damned such good, decent and God-loving people to eternal hellfire just because they didn't believe in Christ as their savior. I know she struggled with that and asked the pastor about it. He said that, although he believes salvation can be achieved only by those who believe in Jesus Christ, he wouldn't tell God that he can't save others. That sounds like a pretty good example of double-talk to me.

But she didn't want to go into a deep discussion about religion, especially my disagreements with Church doctrine. It was not that it would unduly affect our marriage and relationship; we respected each other and would respect each other's right to his or her religious beliefs. She simply didn't want to argue about religion. I respected that, explained it to the pastor during our telephone conversation and, therefore, made it a requisite for his visit.

But he didn't honor my request. Shortly after his arrival, and a few solemn pleasantries, he launched into a discussion about my heretical ways, asking my wife if she had read my material. When she replied that she had not he said she should and she would be shocked. I was a bit surprised that he had betrayed a trust by doing what I had asked him not to, but I didn't bear him any ill will and wasn't angry. I liked him a lot and still do. He is a good, kind and compassionate person, albeit somewhat closed-minded. I expect he was trying to enlist my wife to get me to "come to my senses."

As long as the topic of religious discussion had been opened, I proceeded to ask him questions about Bible infallibility and other Christian dogma. It was the same old routine. The answers were a repeat of Christian doctrine, often quoting St. Paul, but never Jesus Christ.

The subject of salvation came up--about the Christian teaching that God condemns all people to hell who are not Christians. I said to the pastor that I knew there are Christians who did not accept that doctrine, even in his own congregation. But none had the courage to stand up and be counted. By definition they would be labeled heretics, as I had been. I told him that my wife did not accept that doctrine and had held her beliefs longer than I. At that point she queried him about such a narrow doctrine. That is when he made the comment that, although he believed there is salvation only for those who believe in Jesus Christ, he was not telling God that he couldn't save others. It seemed a devious answer to me.

During the ensuing discussion I told the pastor that I was not challenging Church doctrine just for the sake of dispute, or to prove anyone right or wrong; my purpose was to do something about the incredible indifference, unkindness, hatred and terrible violence to which we human beings subject each other. It seemed to me that a major reason for the degeneration of the world was the failure of the Christian Church to teach the true message of Christ; that we must show love and forgiveness one to another, as the requisite for gaining salvation and heaven. That love is all-important to God.

He then made the comment that perhaps I "didn't really understand the concept of love for one's fellow man because my writings were arrogant, rigid, harsh, contemptuous and completely lacking in love." I was a bit taken aback, for most of that simply isn't true. No one who truly knows me would ever call me "contemptuous of others" or "arrogant." I acknowledged that some of my writing was harsh, although I would prefer to call it aggressive and that was in response to the harsh treatment that I received at the written hand of Christian ministers, as well as their refusal to answer my questions and address my concerns about Church doctrine. And, although some of my comments may be sharp and stinging, I had not criticized any of them personally as some of the ministers had done to me.

There may be the *appearance* of anger in my writing, which, of course, is not compatible with the philosophy of kindness and forgiveness that I say we should all live by. However I can say that I felt no anger whatsoever as I was writing this text, or even in my exchange with the ministers I was questioning. Anger is gone from my life, even "righteous" anger. I have no animosity toward the theologians, politicians, doctors and others with whom I disagree. To me anger is violent displeasure and belligerence over a supposed wrong, usually accompanied by an impulse to retaliate. I feel none of that. My feeling about what I have expressed is in opposition to, and a difference of opinion about things and beliefs, sometimes conveyed with emphasis, which seems only appropriate if one feels strongly about those differences.

I said to the pastor that, "Perhaps you see my writing as contemptuous and arrogant because it criticizes your beliefs, and what you teach, and you are unable to accept or even examine that criticism with an open mind." I said, "My writings are not rigid, unlike your teachings." I've told you that "I believe I am right in the beliefs that I have expressed and have given you a great deal of scriptural reference to support those beliefs, especially words that are attributed directly to God and Christ. Yet, I told you that my mind is open and I am willing to change my beliefs if you or anyone can show me where I am wrong. But no one has done so. You have pretty much just brushed me and my questions aside.

"I'm sorry to say that it is *your* teaching that is rigid and arrogant, pastor. When you presume to talk for God, teaching that all who do not believe as you do are damned to hell by God; when you teach that little babies who die without 'baptism' or knowledge of Christ are condemned to eternal hellfire by God, that is really arrogant!

"As to love, my writings are full of it. I have expressed over and over again that we are to show love, kindness, caring, mercy and forgiveness to one another, that we are to love one another as Christ commanded us to; that we are to love our neighbors as ourselves and that love for our fellow man is the expedient that resolves all problems and makes us right with God."

He replied, "It was one thing to write of love and another to really express love." I told him that, "Anyone who really knows me knows that I express and live the love I write of. You don't seem to know me at all." As I recall, the visit pretty much ended there. The pastor said something to the effect that nothing was being resolved. He hoped that my heretical ways would not destroy our marriage.

After he left I opened the manila envelope containing his official reply to my formal request for answers to questions and concerns about Christian doctrine. It was pretty much what I had expected although I had hoped he would be more responsive to my questions and concerns. He answered not one question, nor did he address any of the concerns I raised. He simply dismissed them all by saying, "I can't respond to them because you would not accept certain scriptural writers that I might quote" (namely, St. Paul). It was a total "cop-out" if ever I heard one.

He simply laid out established Church doctrine, using St. Paul almost exclusively for his reference. I noted that he quoted Paul eight times concerning salvation, eternal life and getting to heaven, yet *not once* did he quote what Jesus Christ had to say about those issues. To his credit there was no name calling or damning me to hell, as other ministers had done. The closest he came was to say I was in danger of divine judgment for being a critic of scripture and not accepting it in its totality.

He said that I "had brought dismay and concern to him and others in the congregation"; that I had "upset them and tried to deceive them." In my reply I told him that "I had never attempted to deceive anyone. I was truly sorry if I had caused dismay, concern and upset to them. I had never intended to do so. My only intention was to find answers to my questions and doubts about Christian doctrine."

I said, "I had come to you in good faith. Perhaps you recall my deep concern, during our discussions in your office, about what is happening to us and our world, especially the children. I felt that the Church was not teaching Christ's true message of love for one another, so as to make the world a better place and do what God wants us to do. I believe it is your responsibility to address such concerns of a parishioner, but you did not. In my opinion, you failed in that duty."

He made it quite clear that I was a disruptive influence and not welcome in their midst. Although they had not terminated my membership in the congregation, he had said during his visit that "the door is closing" in that respect.

As I honestly did not wish to cause any further dismay or disruption within the congregation, I advised the pastor that I was resigning my membership and leaving the church. Also, that I had made a decision that I really didn't want to belong to an organized religious denomination that teaches such counterproductive doctrine as man being totally depraved with only evil and darkness in his heart; that believes it is God's justice to kill babies and little children of men who are the "enemies" of God's people; that refuses to teach people to obey all things that Christ commanded, and teaches that God condemns to hell all people who are not Christians.

At that point, having severed all connections to organized religion, it was clear to me that any further attempt to bring about change by challenging the religious authorities was futile. Their stonewalling had defeated me. However, it *totally* convinced me that Christian doctrine was badly flawed, even to the point of preventing humanity from achieving spiritual growth and peace and harmony on earth.

But I was not disheartened nor discouraged. Neither of those adjectives describe me any longer. I simply knew that I had to find another forum for my belief that dramatic change is necessary in many areas of our understanding, if we are ever to solve the problems of the world and bring peace and harmony to this potential paradise that God gave us as a temporary home. Not the least of these is religion.

Hence the reason for this work. It is a book about my excommunication, which you now are familiar with and which will give you a little insight into my personality and from where I am coming. It is about religion and spirituality, life and death, sickness and health and the true nature of humankind. But, most of all, it is about transformation, changing how we think about all those things, which, if accepted, will modify human behavior for the better.

Chapter Three

CHANGE

This book speaks to the needs of people living in a decaying world fraught with stress, uncertainty, anger, violence and despair. It is not about change in the usual sense that is proposed by sociologists, government experts and "think-tank" conservatives. We cannot resolve the problems of crime and violence by putting 100,000 more cops on the streets of our cities, building more prisons, enacting tough gun control, legislating longer prison sentences, or even by creating jobs and removing social ills that contribute to crime and violence.

We will never curb the drug problem through use of catchy phrases like "just say 'no' to drugs," or through education, interdiction or even rehabilitation. We cannot reverse the trend of immorality that is becoming prevalent in the world by preaching morality, enforcing discipline, or even by promoting the return to basic values.

Rather than trying behavior modification, which, more often than not, is unsuccessful, we need to alter perceptions. ***Perception is everything***! Once perceptions have been altered, a change in behavior automatically follows. How we perceive many aspects of modern living must be reevaluated. We must change how we look at religion, government, materialism and the nature of our world. We must reconsider our views of man's relationship with the other animals, of medicine and healing, of sex, death, prayer, the nature of God and, most importantly, the nature of our own being! All of those subjects will be examined throughout this text.

For example, we have been conditioned all of our lives to think that it is man's nature to sin, it is human to err and that we are only mortal beings. When you really think about it, isn't it just as natural to do good? Think about all the people who lead decent honorable lives, doing good for others. A great number do so, even those without religious beliefs. Is there really "not one iota of goodness in man, but only evil and darkness in the hearts of men,"[1] as the great reformer Martin Luther said? The scriptures tell us that we are the "salt of the earth,"[2] that we are the "light of the world"[3] and are to let our "good works shine forth."[4] Although we are told that an "evil man out of the evil of his heart brings forth evil things,"[5] the scripture also says that a "good man out of the goodness of his heart bringeth forth good things."[6] It would seem that sin is not innate in our character, but rather that we have the ability to *choose* whether we wish to do what is wrong or what is right.

The saying that it is "human to err," is the greatest, and most unfortunate, self-fulfilling prophecy in the history of mankind. Is it really impossible for man to rise to perfection? All religious dogma says no human being has ever been perfect or ever will be. That dogma is flawed, for scripture declares that Noah was "perfect in all his generations"[7] and God "found no fault with Noah."[8] We are told to be "perfect as our Father in heaven is perfect."[9] That perfection does not mean never making a mistake; it has to do with our relationship with our fellow human beings. A formula exists for achieving perfection, and it involves that amazing quality called *love.*

Most people believe that we possess a soul that does not die. Scriptures speak of "those that can kill the body but not the soul."[10] We are told that "God sends forth guardians who watch over you and carry away your souls when death overtakes you."[11] Although not proven scientifically, the near-death experience provides very convincing evidence of the body/soul arrangement. The out-of-body part of the experience has been proven beyond doubt. Some part of us--almost certainly our soul, our spiritual self--leaves the body when it dies. If our soul survives after bodily death, are we not then also immortal?

It is also widely believed that our soul in some way emanates from God, and when our body dies, the soul returns to God. Scripture tells us that "Guardians carry away your souls without fail when death overtakes you. Then are all men *restored* to God, their true Lord."[11] We are told that our "bodies are the *temple* of God,"[12] and that "the Kingdom of God is *within you*."[13] Scripture says we are created in God's *likeness*. If God is within us in some manner, such as our soul, which originated from God, and we have the qualities or characteristics of God, being made in his likeness, then are we not divine as well as human?

To entertain such claims of immortality and divinity is heresy in most religious denominations. It invites ridicule, denouncement and even excommunication, which, of course, happened to me. Yet, to deny the divine and immortal nature of man is to deny scripture.

What if we *were* to perceive our total being as immortal and divine, as well as mortal and human? What if we were taught from an early age that, being created in God's likeness, we possess the characteristics of love, goodness, kindness, compassion and forgiveness? What if we perceived that we have the complete ability to manifest goodness rather than evil in our conduct and that God expects that of us in order to be right with him? Who could deny that human behavior would be significantly altered and the world a much better place, if not the paradise that was intended for us?

Is society's perception of human sexuality accurate? Is sexual activity as natural and essential to our well-being as eating and sleeping, as is generally suggested? Is it natural and okay for young teenagers to indulge in the casual sex that is so prevalent among them such that we need only to educate them about "safe" sex? Are we really "sexual beings" who must always respond to our sexual urges? Or are we beings who can control our sexual activities, choosing to act morally and responsibly in our sexual conduct? Isn't the current sexual behavior in our society a learned behavior? The empirical evidence certainly supports these last two perceptions as accurate.

Certainly sexual activity is not essential to good health and mental well-being. There are those who go through life without it and yet are healthy happy individuals. The sexual activity considered the norm among teenagers today would have shocked society fifty or sixty years ago when abstinence was considered the norm. Teenagers then were much happier and more well-adjusted not having to worry about pregnancy or contracting some sexually transmitted disease. We can only conclude that teen sexual activity today is a learned behavior, which is more detrimental than beneficial to their well-being.

Also, we do not desire or lust after a parent, child or sibling. There are a few who do; however, for most of us the idea is repugnant. Why is that? Most certainly because it is a *learned* behavior; we have been *conditioned* to perceive incest as wrong and, perhaps, even genetically dangerous. Surely, sexual behavior is as much a manifestation of psychology as it is of physiology. Indeed, we have fostered the promiscuity and loose sexual morals that are prevalent in society through false perceptions about sex! Clearly we need to teach a new understanding of human sexuality.

What of the animals other than human, such as our feathered and four-legged friends? Is our perception of them as "dumb" animals really accurate? They have intelligence and can reason. They can use tools and construct things. Animals can communicate, not only with one another but with humans. Of course, their abilities in these areas are limited to a level lower than that of the human animal. They have emotions and feelings. They can exhibit love, caring and even forgiveness. Animals express joy and happiness, as well as grief, despair, loneliness and even hatred and anger. They most certainly feel fear and pain.

Is it really okay to take them from their natural environment and imprison them in cages and zoos for our viewing pleasure? The wolf does not pace the confines of his cage because he is happy with his shelter and the food he doesn't have to work for. He is exhibiting despair and loneliness at being separated from his kind and most likely his life-long mate.

We are also told in the scriptures that man is to have dominion over every living thing that moves upon the earth. Those who oppose the position of animal-rights activists usually cite that passage, interpreting dominion to mean that we can control animals and use them as we see fit for such things as food, clothing and laboratory testing. Governments have dominion over people. Does that mean the government has the right to cage people or torture them? Of course not! Nor does man, the human animal, have the right to do those things to the lesser animals. Dominion carries with it the responsibility to care for and see to the well-being of those being ruled. So it should be with man's dominion over animals.

You probably know that *foie gras* (pate') is made from goose liver. But do you know how it is "harvested?" A tube is shoved down the bird's throat and then large amounts of salted fatty maize are forced into the stomach with a pressure pump. An elastic band is affixed to the neck, loose enough to allow breathing, but tight enough to prevent the goose from regurgitating. This force-feeding is done three to four times a day for about three weeks. It results in the liver swelling to ten times its normal size, providing the producer with a large, fat, liver, which he can market for good profit. Side effects to the goose are pain, trauma, esophagitis and even cirrhosis and rupture of the liver. How cruel and foolish to cause so much pain to an animal to produce something that is 85% fat and very harmful to the human who consumes it. The bottom line is profit and pleasure to the palate.

Many have seen the pictures of how calves are treated so as to produce tender veal. The infant calves are taken from their mother before they have a chance to suckle colostrum, the natural antibody substance that most mammals secrete when nursing their newborns. They are shipped to veal barns and confined to the "notorious veal pens" with slatted floors where they cannot turn around or get proper exercise. Such movement would tend to toughen the meat. They are fed only liquid formulas laced with *unnatural* antibiotics, which leave high levels of drug residues in the veal that the consumer eats. After 16 to 20 weeks, barely able to stand, due to their diet and lack of exercise, they are shipped to the slaughter house. It doesn't seem right to treat animals so cruelly for the sake of monetary gain and eating enjoyment..

What about using animals for testing? "A trusting dog is strapped into an unyielding steel restraining device. Then a lab technician forces a hose down the helpless dog's resisting throat and pours a caustic brew of harsh cleaning fluid into the trembling animal's stomach. The terrified dog whines in fear and pain as the chemicals sear and burn."[14] Is that acceptable to you? How can a person treat "man's best friend" and other defenseless animals in such a cruel and heartless manner?

Perhaps most detrimental to the human race is the false perception of religion. Karl Marx said that "religion is the opiate of the masses."[15] In that religion often dulls or deadens people to reality, that is true. Religion is considered as something desirable to have. Most parents express a desire to raise their children in some religious faith; yet if we honestly analyze the effect that religion has had on humanity, we would have to conclude that religion, particularly organized denominational religion and its man-made dogma, has caused humankind a great deal of grief. It is undoubtedly the greatest barrier to peace and harmony among men. It has stifled man's spiritual growth.

The great tragedy of religion is that it has divided the human race, causing discord and enmity among mankind when it should be uniting people in harmony with one another and with God. It is a major cause of disunity and conflict. When a religion proclaims that it is right, all others are wrong, and their followers are damned to hell, the obvious result is distrust, suspicion, anger and hatred.

Generally, religions believe that God is perfect in love, mercy, forgiveness and *justice*. How then is it possible for God to condemn, to eternal hellfire, a child or anyone who has never heard of, has never been taught to understand about a Christ, Muhammad, Moses or Buddha? When a religious group teaches that everyone must believe as they do to be saved, they are proclaiming that those who do not are not saved. They are condemning to hell anyone who is not of their religious persuasion. It should give any thinking person cause to wonder about any religion that proclaims that God condemns to hell all who do not believe as that religion does.

There has to be a logical, inescapable conclusion that all religions cannot be right. I believe that all, without exception, are flawed. The basics of most religious faiths are the same, dealing with a loving relationship between human beings. One of the greatest commandments that God has given to all the religions is to love and care for one another. Almost all hold to that tenet. Then they make the mistake of adding man-made doctrine and laws, or interpreting God's basic laws and instructions to meet their own requirements or beliefs.

Because religious leaders and theologians have distorted and added to God's truths and made false claims that theirs is the only true religion, the people are at odds. There is non-acceptance of one another. We call one another less-than-flattering names such as heathen and infidel and sometimes much worse. We even become violent and kill each other over religious beliefs. It is interesting to note that the violence is not over basic religious beliefs about God and love; rather, it is over the man-made dogma: You must believe in what *we* say about religion; you must worship the way *we* do, or you must believe in and follow *our* prophet.

When we closely examine the doctrine of the world's religions, it is very clear that much of it is in error, fostering guilt, low self-esteem, suspicion, distrust, alienation and even violence and death. It is not really necessary to examine all religious doctrine to see that this is so. We can use as an example the two great religions of Islam and Christianity. They are perhaps the two most flawed and rigid religions of the world. Their faulty dogma sets the tone for the disunity that plagues the world.

For example, they both claim to base their dogma on their infallible scriptures, the Bible and the Koran. Christianity, in general, teaches that the Bible is the authoritative word of God and without error. Although the Bible does indeed contain the reliable word of God, it also contains the *unreliable* word of man. One version of the Gospel says one angel was at the tomb of Jesus Christ. Another says there were two. *Obviously, both cannot be true.* One Gospel says Christ's ascension occurred on Easter Sunday night, after meeting with the disciples. Another tells of the ascension taking place forty days after Easter. *Both cannot be correct.*

We have seen the psalmist's words, recorded in the Old Testament, about the Babylonians who razed Jerusalem--"Blessed is the man who destroys you. Blessed is the man who takes your *babies and smashes them against the rocks.*"[16] To believe that those are the words of God and that God would bless the soldier who smashes his enemy's babies against the rocks in vengeance against the father, is not rational. We will see that the Bible contains many errors.

Muslims believe that every sentence, word and even every syllable in the Koran is also the unfailing word of Allah. When one closely examines the Koran, it is clear that this cannot be so. The Koran says it was *all* given to Muhammad in *a* (one) night. History records that it was given over a period of years, as most Muslims believe. Surah 23:94 says, "Requite evil with good." Yet Surah 42:35 says, "Let evil be rewarded with like evil." In the context in which these statements are given, their meaning is as stated. Obviously, *one is in error.*

The Koran states that Allah *leads* unbelievers (all non-Muslims) to ruin and hell. How can one believe that those are the words of a merciful and forgiving Allah, who states elsewhere in the Koran that if an unbeliever repents and mends his ways, he will be forgiven and receive his reward in paradise? There are many other errors and contradictions in the Koran. Just as with the Bible, God's word *is* in the Koran, but so is the fallible word of man. For the Christian Church hierarchy and Islamic leaders to cling to the doctrine of scriptural perfection, in the face of absolute evidence to the contrary, is intellectually dishonest as well as detrimental to the unity of the human race.

The dogma of the Christian Church concerning the nature of God, the nature of man and the way of salvation is not the teaching of Jesus Christ. The Church has strayed far from his instructions. Islam's claim that one must be Muslim and follow Muhammad in order to achieve paradise is *not* the lesson of the Koran. This book will provide evidence, sufficient for any reasonable and open-minded person, that these things are true. If peace and harmony on this earth are to be achieved, we must change our perception of religion and bring about a drastic reformation in organized religion's dogma, teaching *only* the basic truths about love, caring, goodness, compassion and forgiveness, which are common to all religions.

This book may alarm, even anger, some people because radical change is frightening and the truth often hurts. Many will perceive it as a threat to their livelihood. However, when the changes to perception that are proposed in this work come to fruition, all offense and anger will cease and no one will have to be concerned about his or her well-being. You are challenged to read this book with an open mind. Don't continue to accept blindly everything you have been taught. In the light of what you read here, search for knowledge and *see for yourself* what is right.

Unless we change our ways, the frightful deterioration of our world and the violence to its inhabitants, that is occurring today, will surely accelerate. What you are about to read in the next chapter is very negative, pessimistic and discouraging. I am a positive person and have a great dislike for negativity and pessimism, but at the same time one cannot ignore reality, and what you are going to read is stark reality. I feel it is absolutely essential that you be made completely aware of the terrible conditions that beset us. There are those who are somewhat aware. Many are in denial, believing that our America is the greatest nation in the world and that our troubles are only a blip on the screen of continuing prosperity and greatness. Many would like to think that we will somehow struggle through all the trials and tribulations without serious consequences or that it "won't happen to me," but that is wishful thinking. After you have read the next chapter, put your imagination to work and picture those problems multiplied two or four fold. It is surely going to happen unless we alter our perceptions and, thusly, our behavior.

Chapter Four

ARMAGEDDON OR A GOLDEN AGE?

Which is it to be? What *is* the destiny of our world? Is it to be chaos and destruction, or will the pendulum swing and a new age of peace and harmony be ushered in? Or do we even have a choice? Many religious fundamentalists believe not; that the end of the world is a given fact foretold by the scriptures. References to the *end* abound in the scriptures: "I am with you always even unto the end of the world."[1] "Heaven and earth shall pass away, but my words shall not pass away."[2] "But the end shall not yet be. For nation shall rise against nation, and kingdom against kingdom; and there shall be earthquakes in divers places, and there shall be famines and troubles: these are the beginnings of sorrows."[3] "I saw a new heaven and a new earth; for the first heaven and the first earth were passed away."[4]

Given all the natural disasters that have recently occurred-- the San Francisco area earthquake of 1989, the storm of the century that occurred over the eastern United States in 1993, the Great Flood of '93 that befell the U.S. Midwest, the famines that are decimating parts of Africa, the "Great" earthquake of 1994 that rocked the San Fernando Valley in California and the disastrous affects of "El Nino" around the world--wide speculation exists, especially by those religious fundamentalists, that the end is not far off. From church pulpits, and in everyday discussions about these calamities, it is not uncommon to hear comments about these disasters as signs that the end is near. For a large part of this century, there has been prediction and speculation that the turn of the century will bring the great cataclysm signaling the "end."

Many psychics have predicted that great turmoil will begin to escalate just prior to the turn of the century, notably in the last half of the 1990s. Early in this century Edgar Cayce, who exhibited remarkable psychic abilities, that have been well documented, predicted great upheavals for that period of time. Five hundred years ago, Nostradamus made numerous predictions, which he recorded in what are known as quatrains. According to scholars who have interpreted them, he was amazingly accurate, both by event and by date, predicting such things as both World Wars, the downfall of communism, the assassination of John F. Kennedy, the fall of the Berlin Wall, the rise and fall of Napoleon and Hitler, the invention of the submarine and the airplane, the use of the atomic bomb and many others. One scholar said that Nostradamus, in his predictions, was "right on the money." A prediction yet to come about concerns a great catastrophe and destruction in 1999. It is interesting to note that some psychics qualify their predictions with the conditional phrase, *"unless we change our ways."* Nostradamus emphasizes in the quatrains that we can change these things *if we choose to.*

On the other hand, equal if not greater support can be found in the scriptures for a "golden age that is to come." It is also interesting to notice that these references to a golden age are also qualified with a condition, namely that when the *world is full of the knowledge of God*, it will come about. To be found is reference to a "peaceable kingdom" that is to come. "In that day the wolf and the lamb will lie down together, and the leopard and goats will be at peace. Calves and fat cattle will be safe among the lions, and a little child shall lead them all. The cows will graze among the bears, cubs and calves will lie down together, and the lions will eat grass like the cows. Babies will crawl safely among poisonous snakes, and a little child who puts his hand in a nest of deadly adders will pull it out unharmed. Nothing will hurt or destroy in all my holy mountain, for as the waters fill the sea, so shall the earth be full of the *knowledge of the Lord.*"[5]

Many are aware of the Lord's Prayer, in which we are instructed to continually ask that God's "kingdom come and his will be done on **earth** *as in heaven."* Everyone who believes that heaven exists also believes that there is no sorrow--rather, only love, joy and peace there. Clearly then, according to the Lord's Prayer, that condition is to exist also on earth. It would be foolish for us to pray continually for that condition to be done on earth if world conditions are supposed to deteriorate until our planet is finally destroyed, either by man or by God.

A strong case could be made that all those references to the end of the world could mean the end of the world *as we know it.* When "the world is full of the knowledge of the Lord," that is, when we understand God, what he expects of us and live accordingly, then there will be no more harm or destruction. This world that is currently filled with sorrow and violence will become a world of peace and good will. Some theologians say those references to the end of the *world* were incorrectly translated; that the correct translation is end of the *age.* This old age of violence, disbelief and ignorance will be ushered out and a golden era of knowledge of God, peace and harmony will begin.

A new *age* could explain that scriptural reference: "I saw a *new* heaven and a *new* earth, for the first heaven and the first earth were passed away." The new heaven and earth will be merged in some manner so that "God's will is done on *earth* as in heaven." Genesis does imply that in the beginning God separated the heavens and the earth. Is it really believable that God would destroy his own creation, especially the beings that he made in his own "likeness" and whom, he has said, through the scriptures, he *loves* unconditionally? Or is it man who is going to do the destroying? It might be possible for us to destroy the earth. We're doing a pretty fair job of it right now with over-population, resource depletion, war, environmental destruction and possibly nuclear devastation. But man couldn't destroy the heavens. Or could he?

Perhaps we *do* have a choice; we can change our ways and learn to do what is good and right, or we can continue on our present course toward some global cataclysm. It would seem that the latter "Armageddon" scenario is being played out. Just during the last few years it is quite clear that man and nature are becoming more and more violent. The frequency and magnitude of natural disasters are increasing.

The three most devastating in United States history occurred during a twelve month period in 1992 and '93. Hurricane Andrew devastated south Florida in September of 1992. Then in March of '93, a giant blizzard, called a "killer storm" and "storm of the century," blanketed the eastern half of the United States with rain, snow, hail and sleet. In the summer of 1993 relentless rain inundated the Midwest, causing the worst flooding in U.S. history.

Globally the picture is similar: a tidal wave hits Japan; consecutive typhoons strike the Philippines; earthquakes rumble around the world; volcanic eruptions occur in Madagascar and Montserrat; drought and famine are more common; monsoons cause devastating floods in southern Asia, and unusual flooding and mudslides occur in parts of Europe.

Although man has exhibited violence throughout history, the intensity and savagery of it seems to be mounting. We are witnessing unspeakable horrors. In Brazil, merchants hire gunmen, usually off-duty policemen, to hunt and kill homeless children because they steal food for survival. Despots, out of greed for material wealth and power, have systematically withheld food, starving tens of thousands to death. During one period, in Somalia, one thousand children were dying every day from starvation.

Armageddon or a Golden Age? 57

Dorothy St. Germain, an American doing hospital work in Somalia, said conditions reminded her of a horror movie in which "skeletons emerge from their graves to terrorize the living." She goes on to speak of "emaciated children who can barely lift their arms to wave off the flies. Mothers, with little to give but comfort, nurse babies who appear more dead than alive. Reed-like children moan and suffer from the life-draining effects of dysentery." Georgie Anne Geyer, a reporter who had visited Somalia, spoke of the thirteen-year old boy who, "thought dead and was being buried, opened his eyes and two tears rolled over his cheeks!" What cruel and vile behavior on the part of man to deliberately cause such suffering!

The bloodletting and carnage in Bosnia has been atrocious. There was shelling, killing and mangling of scores of innocent civilians in the market place as they looked for food to sustain their lives. Hospitals were deliberately shelled and little children fleeing in buses from the violence were fired upon and killed. In Rwanda, the killing reached holocaust proportions as the people shot and hacked one another to death, exterminating half a million lives. It is almost beyond belief that human beings can intentionally do those things to one another.

Elsewhere, in everyday life, children are killing children, parents are murdering their children, children are slaying their parents and teenagers are killing one another because the other has something they want or because they are "in their face" or just because it's *fun!* The scenario of a disturbed, angry, fired or laid-off employee returning to his work place and using an automatic weapon to kill his supervisor and fellow employees is becoming all too common. The frightening aspect of this violence is that these are not hardened criminals but ordinary everyday citizens, most of whom had never exhibited violent behavior.

Even the animals seem to be more violent. Domestic animals such as dogs are attacking people more frequently, and without apparent provocation. In Southeast Asia, groups of leopards and bands of elephants have been on the rampage against people and villages.

The world is in serious trouble. J. B. Say, a French philosopher, wrote that, "It is impossible to avoid a precipice when one follows a road that leads nowhere else." The world has been following the road of moral, political, economic, financial, environmental and spiritual irresponsibility for too long. Most haven't even recognized that we are on such a road.

Nations and people are splintering world-wide. Corruption, immorality, violence and hatred abound. Unrest and the spilling of blood are present everywhere. As of this writing, there are 42 wars of some kind going on around the globe. Incredible sums of money have been spent on weapons of war and preparing for "defense." At the height of the Cold War, it has been estimated that the world was spending about $750,000,000,000 (three quarters of a trillion dollars) annually so as to be prepared for armed conflict. An *obscene* amount, by any standard! Even today, with the breakup of the Soviet Union and the end of the Cold War, that amount is undoubtedly close to half a trillion dollars!

If the nations of the world would spend as much time, effort and money promoting peace as they have preparing for war, much of the evil and aggression that has arisen likely would have been prevented. The nations of the world suffer the delusion of, and are besieged by, a "military-might-equates-to-national-security" mentality. Nothing could be further from the truth. The opposite is true. It should be obvious that the more the world has armed itself over the years, the greater the danger has become!

President Eisenhower said, in 1953, "Every gun that is made, every warship launched, every rocket fired, signifies, in the final sense, a theft from those who hunger and are not fed, those who are cold and are not clothed. This world in arms is not spending money alone. It is spending the sweat of its laborers, the genius of its scientists, the hopes of its children. This is not a way of life at all in any true sense. Under the cloud of war, it is humanity hanging on a cross of iron." By our continued manufacture of weapons of war, we are indeed crucifying the world!

Many "civilized" nations have contributed to the proliferation of the weapons of war, which has made the world an armed camp, a veritable powder keg that could explode, triggering an Armageddon-like cataclysm. A prime example is the Middle East. According to some interpretations of the biblical Book of Revelations, that is where the final battle of Armageddon is to take place. The stage has certainly been set there. There is great hatred and enmity between the Jewish people and the Arab nations that surround them. The rest of the world, for political and sometimes ideological reasons, has lined up on one side or the other and helped arm both camps to the teeth. There is right and wrong on both sides. All the factions in the Middle East need to be reminded of and reexamine their basic religious beliefs, that they "cannot know and love God until they love and want for their brother what they want for themselves." *To God they are surely **brothers to one another**!*

Economically and financially, there is great distress around the world. Although there is great wealth to be found, massive poverty also abounds with hundreds of thousands of people starving to death each year. The "Asian Economic Miracle," which world economists expected to continue indefinitely, quickly became the "Asian Crisis" in 1997 as unjustified high-flying financial markets ran headlong into the reality of corruption and debt. Substantial danger exists that a number of nations there as well as elsewhere in the world, will suffer chaos and possible anarchy as their economies slide into depression.

Although the United States is enjoying great prosperity as of this writing, in 1998, we are not immune from such a happening. Our country is awash in a sea of red ink. Credit card debt is at an all-time high. Over one million Americans filed for personal bankruptcy in 1997, a thirty-percent increase over the previous year. Mortgage delinquencies are on the rise.

We have become the largest debtor nation in the world, with the national debt standing at $5.5 trillion. Not only have we had to borrow huge sums just for everyday government operation, we don't have the money needed to resolve some very serious problems this country is facing. The U.S. infrastructure of roads, bridges, dams reservoirs and waterways is crumbling, requiring over $1 trillion just to bring it up to standard. The disrepair and safety of our nuclear weapons plants are in crisis and need $150 billion to correct. AIDS, crime, drugs, homelessness, health care and environmental cleanup are all reaching crisis proportions requiring hundreds of billions of dollars just to halt the tide.

Although the annual deficit has declined due to increased economic activity, the budget is far from balanced. The Administration's and Congress' claim that the budget was near balance in 1998 was nothing short of deceit because it did not take into consideration borrowing from the Social Security Fund. The government has recently been collecting $60 to $70 billion in surplus Social Security *contributions* each year to make sure that the Fund will remain solvent, especially when the baby-boomer generation comes of retirement age shortly after the turn of the century. That money is supposed to go into a trust fund, but it does not because the government uses it for operating expenses and issues the Fund *pieces of paper* in the form of government bonds.

But those are very unusual bonds; they can't be marketed. And because Social Security cannot sell them, the government has designated them as *non-government debt!* What do you think is going to happen when the need for those surplus funds arises? The government will have to borrow more *cash* from the taxpayer to redeem their IOUs to the Social Security Trust Fund.

Further, talk about how to spend the "coming budget surplus" is only political rhetoric based on that devious accounting and overly optimistic economic predictions. U.S. economic growth and government income will likely decline as a result of the Asian crisis. As global markets are intertwined, the U.S. and other world economies are likely to catch cold from the "Asian Contagion;" perhaps even pneumonia. There is a saying that "the business cycle hasn't been repealed," that is, economic growth fluctuates. It runs the gamut from a booming economy to stagnation to recession to depression. Recession, and probably something more severe, is conceivably in the offing. When money and power become top priorities for people and nations, disaster is sure to follow.

In parts of the world, religious fundamentalists, who use violence as a means to the end, are on the rise. Although the Cold War between the United States and the former Soviet Union is over and the threat of a nuclear holocaust diminished, there is great concern about accountability of nuclear weapons. A strong possibility exists that nuclear weapons from the former Soviet republics have been acquired by countries that harbor and support terrorists, who might not hesitate to use them. The probability for world-wide political, social, economic and financial upheaval is very high.

All of these conditions will surely accelerate into an Armageddon-like scenario unless we change our ways.

Chapter Five

MATERIALISM AND SPIRITUALISM

Putting it all on a religious or spiritual basis, we can then understand why the world is in such a hell of a mess! The scriptures tell us that we are to "Seek first the Kingdom of God and his righteousness and then these things (material needs) will be added unto us."[1] That means that our first priority is to understand God and what he expects of us and when we do, the things we need in life will accrue to us.

We are also told that "The destiny of those who do not listen to God is destruction. Their god is their stomach and their glory, their shame."[2] This aptly describes much of the world! Yes, materialism is the god of many. It is certainly a "look-out-for-number-one" world.

We admire and envy those who are affluent and live in opulence. How often we hear, "Oh how nice it would be to be rich or win the lottery." And when wealth is achieved, it is often hoarded, rather than used to help those who are less fortunate. Acquiring wealth is not wrong. It is the storing up of more than we can possibly use while others are in need that is inappropriate.

That is what the scriptures mean when they admonish us not to "store up treasure for yourselves here on earth rather than in heaven."[3] We are indeed our "brother's keeper." We must not be indifferent to those who are poor and in distress. We are to use our means to help them, and when we do, we store up treasure for ourselves in heaven.

A message basic to all religions is to love, care for and be of service to one another without thought of remuneration. And that service is to be directed to those in need who cannot pay, rather than those who can. Scripture tells us, "When you put on a dinner, don't invite your friends, relatives or rich neighbors for they will repay you in turn, but instead invite the poor, the crippled, the lame and the blind for they can't repay you and then you will receive your reward in heaven."[4]

But we don't do these things. Materialism is our first priority rather than spiritual values. We *do* store up treasure for ourselves here on earth while others are homeless, sick and starving. We concentrate on making it in the world of materialism, and if we have time along the way we might look into what God is about and what our relationship with others should be. Our priorities are completely out of whack. We pay exorbitant salaries to people who can bring in the big bucks, but won't spend adequate funds to properly educate our children. We spend billions of dollars on weapons of war and space programs, but often do not feed the hungry, shelter the homeless or take care of the sick. How can we possibly defend the expenditure of hundreds of billions of dollars spent on space exploration when tens of thousands of children here on earth are dying each year from starvation and sickness? It is unconscionable that we have so misplaced our priorities!

In February 1997, our space agency spent an additional $347 million to install a more powerful camera in the orbiting Hubble telescope which will enable the scientists to see farther into space, exploring more of the universe. It is incredible that such tremendous amounts of money are being expended, just to observe more of what they already know, when the children are starving to death. The administration, Congress and the space agency need to be asked this question: "What is more important, to explore space or relieve the suffering of the children?"

To peer through a multi-billion dollar telescope that has been hoisted into orbit, thinking we are going to "see the beginning of the universe" is foolish. It is not likely that the scientists will ever "scientifically" discover how the universe was created. They are wasting their time and our money trying to detect its origin. To indulge our hobby of astronomy and aspire to "go where no other man has gone before" is okay and perhaps even admirable if funds were left over after we have taken care of the needs here on this earth. We try to justify all these actions by claiming free enterprise, prestige and national security. You can be sure that God doesn't accept *those* excuses! When one really analyzes all the scriptures, it is clear that indifference to the plight of others is the great sin in God's sight.

Scriptures tell us that God puts great store by the children. We are admonished that mistreatment of the "little ones" will bring dire consequences. We have been told not to deny the children, but to "bring them up in the nurture and admonition of the Lord."[5] Nurture means to raise them with unconditional love, teaching them God's admonition to love others unconditionally, and forgive our fellow human beings. We have failed miserably in that. In raising our children, we need to de-emphasize materialism and teach them spiritual values such as love, compassion and forgiveness--***by example.***

The world's perception of religion must change. We must perceive denominational religion as an obstruction to the unity of people everywhere. It isn't necessary to do away with churches or mosques. Nor do we need to give up Christmas or 'Id al Fita. Church-going and religious festivals can be comforting and uplifting if the participation and observance set the right tone--one of fellowship and serving others as well as insuring that the *true* message of Christ and Muhammad is being taught. Although it has been highly commercialized, Christmas is a wonderful time of year, fostering a tremendous amount of good will among humankind. Still, we need a different perception of Christmas--one in which there is more gift giving to the needy and less to those who are not--an outpouring of aid to everyone who is in need, regardless of the circumstances.

But it *is essential* that the religions of the world cease their folly of using diverse and false religious doctrine to divide the human race. We must realize that inaccurate religious dogma about the innately sinful nature of man is a barrier to man's spiritual growth. Religions must teach God's basic laws that are common to them all: that we are to acknowledge God, that we are to love one another, showing kindness and forgiveness, and that only in doing these things can we achieve unity with one another here on earth as well as gaining salvation and paradise.

There must be a general movement away from religiosity; that is, piety, the rituals and trappings of religion and specific sets of religious beliefs. We need to move toward spirituality; that is, toward understanding the true nature of God, man and our world; that spirit is the vital principle in them all and that we are all spiritually interconnected. We must search for the right relationship that will allow man and all of creation to exist in peace and harmony. It is necessary to understand that love is the way; the true power that can make all things right.

Chapter Six

WINDS OF CHANGE?

There seems to be some movement toward a greater understanding of spirituality and what God really requires of us. Is it a sincere effort by man to *change his ways*, which might result in avoidance of Armageddon and the ushering in of the Golden Age? It is difficult to reconcile such a movement with the degeneration of the world that we see around us. Perhaps it is cyclical, yet with ever upward progress. Sort of two steps forward and one back.

In January, 1994, the San Diego Union reported some statistics about religion indicating there are signs that denominational religion is on the decline while spiritualism is alive and thriving. Organized religion and its dogma are becoming a casualty of dissatisfaction as people don't seem to find what they are seeking in their relationship with God. Religion is losing its influence.

Membership in Protestant churches is ebbing. Corrupt evangelists and a tendency toward materialism are having a decided negative effect. In Catholicism, one third of the young Catholics say they are open to a switch of denominations. There is a shortage of priests in the church. Pedophilia and homosexuality among priests is hurting the church. Of the six million Jews in the United States, only thirty-five percent belong to a synagogue. Only five percent of the Muslims in the United States are involved in mosque activities.

Spirituality does seem to be on the rise. Ninety-three percent of the people in the United States say they believe in

God, or a supreme being. A great spiritual yearning exists among people. They are searching for something that will bring peace and harmony into their lives and among people of the world. It is not enough to go to some denominational church regularly, only to know that your beliefs separate you from other people and that those beliefs provide few, if any, answers to the frustration, despair and violence that is ever increasingly being encountered in everyday life.

The San Diego Union also published an article, "The Me Generation Searches for its Soul," showing how there seems to be a great movement in America of people searching for meaning in their lives. It showed that about half of the nonfiction books on the best-seller list have a spiritual theme and that "The hungry soul of America is devouring anything that smacks of spirituality." James Redfield, author of THE CELESTINE PROPHECY, believes that, "A new, more positive, more spiritual approach to life is truly emerging out there; it's not just something to be hoped for, it's actually happening right now."

Many are beginning to understand that we have to look within ourselves, to some part of the human consciousness, our spiritual self, to find those answers. There are many organizations that are dedicated to research and to helping people find their true selves. The Institute of Noetic Sciences is one such group. Carol Guion, Associate Editor of the <u>Noetic Sciences Review</u>, said in an article, "Signs of a World Awakening," that their aim is twofold: "fostering research on human consciousness and exploring its relevance for human affairs. As we have grown over the last twenty years, we have watched people around the world also growing--individuals awakening to a more profound understanding of themselves, and groups creatively finding ways to link our social, ecological and spiritual visions through action. To broaden awareness of these changes, we report on people, projects, trends and ideas that embody a blend of action and awareness and give us renewed hope for the Earth. They may be, we think, signs of a world awakening."[1]

There are indeed a great number of signs of spiritual awakening. Many peace movements and organizations promoting human rapport have sprung up world-wide since the late 1950s. The "New Age" philosophy and the "Age of Enlightenment" were ushered in during the 1960s. Meditation and self-hypnosis as a means to look to our inner self for answers, and even to look for God, are being practiced by millions of people. Prayer wheels, peace chains and hands across the nation and around the world have been organized with emphasis being placed on saving the environment, saving the children and saving our world.

We see an endless stream of books and other publications dedicated to exploring spirituality, the purpose of life, the nature of the human consciousness, our relationship with one another, with God and many other noetic subjects. Holistic learning centers where the connection between body, mind and spirit is being examined, are springing up around the world. A great deal of research into self-healing and spiritual healing is being conducted with the interesting and remarkable idea that "we are truly self-healing organisms who possess capacities and potentials about which we have only dared to dream."[2]

There is movement toward individual freedom; that is, away from the dominance of institutional entities such as the church, governments and big business. The religious denominations have maintained their power by teaching the belief that they are essential as an intermediary between man and God. In doing so they have kept mankind at "arm's length" from God, from knowing him and from realizing that he is within us and can be called upon personally to enhance our way of living and give us the answers to life's problems. People are beginning to turn away from religion, realizing that it doesn't have those answers.

Government operates in pretty much the same manner, usually striving to be bigger and more intrusive into the lives of its citizens, emphasizing its importance to the well-being of the people. In doing so, government insures its entrenchment. We've heard the saying that big government isn't the solution, but rather the problem. That is most certainly true. More government is not healthy for its citizens as it tends to enslave them to dependency, thereby suppressing individual initiative and man's abilities to do good and to fend for himself. More and more people are becoming aware of the big-brother threat of government, its intrusion into their lives, and are rebelling against it.

Big business, in such forms as "Madison Avenue," also attempts to intrude into and control our lives through media advertisement, usually not to our benefit, but rather to their own in the way of materialistic gain. It promotes such things as smoking, alcoholism, sexual irresponsibility and violence. People are getting fed up with it. Also, in the name of progress and the false altruism of feeding the world, big business has adulterated our food supply with pesticides, fungicides, chemical fertilizers and preservatives. The actual reason is to maximize profits. In collusion with Madison Avenue, we are conditioned and encouraged to consume unhealthy products such as fat and sugar-laden foods, to the extent that most of our diets are extremely poor, which then leads to illness, disease and even death, especially among the children.

But we are resisting them also, insisting on a ban of harmful pesticides and chemical fertilizers not only because of the harmful effects on the food we consume, but due to the poisoning of the soil, the air and our water supply. Many people are going organic; that is, using only food that is grown naturally without the use of artificial growth stimulants and pesticides.

Part of spirituality is getting back to the basics of being closer to God, such as eliminating the middleman--the church--

in our worship and communing directly and personally with God in Nature and in our everyday life. We need to perceive that less government is in our spiritual interests. According to the Old Testament, God did not want the people to have a government, but rather just to live according to his instructions. But they kept pestering the high priest for a ruler, until he finally gave in and anointed them a king, hence, governments came into being. Mankind would be much better off with less government; simply living by the basic laws of God and taking responsibility for our own well-being and relationships with others. Most certainly we would be better off if we lived by God's admonitions such as the one that commands us to love our neighbor as our self.

Music is another sign of the world awakening to spiritualism. Music has been called the international language and given credit for "soothing the savage breast." A great deal of good music promotes the spiritual values of love, peace and harmony. The words of that wonderful song, "What the World Needs now is Love Sweet Love," were never more true. Unfortunately, there is a lot of bad music that is unsettling and violent, with anxiety-ridden lyrics. Certainly we have the right to freedom of speech. But we *do not* have the right to be irresponsible in our speech and our music, thereby causing harm to others.

Perhaps the greatest indication that mankind is undergoing a spiritual awakening is found in the phenomenon of the near-death experience. Those who come back from that experience undergo a profound change in the way they live and think. They look for the good rather than the bad in others. They cease their judgment of others. They project love, kindness and good energy vibes. They often have a "burning desire" to help others. Things like materialism, anger, fear and worry no longer have influence over them.

During their experience they are made aware that love of others is what God expects of them. They are also made aware that they are accountable for their actions in *this* lifetime. The near-death experience researchers have documented over 30,000 cases. Surveys estimate that perhaps as many as eight million people in the United States alone, have had the near-death experience. The peace and good will emanating from that many minds is certain to have a peaceful, benign effect on this world, of which they are an inter-connected part. Surely, it would be contributory to the peaceable kingdom or golden age that is to come.

Clearly mankind has not heard God, has not listened to his prophets, and so God, through the near-death experience of millions of people, is sending us another message that he exists, that he loves us unconditionally, and what he wants us to do in order to be reconciled to him. We are to show love to one another; caring for and forgiving one another. Perhaps the near-death experience will be the impetus for the great spiritual awakening and search for knowledge of God. There does seem to be a movement and yearning to understand our purpose in life, even to change the way we live and, thus, make the world a better place.

Researchers into the NDE and many experiencers themselves believe such a change is under way. Dr. Kenneth Ring, an NDE researcher, has published several volumes on that phenomenon. In his book, HEADING TOWARD OMEGA, he draws some remarkable conclusions. He suggests we are heading toward Omega, the final goal of human development. He says further that "millions of people having the NDE, along with many others who have had similar awakenings, collectively represent an evolutionary thrust toward higher consciousness for humanity at large."

It is my belief that we are proceeding into an age of enlightenment, a higher level of consciousness. Not a consciousness in which we become "wholly spiritually beings" or are able to change at will from physical to spiritual beings and back, as some believe. But simply a greater spiritual awareness of our total nature and the true nature of God and this world we live in which will then lead to that peaceable kingdom; a golden age when God's will is done on *earth* as in heaven, when nothing shall harm or destroy, perhaps not even earthquakes! However, we will not achieve that state of bliss, without greater suffering, unless we change the way in which we think of ourselves.

Chapter Seven

AS WE THINK, SO ARE WE

   Consider a machine so complex and powerful that it can perform millions of calculations per minute. No, not the human mind, but today's super computer. *It was invented by the human mind*--a mind like yours. A mind like yours invented the airplane and the submarine, and put mankind on the moon. A mind like yours discovered the vaccine for polio and cures for many illnesses.

   The human mind has brought forth many things from nothingness into existence, from an idea to an actuality simply through the creative effort of thought. As a man thinketh, so is he. It's true when you think about it. In the same manner that a man's thought concerning flight led to the invention of the airplane, our thoughts concerning ourself bear similar fruit. For us to decide then, is whether or not the fruit of our thought will be bitter or sweet. As we conceive ourselves to be, so we will become by acting upon our thoughts.

   If the human mind can put man on the moon, can it not also do so simple a thing as change the circumstances of one's own life? If we think of ourselves as lacking control over our lives it will come to pass because our actions, reactions and expectations will reflect the attitudes we have implanted in our minds. Similarly, if we perceive ourselves in control of our lives and our circumstances, we will act as if it were true and it will become true through our behavior and desires. As the twig is bent, so grows the tree.

We have the means to control all aspects of our lives. We can choose good health, happiness and good fortune by the thoughts of our conscious mind. Through the blueprint of the human body, God has endowed us with an incredibly powerful mind. But that latent power of the mind is not understood or used by most of us. We refuse to accept God's statement to us that we are "wonderfully and fearfully made" with amazing abilities; even the ability to do miracles. Instead, we accept and believe the words of men that we are innately sinful, basically corrupt and prone to error, and subsequently those characteristics are brought to fruition in our lives.

The scriptures tell us that, "As a man thinketh, in his heart, so is he."[1] What does it mean to "think with your heart?" Also, we often hear the phrase "listen to your heart." We can't think with the muscular organ in our chest that circulates the blood throughout the body, nor can it speak to us. As we think in our heart, means to hold thoughts with deep conviction and determination. For example, if we originate a thought in our mind to make some change in our behavior, then cling tenaciously to that thought, the change will occur. That seems logical, and we generally accept the idea that how and what we think forms the kind of person we are.

But, how is it possible to "listen to our heart?" If, indeed, we can, then there must be something else in our nature besides thought and the reasoning capability of our minds. It wouldn't be conscience, for that can be conditioned. We often think of "heart" as intuition or feeling. Sometimes it is spoken of as the inner self or higher self. Still, all those terms are vague; where does intuition come from and what is the inner self?

It is likely that the soul--the spiritual field of energy given from God, which gives us life and is indestructible--is the inner self, and it provides us with those intuitive characteristics. We'll talk more about the soul and its traits in the next chapter, "The Nature of Man." Whatever "heart" is, it and the power of the mind figure prominently in mankind's behavior, well-being, health and salvation.

If you think you are an inadequate and inconsistent person, if you think you are something less than a good person; and if you think that you must experience unhappiness and failure along the road of life, so it will be. But if you think of yourself as a magnificent human being, wonderfully and fearfully made, as God has told you; if you believe you were created in God's likeness with his qualities of love, wisdom, goodness and compassion; if you believe you have the ability to manifest those qualities in your life; if you think you have the capability to live in accordance with God's instructions, and if you think your life can be filled to overflowing with happiness and good fortune, *so it will be!* As you think, so are you!

We have seen that James Allen, in his inspirational book, AS A MAN THINKETH, has said, "A man is literally what he thinks, his character being the sum of his own thoughts. As a being of Power, Intelligence and Love, and the lord of his own thoughts, man holds the key to every situation, and contains within himself that transforming and regenerative ability by which he may make himself what he wills. By the right choice and true application of thought, man ascends to Divine Perfection."

God has said essentially the same thing about his creation, mankind. "You are wonderfully and fearfully made....You are the light of the world....The Kingdom of God is within you (We possess the godly qualities of love, wisdom, goodness, patience, mercy and forgiveness)....You are created in God's image....Get yourselves new minds and hearts....As you think, in your heart, so are you....Be perfect as your Father in heaven is perfect."

God has indeed created us to be truly magnificent beings of spectacular complexity with fantastically powerful minds. By thought and the power of the mind we can *make ourselves what we will*, as James Allen has said. We can *choose* good health, happiness and success. We can *choose* to let our light shine.

We can *choose* to be good, kind and loving to our neighbor. We can *choose* to "obey and live by every word of God." He has told us we have the ability to do that. We should not doubt him.

With that God-given power, we can stop others and circumstances from shaping our lives. We can take complete charge of our lives. We can embrace the good things in life that lead to happiness and success; choosing good literature, good television fare, good music, healthy and nutritious food and all the things we know in our heart are right and true.

When we implant harmonious constructive thoughts in our minds, they will bring harmony, happiness and good fortune into our lives. We should cease to dwell on fear, worry, anger, superstition and false beliefs. Replace them with thoughts of courage, love, truth and God's instructions and we can move onward and upward to peace, joy and abundance. Through the power of the mind and the thoughts that we implant there, we can change any discord, tumult, sadness and hardship in our lives to harmony, tranquillity and success.

Great desire and belief are the basic powers that allow you to attain your goals. Conviction must always be deep-seated and believed with all your heart and mind. Half-hearted belief never gets the job done. Sustain a belief whole-heartedly, never giving up, doubting or wavering and your belief and aspiration will be rewarded. The latent powers of the mind are becoming more and more manifest as time goes by and we are coming to understand the workings of the mind and its capabilities.

Thought is simply the process of programming our mind and memory. Both harmful and beneficial mind programming is happening to each of us all the time. It is done by parents, peers, ourselves, the church, television and in many other ways. Mind programming is essentially the lifelong implantation of data in the memory of our conscious mind. Its simplest form is basic learning, both what is good for us and that which is bad for us. Sometimes it is done haphazardly through life's experiences. Much of the time it is done deliberately, in a

As We Think, So Are We   79

structured manner, as in formal schooling or through advertising.

We know that almost all deviant behavior in a society is caused by societal failure to instill proper values, beliefs and behavior patterns in its members. Instilling those beliefs, values and behavioral patterns is nothing but mind programming and it is obvious that we have done, and are doing, a poor job of it in our society. We allow media, television for example, to program the minds of our children with violence, loose sexual morals and bad habits such as smoking, drinking and the consumption of unhealthy foods.

It is no secret that if a child in his formative years is told or perceives that he is not loved, not wanted, perhaps that he is no good and will never amount to anything, he will almost certainly turn out that way. On the other hand, the child who is shown a great deal of love, continually reinforced with the encouragement that he can grow up to be anything he wishes, almost always turns out well and is the achiever. All this, again, demonstrates the phenomenal power and effectiveness of mind programming.

Not too long ago, I viewed a television documentary about mentally handicapped individuals with amazing abilities. A young man in his early twenties was severely mentally handicapped. His mother put a piano in his room, thinking it might provide him some entertainment. One day she heard beautiful piano music coming from his room. To her astonishment, her son was playing the piano. He had never touched the keys of a piano before, yet he was playing like a master. She found he could listen to any musical composition, no matter how long or complicated, then sit down at the piano and play it completely and without error. His mind accepted completely what he had heard and, through its fantastic power and capability, was able to transmit that knowledge to his hands, bringing it to reality on the piano.[2] What a wonderful and magnificent demonstration of the ability and power of the mind!

Thoughts planted in the mind are like seeds planted in the earth. With care and nourishment those seeds grow and bring forth after their kind. They can produce sweet fruits and beautiful flowers, but they can also produce weeds and thorns. Likewise, thoughts planted in your mind, given constant attention, nurtured and affirmed steadily, will bring forth the essence of your being, be it beautiful or ugly.

The thoughts that you establish in your mind and hold with deep conviction in your heart can produce love, goodness, mercy and forgiveness in your actions. But certain kinds of thoughts can also produce hatred, anger, cruelty and vengeance. The scriptures say, "A good man out of the good treasure of the heart brings forth good things; and an evil man out of the evil treasure of the heart brings forth evil things."[3] Whatever we store deep in the memory of the mind, and believe with certainty, is what we will bring to fruition in our lives.

Mankind is capable of both good and evil. We can choose the one we wish to manifest in our behavior by the simple expedient of the thoughts that we fix in our minds. If we put good, positive and godly thoughts in our minds, we will bring forth "good things out of the good treasure of the heart." But should we let our minds dwell on evil, negative and ungodly concepts, we will bring forth "evil things out of the evil treasure of the heart."

Others can plant evil, negative and undesirable thoughts in our minds, but we can choose not to nourish them. By not nourishing them, or by replacing them with good, desirable thoughts, they will die and have no effect on our life. We indeed can exercise complete control of our lives by the power of the mind and the thoughts that we entertain.

Those who constantly dwell on immoral, worldly thoughts are often immoral people who are sunken in depravity and consumed by unrestricted appetites. Their destinies, on earth, are questionable. Those who entertain good, moral, positive and godly thought become molded in a way such that their reward is happiness, success and harmonious living.

You must replace all less-than-godly thoughts that have been implanted in your mind with good, positive and godly thoughts. You must supplant any thoughts of hatred, anger and resentment with notions of love, kindness, patience and contentment. Then will your light shine forth. Harmony and peace between your mind and your soul, between your physical self and your spiritual self will prevail. When you attain that peace and harmony, you will enjoy good health, joy and success. You must always concentrate on those good thoughts. It is the conflict between the less-than-godly convictions of your mind and the basic, natural goodness of your spiritual self that saps your energy and causes illness, unhappiness and failure. Get yourself in sync and your life will improve dramatically.

How can we ensure that we store only good treasure in our hearts? Many of us have tried to do what is good and right, even living according to God's word, but seem to do it only half-heartedly or fail completely. We may even completely accept that God's instructions for living are good and realize we should live by them, only to find that the "spirit is willing but the flesh is weak."

God has told us how we are to do it. He says, "Get yourselves *new* minds and hearts."[4] We are to change what we think with our minds and believe with our hearts. For years you have let all manner of computer hacks have access to your mental computer, programming it with all kinds of negative, harmful thoughts.

You need to take complete control of the programming that enters your mind. Use a code for access--Loving, Good, and

Positive thought. If it's not compatible with that code, it is to be rejected. Use the power of your mind to promote good health, happiness and success in your life. Use your God-given mental power to promote peace and harmony in the world. Use your amazing mind to search for knowledge and truth. Use your mind to create miracles!

Most of us have read about, heard of, or know someone who has experienced a miracle. Some of us have experienced our own. That is, some situation to which there seemed no earthly solution, was eventually brought to a satisfactory conclusion. One of the most frequent involves terminal illness such as cancer. There are those who have had inoperable cancer spreading throughout the body. The doctors have abandoned hope and sent the patient home to die. However, because the patient had absolute, undoubting and unwavering *belief* that he would get better, he was healed. The cell structures within the body were deformed, yet they were returned to normal.

Doctor Gerald G. Jampolsky has written a marvelous book called, TEACH ONLY LOVE. He practices mind/body healing at his Center for Attitudinal Healing in Sausilito, California. He talks about the case of a young woman of 23 who was legally blind. She had a small amount of close vision, but could not function as sighted. As a premature infant, she had been placed in a high-pressure oxygen tank, which resulted in her blindness.

She was active, with the help of her seeing-eye dog, attending college and working at part-time jobs. Having been told, later in life, the cause of her blindness, she felt, as would most people, a certain amount of rage and resentment at the world. She had heard of the Attitudinal Healing Center and became involved with an attitudinal healing group there.

One day she asked Dr. Jampolsky if he thought it was possible for her to regain her eyesight. He told her ***anything*** is possible; the mind knows no boundaries. She began to grasp the idea that the thoughts we put into our minds determine our perceptions. She began to work on positive mental pictures. She began to practice peace of mind, peace of God, unconditional love, forgiveness and listening to her inner voice. Her bitterness began to dissolve and her attitude about herself began to change. Where she had always treated herself as a blind person, she now began to **think** *of herself as normal and whole.*

And the miracle happened; her vision improved so that she was legally sighted during the daytime. She became involved in helping and being of service to others with her new attitude about the holistic approach to health. One day she called Dr. Jampolsky and told him she would like to take him for a drive. He exclaimed, "What do you mean?" She then told him she was licensed to drive and was now sighted for both day and night. Doctor Jampolsky later said it was the happiest time he ever had in a car, even though he cried.

What an extraordinary and wonderful story of love, caring and the miraculous power of the mind. If we can do such things as put cancer into remission by returning deformed cells to normal and restore eyesight by attitudinal healing and the thoughts of our minds, surely we have the power to change and control the behavior of our character. Surely, we have the power to obey God and follow his instructions. Assuredly, we have the ability to manifest the godly qualities of love, goodness, mercy and forgiveness in our lives, and to live in peace and harmony with our fellow human beings and all of creation.

We do all those things by getting ourselves those "new minds and hearts," as God has told us to do. We get them by changing our way of thinking. We do it through the power of the thoughts that we implant in our minds. We do it through the power of love!

To love is the greatest commandment of all. That commandment has been given to all the religions of the world in one way or another. Yet that caring, kind and forgiving love that we are told to show one another is generally not taught in the churches, the schools or our homes. Most unfortunately, we do not teach it to our children, but more often teach them hatred, violence and materialism.

The simple truth is, that mankind can live in harmony with *all* of creation simply by following God's instructions concerning love. Granted, it can be difficult, particularly as we have been conditioned all our lives to believe we cannot live harmoniously. We are continually bombarded with such notions that it is our nature to sin and it is human to err. We are often programmed from cradle to grave to believe we are poor, miserable, inadequate creatures who can't help ourselves. As we think, so we are!

But it is not difficult to follow God's instructions when we change our way of thinking and get ourselves new minds and hearts. We *stop* thinking we are those poor miserable creatures; that it is our basic nature to do wrong and live in discord. We *start* thinking that we are magnificent human beings, created in God's likeness with good qualities and with the ability to live by and keep God's commandment to show love to one another.

Think about it! Isn't it just as easy to love as to hate, to be compassionate rather than being cruel and to forgive instead of bearing resentment and seeking retribution? In fact, it's much easier! And the reward is marvelous! Do you remember the wonderful feeling you enjoyed when you showed love, were kind to, or forgave someone? Try it again and again! Deliberately practice it!

A few years ago, Ann Herbert, of California, saw some graffiti that read, "Random acts of Violence." She decided that kindness was better and coined the phrase, "Random acts of kindness and senseless acts of beauty." It received wide media attention and led to the publication of a book, RANDOM ACTS OF KINDNESS, by Will Glennon. The publishers, Conari Press, held a "random acts of kindness party" where guests told stories of kind deeds that had touched their lives. Will Glennon said, "It was almost magical, the impact it was having on people was extraordinary. People were crying."[5]

Actually Ann, acts of beauty are not senseless, but we know what you mean.

To practice acts of kindness and beauty is a marvelous thing to do. Those who do so understand the *reward* of showing love to others. It makes you, as well as the recipient, feel good and promotes harmony in the world. Difficult as it may seem, we can and should always think love, *kindness*, mercy and forgiveness and practice these qualities in our daily living and actions toward ***all*** others. No exceptions! Let that be your new habit, your new way of life! And when you live like that, think of the effect it has on humanity and the world! God says, "a little leaven leavens the whole loaf." God's wisdom is impeccable!

Through the power of our minds, God has given us the capability to implant righteousness in our hearts and live as he desires us to. He has given us the ability to promote peace and harmony on earth. There is an old Chinese proverb that says:

> *If there is righteousness in the heart, there will be*
> *beauty in the character.*
> *If there is beauty in the character, there will be*
> *harmony in the house.*
> *If there is harmony in the house , there will be*
> *order in the nation.*
> *If there is order in the nation, there will be*
> *peace in the world.*

By the creative effort of thought, we get new minds and hearts, and shape all aspects of our lives. By the effort of thought we create goodness, peace and harmony in our character, our homes, the nation and the world. By the power of our thoughts we live in accordance with God's instructions, creating the way of life that he has always intended for us.

By the power of thought God's will is done on Earth as in Heaven! AS WE THINK, IN OUR HEARTS, SO ARE WE! But before mankind can effectively and permanently achieve these goals we must discard the notion that it is our nature to sin and err.

Chapter Eight

THE NATURE OF MAN

Are we no more than a bag of water and bones; a mortal "assembly of nerve cells and their associated molecules," as some contend? And when that "assembly" disintegrates in death, is that the end? Or is there more to us than just this physical, mortal body? What do we know about the nature of the human consciousness? We usually think of it in terms of the physical body and/or in abstract terms such as awareness, intellect, thought, mind and perhaps soul or our true spiritual self. One near-death experiencer has said, "Know this, that we are not our body." In that we are more than just the body, that is true. However, our true being is mind, body and soul. They are the sum total of our being.

Most of us believe that we *are* both body and soul. We know the physical body dies and have reasonable proof that the soul does not. The scriptures of almost all religions speak of this arrangement. For example, the New Testament of Christianity speaks of the *body* and the *soul.* It says don't fear those who can kill the body but not the soul. Jesus Christ said to the thief on the cross next to him, "Today you shall be with me in paradise."[1] That could only have been possible if their souls separated from their physical bodies which were to die and be buried.

Islamic scripture has many references to the body *and* the soul. "Do not say that those slain in the cause of God are dead. They are alive, but you are not aware of them."[2] The Koran says, "He sends forth guardians who watch over you and carry away your souls without fail when death overtakes you. Then are all men restored to God, their true Lord."[3]

The scriptures of the Eastern religions such as Hinduism, Buddhism and Taoism are replete with references to the soul of man that does not die but lives forever. It is a belief that is almost universal in the Orient. The Bhagavad Gita, epic scripture of the Hindus, speaks of the soul thus: "It is not a thing of which a man may say, 'It hath been, it is about to be, or is to be hereafter, for it is without birth and meeteth not death; it is ancient, constant, and eternal, and is not slain when this its mortal frame is destroyed'....The weapon divideth it not, the fire burneth it not, the water corrupteth it not, the wind drieth it not away; for it is indivisible, inconsumable, incorruptible, and is not to be dried away; it is eternal, universal, permanent, immovable; it is invisible, inconceivable, and unalterable; therefore, knowing it to be thus, thou shouldst not grieve!"[4]

The Tao Te K'ing, written sometime before 500 B.C. by Lao-tze, the founder of Taoism, speaks of the creator of the heavens and the earth and how all the souls that he also created shall live forever: "There is something which existed before Heaven and Earth. Oh how still it is, and formless, standing alone without changing, reaching everywhere without harm. It appears to be everlasting. Its name I know not. To designate it, I call it Tao. How unfathomable is Tao! All things return to it. Not visible to the sight, not audible to the ear, in its use it is inexhaustible.

"Tao produces all things; its Virtue nourishes them; its Nature gives them form; its Force perfects them....It is the beginning of Heaven and Earth....it is the Mother of all things....He who acts in accordance with Tao, becomes one with Tao. Being akin to Heaven, he possesses Tao. Possessed of Tao, *he endures forever.*"[5]

Take note of how the scriptures are in agreement. The New Testament says, "Don't fear those who can kill the body but not the soul." The Bhagavad Gita, in beautiful prose, says of the soul, "It is ancient, constant, and eternal, and is not slain when this its mortal frame is destroyed. The weapon divideth it not, the fire burneth it not, the water corrupteth it not, the wind drieth it not away...for it is eternal." The Koran says the soul is restored to God, and the Tao Te K'ing tells us that all things return to it (Tao/God).

How is it possible for any reasonable person to deny the existence of man's soul, that it never dies but lives forever and is eventually restored to its creator? Surely we must conclude that man's essence consists of both body and soul! And because man's soul is eternal, then it must be acknowledged that we are immortal. Would not a greater awareness of that result in a change of our ways so that we live and act in accordance with what God expects of us?

THE PHYSICAL BODY AND THE CONSCIOUS MIND

What are the characteristics and qualities of these separate, yet intertwined, entities we refer to as body and soul? We know the physical body quite well, but not completely. Through the medical wonder of ultrasound, we observe it almost from conception, monitoring its progress in the womb. We are well acquainted with the birth process, see the child grow to maturity and then watch the body decline into old age. How familiar we are with death; yet still do not understand it and look upon it with fear and even loathing, when we should not.

One obvious capability of the physical body and the conscious mind is the capacity for incredible wickedness. Throughout history predators, autocrats and tyrants such as Stalin and Hitler, as well as others closer to home, have inflicted terrible cruelty on humanity. Look at the carnage in this country from crime, and the violence in the Middle East due primarily to religious differences. Consider the frenzied manslaughter in Rwanda generated by political and racial differences.

Think about what has happened in Bosnia-Herzegovina. The ethnic cleansing of the Bosnian Muslims by the Serbian Christians is a prime example of the hatred and violence brought about because of religion, as well as vengeance for what the Muslims did to their forefathers five or six decades ago. Of course, the Muslims there are not innocent either, perpetrating similar atrocities against the Serbians.

You could ask both the Christian Serbs and Muslims if it isn't better to be kind than cruel. I'm sure they would all agree. The Serbs would say that they believe in Christian values such as forgiveness. The Muslims would agree their religion teaches that they must do good and forgive, so as to achieve paradise. Most would probably agree that it would be foolish to hold someone responsible for something that their great grandparents did sixty years ago.

Yet, there they are, completely ignoring all those things they say they believe in; killing and maiming one another, even the children. Isn't a person a hypocrite if he or she doesn't practice what they believe? They would probably agree with that, too. The problem is that they, like most people, don't understand the power of the mind. They believe in love, kindness and forgiveness, but those kinds of thoughts are held in the mind only fleetingly. The thoughts of anger, hatred and vengeance are *dominant* and therefore control their actions. It is those kinds of mental seeds out of which chaos grows.

In Somalia, men greedy for material wealth and power, systematically withheld available food, starving their fellow human beings to death. During one period, one thousand children were dying every day from starvation in Somalia. Around the world, *hundreds of thousands* of our children are dying every year from the effects of lack of food.

Think of those thousands of homeless children in the streets and sewers of the big cities of Brazil who have to steal from the merchants in an effort to stay alive and then must evade the gunmen whom the merchants hire to hunt them down and *exterminate* them like rats! What monstrous human cruelty and injustice! How can governments allow these things to happen?

How do we explain all the evil that humans inflict on one another? Christian Church dogma says it is the result of the innately sinful nature of man. We have seen how, in the 16th Century, the secular and religious authorities of Europe established the Augsburg Confession, which has declared that "Since the fall of Adam all men who are born according to the course of nature are conceived and born in sin. That is, all men are full of evil lust and inclinations from their mothers' wombs and are unable by nature to have true fear of God and true faith in God. Moreover, this inborn sickness and hereditary sin is truly sin and condemns to the eternal wrath of God all those who are not born again through Baptism and the Holy Spirit."

We have also noted Luther's characterization of humankind that, "there is not one iota of goodness in man, but only evil and darkness exists in the heart of man." This is the basis of much of Christian doctrine; that man is corrupt and depraved, and can do nothing by himself to change that condition. It is only through belief in Jesus Christ as Savior and Redeemer and the power of the Holy Spirit that man can do good.

We have taken note of how the Christian theologians cited the scriptures as justification for the doctrine concerning the depraved nature of man. They began with the story of Noah and the Flood wherein God said he was going to "destroy *all* living things upon the earth, both man, and beast and the creeping thing," because "all flesh had become corrupt....because of the wickedness of man....every imagination of the thoughts of his heart was only evil continually."[6] Can we see the error and contradiction there? If all flesh had *become* corrupt, there had to be a time when it was *not* corrupt.

It could not be that God was talking about all men being corrupt since Adam's Fall in the Garden of Eden, for the book of Genesis says that God had "respect for Abel,"[7] the son of Adam. Certainly God would not respect him if he were corrupt, wicked and evil continually! What of Noah himself, whom the scriptures say, "was perfect in all his generations," and of whom it is said that God "found no fault with Noah?" Also, what of the animals? How was it possible for them to become *wicked* and *corrupt*?

But if all of this is true; if the decree of the Augsburg Confession that all men are full of evil lust and inclinations from their mothers' wombs is factual; if Luther was right and if all the scriptural references to man as abominable, filthy, lascivious and wicked are the literal, infallible word of God, then that explains Hitler, Stalin, Rwanda, Bosnia-Herzegovina, Somalia and all the other carnage that man commits around the world, doesn't it?

But wait! What about all the empirical evidence that supports the ability of man to do good without the benefit of Christian beliefs? If man has only evil and darkness in his heart, as Luther says, is lustful from conception as the Augsburg Confession decrees, and can overcome that condition only through the enabling relationship with Christ, baptism and the power of the Holy Spirit, why is it that non-Christians can live good decent lives? According to Christian doctrine about the nature of man, non-Christians, being evil and corrupt, without having been baptized, without faith in Christ or belief in the Holy Spirit, can live only wicked and immoral lives. There can be no good, decent people other than Christians!

But we know that is utterly false, don't we? Most of us personally know, or know of, a number of non-Christians, such as Muslims, Buddhists and Hindus, or perhaps even atheists who are wonderfully good, kind, worthy and respectable human beings, perhaps more so than many Christians we know.

Even entire non-Christian societies live in the spirit of God's instructions to show love and do good to one another; sometimes much more so than most Christian societies. We all know of the immorality, corruption, violence, killing, child abuse, drug abuse and indifference that is occurring in our country, a nation that counts itself as being 84% Christian.

Why do you suppose that is? Most Christians are not aware of the fact that in Tibet, a nation that is almost 100% non-Christian, kindness, goodness, peaceful demeanor, caring and brotherly love have greatly subdued all of these terrible wrongs.

Although most Buddhists have not been baptized, do not believe in the Holy Ghost and know little or nothing about Christ, many live in accordance with his teachings. They believe in and live by the code of love and forgiveness. They believe in living in peace and harmony. They believe in goodness and kindness toward all others. Their philosophy is: "Hatred does not cease by hatred at any time; hatred ceases by love. Let a man overcome anger by love, let him overcome evil with good. If someone curses you, you must suppress all resentment and make the firm determination that your mind shall not be disturbed, and no angry word shall escape your lips. You will remain friendly and kind, with loving thoughts and no secret spite. If then you are attacked with fists, with stones, with swords, you must still suppress all resentment and preserve a loving mind."[8]

Not only do Buddhists believe these things, most practice and live by them. You may have noticed their credo is remarkably similar to the instructions Christ gave to us: "Love your enemy; do good to them that curse and revile you; don't get angry with your brother; turn the other cheek and love one another." All Christians should ask themselves and their pastors the following question. Given the Christian teaching that all men are evil and corrupt and can only live decent honorable lives through baptism, faith in Christ and belief in the Holy Spirit, how then do the non-Christian Buddhists do so? When you come up with the correct answer, then will you understand the nature of man, comprehending, finally, why Christians can commit atrocities and why non-Christians can do good! You will find that it has nothing to do with the dictates.

What of the preponderance of scriptural evidence that belies Christian doctrine regarding the depraved and innately sinful nature of man? Why were Noah and his sons saved after God had declared that he was going to destroy all men because *all* flesh had become corrupt.

If we examine the scripture with an honest and open mind, the answer is quite clear. Noah found grace in God's eyes because "Noah and his generations were perfect; Noah walked with God." That can only mean that Noah walked in God's ways and his actions were pleasing and acceptable to God. The Good News Bible says in Genesis that, "Noah had *no faults* and was the only good man of his time, he lived in fellowship with God."

Farther along in Genesis, God says to Noah, "I have found that you are the only one in all the world who does what is right." In the King James version of that message, God tells Noah that he "sees *Noah's righteousness*." This does not mean that Noah had never done anything wrong. It means Noah obeyed God and lived in accordance with his instructions. And, if he did fail, he repented, expressed his sorrow for the wrong he had done, turning again to God's ways. Noah was thus considered perfect in God's sight.

The theologians and ministers like to quote Psalm 51:5 to support the doctrine of original innate sin where King David says, "Behold, I was shapen in iniquity; and in sin did my mother conceive me." They took that out of context, just as they did in the matter of Noah. They completely ignore David's following words which belie the doctrine of original sin and total corruption of man.

After David had sinned by coveting Bathsheba, the wife of Uriah, he said to God, by way of penitence, "You desire truth in the inward parts."[9] How could there be truth in the heart if there was total depravity there? David goes on to say, "Purge me with hyssop, and I shall be clean; wash me, and I shall be whiter than snow."[9] He asks God for a *clean heart* and a *right spirit*.

Clearly then, David expected to be pure in heart again. How was that to be accomplished? He couldn't be washed pure as snow by the blood of Christ, as the ministers like to say, because that blood hadn't been shed yet. He couldn't be clean and pure simply by believing in the promise of a savior and shed blood, because David couldn't possibly have understood the cross and Atonement as it is taught by the Christian Church today. The only possible way would for David to be "clean" again would be to have a change of heart, turn from his sin, return to God's ways and obey God. David even says that he will then "teach transgressors God's ways, and *they will be converted.*"[9]

In saying that man is totally corrupt, the Church dismisses, even denies Jesus Christ when he says "Blessed are the pure in heart."[10] They explain those words of Christ by saying we are pure in heart when we believe in and accept the crucified Christ as our savior. But that is not a valid premise, for according to Christian dogma, Christians are still innately sinful even *after* acceptance of Christ; there is still sin in their hearts. But Christ says there *are* those who are pure in heart. Where there is purity of heart there can be no sin and certainly not depravity or corruption.

The empirical and scriptural evidence that man has the ability, of his own volition, to do good as well as evil, is overwhelming. From life's experiences, we know that we are capable of extraordinary goodness. Witness the many who have dedicated their lives to helping others. Look how people respond automatically in times of crisis, particularly when another person's life is in jeopardy. In times of natural disaster, wide concern is shown for the welfare of those involved through an outpouring of support in the way of money, food, clothing, medical supplies and prayer. Man is even willing to give up his own life that others might live--his sacrifice not being guided by his religious persuasion. .

It is clear that man's wickedness is not innate, but rather learned. The Church acknowledges that sin is *willful* disobedience to God. It is not possible for a new-born child to be *willfully* disobedient to God! To say that newborn babes or little children are lustful, wicked and depraved is ludicrous. The Christian doctrine of "original sin" is badly flawed. The Church teaches that Adam disobeyed God in the Garden of Eden, and as a result of that "sin," Adam caused mankind's great "fall" from God's grace. Because Adam sinned, we as descendants are all sinful from the moment of our conception. Not one of all mankind is righteous. We can only be rescued from that fallen-from-grace condition by God's punishment of Christ for our disobedience. St. Paul claimed that "through one man, Adam, *all* men have fallen from God's grace and are damned to hell by God; and *only* through one man, Jesus Christ, are all men saved from God's wrath and condemnation."[11] That philosophy is not only errant but quite bizarre!

This means that all people who lived and died before Christ appeared as a savior were not rescued from their fallen-from-grace condition. They died in their sinful state and are all damned to hell and eternal punishment by God. Are we to believe that our wonderful, loving God condemns his people to eternal hellfire by reason of ignorance of Christ? That cannot be. God certainly wants us to do what is right and good, but he doesn't condemn us to hell and eternal punishment if we fail. Throughout the scriptures, through all the prophets and in the Gospel, through Christ, God continually told the people to cease their wrongdoing, obey him, do what is right and good, and they would become righteous and live in his good graces *again*.

All the prophets were counted as righteous by God. In Genesis, we saw that Noah was righteous and God found no fault with him. There are numerous references throughout the

Old Testament to those who were righteous with God--Abraham, Moses, Elijah and David, to name a few. The New Testament speaks of *many* a righteous man who longed to see the time of Christ. To declare that *all* men have fallen from God's grace and that *none* is righteous even contradicts Christ himself who spoke of the "righteous" and the "pure in heart" and who said that he didn't "come to save the righteous but the sinners."[12]

Think further about that notion of original sin. According to Christian teaching, God told Adam and Eve they could eat the fruit of all trees in the garden except from one specific tree in the center of the garden. Came the devil in the guise of a snake, carried on a conversation with Eve and convinced her it was okay to eat the fruit that God had forbidden. She partook and gave it to Adam as well. Now God had created Adam and Eve in perfection, but the instant they ate the fruit, they lost that perfection, and sin became innate in their character. Then all descendants of Adam and Eve were born in that imperfection with *their* character sinful and unclean.

Let's analyze what supposedly occurred in the Garden of Eden. God had created man and woman in perfection and placed them in a garden of paradise. He wanted them to remain perfect. Yet, knowing that his creation was subject to temptation, he planted a tree in the garden whose fruit, when consumed, would instantly turn his creation into an imperfect being. Most of us would have left that tree with its debilitating fruit out of the garden. It's strange that God didn't think of that.

But let's go on with this myth. Then God, who is omnipotent and could have barred the devil from the garden, made another mistake and allowed the devil access to paradise. Perhaps he forgot, or didn't recognize, the devil in that disguise as a snake. Then there is the miracle of a snake that could talk, even though it didn't have the physiological features required to form speech. What about those amazing magical properties of the fruit that, once eaten, could turn a perfect, sinless human being into an innately sinful being?

To top it all off we find that God was negligent and uncaring. Being as powerful as he is, it would have been a simple matter to reverse man's imperfection and start over, rectifying his mistakes with the poisonous fruit and allowing the devil to accost Eve. But he didn't, and thus let the process of "original sin" proceed so that all of humanity would sin, requiring him to damn them all to hell and eternal punishment until he came up with some plan of redemption.

Surely, anyone can see how foolish the concept of original sin is! It demeans God, depicting him as a bumbling, inefficient, even cruel creator. Of course God is none of those things, as we all would agree. Whether metaphorical or reality, the Garden of Eden and the Christian interpretation of the events that transpired there, when seriously analyzed, raise questions about the validity of that Christian doctrine. As God is perfect and could not possibly concoct such a flawed plan, we can only conclude that the Christian teaching of what happened in the Garden of Eden, as well as the concept of original sin, is errant and that man is not innately sinful. It is most likely that the Garden of Eden and the events that happened there were simply a story of disobedience to God, an exercise of free will by man to choose either obedience or disobedience.

Adam was created in perfection, but had the free will to choose obedience or disobedience. He chose to disobey God's instructions not to eat of the fruit of that specific tree. We are all created in perfection without the knowledge of sin, but when we are old enough to *understand* the difference between right and wrong, we have the free will to choose just as Adam did.

To believe and teach that God created us in the learned image of Adam is to desecrate God's creation--man! It is a denial of God's wisdom and omnipotence. Besides, we all know learned characteristics cannot be inherited. God *does not* create imperfection! We are created *without sin;* born in perfection, pure and innocent as little children. Later we *learn* to sin. Through our own conscious thoughts and subsequent actions we have made ourselves imperfect.

Through that same power of mind and thought we can reverse that imperfection and choose to do what is right and good, thereby becoming, once again, righteous with God. This is what God means when he said to get ourselves new minds and hearts; turn from our wrongdoing, do what is lawful and right, and then we shall be right with him. It is called repentance. This is what Christ meant when he said we must be born again and become as little children. Not childish but childlike, pure and innocent. And we don't have to worry if we should fail again, for God will forgive us if we forgive others, showing love and mercy to one another. That is the gospel of Jesus Christ.

The nature of our physical self, our conscious being, is quite clear. We are not the inconsistent, inadequate, poor miserable sinner who is, by nature, sinful and unclean, and unable to do anything by himself to change that condition. We are not rotten and depraved, with only evil and darkness in our hearts. Our physical self is capable of both good and evil, with the power to choose to manifest the good and avoid or suppress any tendency to do evil.

There is a very interesting dialogue in John Steinbeck's EAST OF EDEN where Steinbeck, in his inimitable way, reflects on man's abilities when it comes to doing what is right and wrong. Lee, Adam's Chinese servant, was engaged in a conversation with Adam and Samuel, telling them about his study of the Old Testament in a group that included some elderly Chinese gentlemen and a rabbi:

"After two years we felt that we could approach your sixteen verses of the fourth chapter of Genesis. My old gentlemen felt that these words were very important too--'Thou shalt' and 'Do thou.' And this was the gold from our mining: '*Thou mayest*.' 'Thou mayest rule over sin.'

Samuel said, "It's a fantastic story. And I've tried to follow and maybe I've missed somewhere. Why is this word so important?"

Lee's hand shook as he filled the delicate cups. He drank his down in one gulp. "Don't you see?" he cried. "The American Standard translation *orders* men to triumph over sin, and you can call sin ignorance. The King James translation makes a promise in 'Thou shalt,' meaning that men will surely triumph over sin. But the Hebrew word, the word *timshel*-- 'Thou mayest'--that gives a choice. It might be the most important word in the world. That says the way is open. That throws it right back on a man. For if 'Thou mayest'--it is also true that 'Thou mayest not.' Don't you see?"

"Yes I see. I do see. But you do not believe this is divine law. Why do you feel its importance?"

"Ah!" said Lee. "I've wanted to tell you this for a long time. I even anticipated your questions and I am well prepared. Any writing which has influenced the thinking and the lives of innumerable people is important. Now, there are many millions in their sects and churches who feel the order, 'Do thou,' and throw their weight into obedience. And there are millions more who feel predestination in 'Thou shalt.' Nothing they may do can interfere with what will be. But 'Thou mayest'! Why, that makes a man great, that gives him stature with the gods, for in his weakness and his filth and his murder of his brother he has still the great choice. He can choose his course and fight it through and win." Lee's voice was a chant of triumph.

Adams said, "Do you believe that, Lee?"

"Yes, I do. Yes, I do. It is easy out of laziness, out of weakness, to throw oneself into the lap of deity, saying, 'I couldn't help it; the way was set.' But think of the glory of the choice! That makes a man a man. A cat has no choice, a bee must make honey. There's no godliness there. And do you know, those old gentlemen who were sliding down to death are too interested to die now?"

Adam said, "Do you mean these Chinese men believe the Old Testament?"

Lee said, "These old men believe a true story, and they know a true story when they hear it. They are critics of truth. They know that these sixteen verses are a history of humankind in any age or culture or race. They do not believe a man writes fifteen and three-quarter verses of truth and tells a lie with one verb. Confucius tells men how they should live to have good and successful lives. But this--this is a ladder to climb to the stars." Lee's eyes shone. "You can never lose that. It cuts the feet from under weakness and cowardliness and laziness."

Adam said, "I don't see how you could cook and raise the boys and take care of me and still do all this."

"Neither do I," said Lee. "But I take my two pipes in the afternoon, no more and no less, like the elders. And I feel that I am a man. And I feel that a man is a very important thing-- maybe more important than a star. This is not theology. I have no bent toward gods. But I have a new love for that glittering instrument, the human soul. It is a lovely and unique thing in the universe. It is always attacked and never destroyed-- because 'Thou mayest.'"

We can indeed consciously choose our course, making the decision to do what is right and good, rather than that which is wrong and evil. When we do so, cooperating with the perfect uniqueness of our soul, then all possibilities are opened to us.

THE SOUL OR THE SUBCONSCIOUS

What of our other half, our spiritual self, our soul, that which the "sword cannot cleave and which neither fire nor water nor wind can destroy, but which is eternal, unalterable and incorruptible?" What is its nature? What is its relationship to our physical self? What is its purpose? When do we acquire it? We have concluded, and most people believe, that, in some manner, it emanates from God. We have a preponderance of evidence from all the scriptures of the world that it does not die, but survives the death of our physical body and at that time, in some manner, returns to God.

As it emanates from God and is universal, *unalterable* and *incorruptible*, as the scriptures say, then it must have God's characteristic of perfection, to include love, compassion, forgiveness and perhaps omniscience.

When the soul separates from the body at the time of the body's death, it appears to retain all the memories, intelligence and experiences of the physical body and mind. During the near-death experience, those who undergo this phenomenon, find themselves out of their physical body usually looking down at it or going through a tunnel and/or arriving in some ethereal heavenly place. At all these times they are aware of every aspect of themselves and their past life, with the exception that they have a new and different type of body. It may be that, at the time of death of our physical body, the mind--that intelligent field of energy that we create--merges with the soul--the field of energy given from God--to form our new spiritual self.

We can then reasonably conclude that the soul, being intertwined in some way with the body and mind, has undergone and taken on all the experiences and development of the physical body and mind. But that does not mean that it has become changed or corrupted by any wrongdoing or bad things that the physical self has chosen to do. It remains *unalterable* and *incorruptible* as scripture tells us.

The soul does have very important and vital functions. As scripture says, the soul is invisible and, as such, is spirit. And as spirit, it is of God. The scripture says, only the spirit gives life. When the soul leaves the body, the body dies. Therefore, it is our soul, which flows out from God, in the form of spirit, that gives us life.

We humans are co-creators with God. Man and woman provide the sperm and egg that are the beginning of a human being. God imbues it with a soul that gives it life and guides its growth. Woman nourishes it. Medical science understands the process of conception and the formation of a fetus. But they don't have the slightest clue as to *what* makes that embryo grow from a fertilized egg into the incredibly complex human body. They generally accept that DNA is the blueprint, the memory that is responsible for *how* it grows, but still cannot explain the force that causes the cells to divide and form into organs, limbs, blood vessels and the massive network of nerves that constitute the human form.

There has to be an intelligence that does that. That intelligence is God, Brahma, Allah, Tao, the Supreme One, the primordial Being or however we wish to designate the Creator. It is God within us in the form of an intelligent field of energy called our soul, inner self, the Atman, or often thought of as the subconscious. As the Tao Te K'ing says, "God produces all things, he gives them *form*, he *perfects* them. Each human body has its own soul which gives it life and guides its growth." So it is with the fetus. The mind of the mother does not know how to *form* and *perfect* the human creature that is growing within her. Nor would it be reasonable or logical to believe that the mother's soul guides the growth of the fetus until the first trimester or until birth, at which time the mother's soul leaves the fetus and God imbues it with its own soul. Surely, the fetus has its own soul which guides its development from the moment of conception. But it is likely that the fetus is not aware--it has not yet developed a ***conscious*** mind.

In addition to giving the physical body life, the soul has other functions that are indispensable to our total being. Not only does it direct fetal growth, but growth after birth to maturity. Usually through the mechanism of the brain, the soul controls the heart rate, breathing, hunger, thirst, sleep, wakefulness, sexual drive, functions of the liver, kidneys and all other organs, as well as the entire nervous system. It regulates blood pressure, blood-vessel dilation and constriction, all senses, chemical balance and metabolism.

The human body is an astounding machine without equal. We are indeed magnificent beings. We simply take our bodies and abilities for granted, not realizing how wondrous they really are. The construction of the human body and how it functions is marvelous. It is made up of trillions of cells, which are continually replaced by new ones. Scientists know that we are constantly renewing our cells, thereby creating new bodies. As we breathe we take in atoms that combine with the food we eat and the water we drink, forming new cells in every part of our body. We are constantly being renewed.

Another marvelous facet of our being is the mind. It has generally been misunderstood; where it is located and what it consists of. It is usually associated with the brain, and thought of as originating there. It is considered one entity, yet with two distinct capacities, the conscious mind and the subconscious or unconscious mind. It has been estimated that the conscious mind comprises about twelve percent of the mind, with the subconscious mind making up the remaining eighty eight percent. How anyone could determine such a statistic is a mystery. It has been thought that the subconscious mind is the storehouse of everything we have ever learned and is the part of our mind that controls our behavior. Although it is almost surely associated with the brain, it is not likely that the rest of the above is true.

We cannot know, for sure. However, through modern research, quantum physics and logic, we can draw some reasonable conclusions about the mind. It is believed that the mind is not confined to the brain, but can affect the cells of the body. Our body is a thinking body; all cells having thought receptors and being cognizant of what is introduced into the body both by thought and by physical or chemical means. Scientists know that there are receptors on all cells that receive messages from the thought process. When we *think* we cause chemical reactions.

For example, when we entertain the thought of danger, certain cells in the body immediately spring into action and produce adrenaline, which increases the speed and force of the heartbeat and thereby our ability to react more quickly and forcibly to the danger. Adrenaline dilates the airways to improve breathing and narrows blood vessels in the skin and intestine so that an increased flow of blood reaches the muscles, allowing them to cope with the demands of strenuous use.

This is one of the many wondrous functions of the body that the Creator has designed in order to help ensure our survival. That particular function of producing adrenaline is one in which we participate with our conscious mind. There are others that are automatic and of which we are unaware. The body has numerous mechanisms to measure bodily activities such as blood pressure, temperature and changes in chemical composition, brought about, for example, by the ingestion of food. If the body becomes hot, adjustments are automatically made in blood vessels and skin to provide cooling. If cold, the blood vessels contract in order to preserve heat.

Other protective functions of the body involve the ability of the red and white blood cells. If the intake of oxygen is impeded by loss of blood during injury, or because of lung disease or perhaps due to an ascent to high altitude, the brain, having received a signal from the affected areas that something is amiss, immediately notifies the bone marrow to go into action. The marrow, which is responsible for production of the red blood cells, rapidly increases output in order to boost the number of oxygen-carrying cells in the blood. The normal blood cell count is about 5 million per cubic millimeter. In the situation of ascent to high altitudes, the blood cell count, after a relatively short stay, can be as high as 10 million per cubic millimeter.

In the event of injury, the cells at the site of the injury literally send out a call for help by releasing substances which send signals to other parts of the body. The blood vessels expand, allowing a greater flow of blood to the injured area to increase the amount of clotting agent at the site, while at the same time constricting the blood vessels in the immediate vicinity of the severed flesh in order to assist in the clotting efforts. White blood cells, present everywhere in the body, are called to the injured area and, aided by the increased flow of blood to the area, increase their number to more effectively fight any intruders such as bacteria that cause infection; as well, they clean up the fragments of damaged cells by literally engulfing them.

Obviously an intelligence exists within us that is carrying out all these automatic activities without our cognizance. It certainly isn't our conscious mind, for then we would be aware. When we sleep, or should we be in a coma, our conscious mind is not functioning, still involuntary actions such as heartbeat, breathing and functioning of the organs continue unabated. When the soul leaves the body at the time of our "death," all of these automatic functions cease. We can conclude then that it is the subconscious or soul that is the intelligence, the force that is responsible for sustaining our life.

The conscious mind is generated by the physical self. As our bodies grow and expand from birth so it is with the mind. Clearly the newborn infant does little if any thinking or reasoning, obviously because the conscious mind is undeveloped. The babe survives, compliments of the soul, which keeps the body functioning. An example would be the instinct to cry when it is hungry or, perhaps, ill. As the child grows, the mind develops by experience and learning. It stores knowledge in the memory of the conscious mind.

It has been thought that the subconscious mind is the storehouse of everything we have learned, but it is not. All of life's experiences are stored in the memory, a function of the conscious mind. We experienced them with the conscious mind and recall them with the conscious mind. Neither is it the subconscious mind that controls our behavior, as is popularly thought. It is our memories and the thoughts of our conscious mind that determine our actions. Nor can we program the subconscious, through hypnosis, so as to change our behavior. The subconscious or soul never changes but is *unalterable* and *incorruptible*, as the scriptures tell us. It is the *conscious mind* that we program through experience, repetition and memory. When we program it with new experiences or new thoughts, when we change our perceptions, and when we suppress old memories with new ones, then changes in behavior occur.

We have only one mind, the conscious mind. It is an intelligent field of energy that *we* create, just as the soul is a field of energy that God has created. After all, we are made in God's image; he creates, and we create. We create such things as offspring, music, literature, concepts, neuro-peptides, mind and thought. Our mind is most likely seated in or associated with the brain, developing from childhood as the brain grows, absorbing learning and experience through all our senses which are connected to and coordinated through the brain. When we receive a blow to the head that renders us *unconscious*, the effect of the blow on the brain causes the mind to dysfunction. A lack of oxygen to the brain can also result in the loss of consciousness. These are reasonable indications of the association of the conscious mind with the brain.

There is indeed a mind-like intelligence that is in every cell of the body. But it is not the mind, either conscious or subconscious. It is our soul, a separate entity, given from God, indestructible, that gives life, forming and perfecting the body, sustaining it through the constant production of new cells. It is the dynamism behind all these involuntary actions such as heartbeat, breathing and other organ functions. It is the life force that knows how to heal.

Although the soul may influence us by means of its intuitive characteristics, what we call "heart," it cannot dominate our physical self but is generally subordinate to the mind. It cannot override the decisions we make with the mind, such as to do wrong. That is the free will that God has given us. Yet, the soul is the master in controlling the vital functions of the body. Although we can vary our breathing and heart beat, with thoughts of the mind, we cannot cause them to cease.

The mind and the soul are two separate entities that possess and control our bodies. The soul is the constant always working toward our good. The mind is the variable that causes difficulties in our lives, such as illness and lack of well-being. When we get our mind in sync with our soul, then we can enjoy good health and even bliss. In the chapter on health, healing and medicine we will examine how the mind, working with the soul, can produce perfect health and bring about miracle cures.

With our total being we are capable of amazing things. We can accomplish incredible good or great evil. We can make our lives a complete joy or a veritable hell. Humankind can destroy the earth or make it a paradise. How we perceive our nature and think with the mind determines which it will be.

There has been a great deal of reference to God so far in this text, and even though 90% of the people on earth believe in God or some supreme spiritual being, there is no scientific proof that such a being exists. Is there really a God? Is there any evidence of his existence?

Chapter Nine

DOES GOD REALLY EXIST?

At one time or another we all have looked up into the night sky and gazed upon the vastness and majesty of the universe--perhaps pondering the magnificence of it all; perhaps to wonder how many stars there really are. We may have entertained thoughts of the coming morning light, or mulled the concept of night and day.

When we think of this home planet we call Earth and how it rotates on its axis causing night and day, do we really understand the tremendous significance of it? If the Earth did not rotate, one side would be in continuous darkness while the other would always be light, making much of the world uninhabitable. Climates suitable for life would be mainly along the fringes between light and dark.

What makes the Earth continue to rotate at a constant speed without slowing down? Scientists recognize no such thing as perpetual motion. Even if we accept that it was sent spinning into space as the result of some big bang, and even that it is spinning in the giant vacuum of space, it has an atmosphere that causes friction, which would tend to slow the speed of rotation over time. Further, the earth is not a perfect sphere but is irregular, with high mountains and deep valleys and fissures that would result in a wobbling effect, also causing a slowing of the rotation. Obviously some unknown force maintains the constant speed of rotation.

Isn't it amazing that, as we rush through space rotating around that axis at over one thousand miles per hour, we have force and gravity must surely give you cause to wonder. And what about gravity? We know it exists and what its properties are, such as its force being relative to mass and density, but man cannot create gravity, and the scientists don't have the faintest idea as to the force that causes it.

More remarkable still is the fact that we are hurtling through space in an orbit around the sun, covering 583 million miles each year at a speed of 67,000 miles per hour! Isn't it incredible that the Earth is situated at just the right distance from the sun creating temperatures and climates suitable to life? Consider the fact that the Earth is tilted on its axis just enough to give us seasons, without which our planet would become vastly different and virtually unrecognizable?

Have you really given serious thought to how this inconceivably ordered universe came to be in the first place? Did it just evolve over billions of years, or was it created? Some say it has always existed and, through evolution, has changed and continues to change over millions of years. Others say it came into existence by chance or accident. Some explain it away with the "Big Bang" theory: "In the beginning, there was not time, no matter, not even space. Then, in some unfathomable way, a universe emerged from a dimensionless point of energy. In the wild first second, the hot, nascent universe inflated to the size of our solar system. At three minutes, the expanding universe became a fusion bomb, synthesizing hydrogen, helium and lithium nuclei from a hot, dense soup of elementary particles."[1]

But these theories raise questions and provide no reasonable answers. Where did the materials, those "elementary particles," come from in the first place? You can't make something out of nothing. What caused that original Big Bang explosion? There was no lightning, no spark. Where did the energy come from? How did that hot, dense soup of elementary particles and the hydrogen, helium and lithium nuclei form into the massive bodies we know as stars and planets, each with its complex composition of gasses, liquids and solids? How did they come to be arranged in those orderly solar systems and galaxies?

Given modern scientific standards, the scientists don't have a single clue as to the "unfathomable way" or the origin of the "dimensionless point of pure energy" that, they say, caused the universe to emerge.

Even if we accepted such ideas, how do they explain the universal laws of science that hold everything, from the stars to earthly microscopic organisms, in wonderful order and harmony? Explosive creation from nothing and evolution by chance would dictate a universe in disarray and a discombobulation of natural law, resulting in disorder and discord everywhere. When we consider the indescribable magnificence and order of the universe, the marvel of the Earth's rotation, gravity, the Earth's orbit, the changing of seasons and all that these things mean to our very existence, does it really seem reasonable to believe that the universe came into being and evolved by accident or chance?

If we say, "probably not", then was the universe created? And how and by whom? Although it cannot be proved by mathematical calculation or scientific explanation, the evidence of creation is very convincing. To the scientist as well as the layman, the beauty, wonder and order of the universe seem to indicate a grand design planned by some great architect.

It seems as if there has to be a purpose for everything. Nothing is left to chance. All things are meticulously ordered and intricate in design. We continue to discover how beautifully and mysteriously all things are made, from the magnificent stars to the tiny atom. Scientific laws are universal, controlling and holding together everything in the heavens and on Earth. It not only seems reasonable in our minds, but feels right in our hearts to believe that all things were created by some guiding hand, according to plan.

Consider this marvelous Earth. Where did the oceans come from? What is the unending source of all of that life-giving water which, through the mechanics of evaporation, clouds and winds brings rain to the land on which we grow our food? Did it self-generate from a small puddle? Did all that water appear by accident? Is it just a remarkable coincidence that there is a moon in orbit around the Earth, whose gravitational pull helps create the cleansing tides, without which our ocean shores would be polluted, unattractive and perhaps even uninhabitable?

Think of the amazing symbiotic relationship between plant and animal life. Plants use the carbon dioxide that we exhale and in return help produce oxygen that is essential to sustain all animal life, including the human animal!

Again, is it reasonable to believe that this wonderful congruity and the extraordinarily complex forms of life on earth simply shook out of a dice cup at random? And what of the most complex life form of all--Man? Did we truly evolve from an amoebae to a multi-celled creature to a fish to a lizard to a four-legged land animal to a two-legged, upright mammal to an ape and to man in his present form?

Without needing to go into detail about Charles Darwin's Origin of the Species, we can say that modern scientists now agree that evolution through natural selection and mutation--the basis of Darwin's theory--is not compatible with evolutionary theories about the earth's beginning. In recent years, the great advancement in knowledge of genes and DNA has caused scientists to estimate it would take about forty billion years for man just to evolve from an ape under the principles of Darwin's theory. And that is many times the Earth's age of 4.5 billion years, as calculated by scientists through carbon dating. So, one part of the evolution theory contradicts another, casting considerable doubt on its credibility.

Further, if we did evolve as Darwin thought, where did the original cell come from? Evolutionists generally say it started from organic molecular materials such as dirt, water, carbon dioxide and perhaps other chemicals. Then through some unknown chemical reaction, caused by sunlight or perhaps lightning (a spark) acting on those chemical components, a molecule was given life.

It is interesting to note that scientists in their modern laboratories under ideal conditions have been trying for years to make life out of organic material and have not succeeded. Even if it were possible to create life from non-living organic material, are we then to believe that a single molecule evolved over billions of years into the incredibly complex form we call the human body?

Let's consider the human body for a moment, particularly the brain, the most complex biological structure known to exist. Among other things, it consists of twelve billion or so neurons or nerve cells, making it a biological computer of awesome capability. Scientists consider it so highly efficient, organized and complicated in design that the latest generation super computers pale by comparison.

Man is unique, and unlike any other living creature. Man is capable of thought, reason, rational choice, love and compassion. Man has a conscience and knows the difference between right and wrong. We possess that ineffable something called "soul." Although the lesser animals possess some of these characteristics, man is the only one who has the capability to develop these traits to the level that allows him to determine his own destiny. Does it seem reasonable that these human characteristics such as soul, conscience, thought and love were produced in the process of evolution?

Evolution cannot be disproved, but neither is there proof that man evolved from an amoeba. The creation and evolution are not necessarily irreconcilable. In reality, it isn't important whether we were made in the process of evolution or created full blown in the form of Adam and Eve. It is only of consequence to those who want to prove their creation beliefs. How we deal with our existence as humans is the real issue. However, as time goes by and man's knowledge increases, in the area of genetics, for example, the evidence does seem to dictate that Darwin and other evolutionists got it wrong about humankind!

If they are wrong, then how did the universe and mankind come into being? When we look upon the splendor and majesty of the universe, the earth's amazingly complex life forms and how they are bound together by order and harmony, it seems logical that such a grand design had to be intentionally created. And if deliberately created, then there must be a creator--a creator whom most of us think of as God.

Most people believe there is a God. Surveys have shown that about 90% of the world's population believe in God, or a supreme being. Some believe through faith, some because it seems reasonable, and some, perhaps, for both reasons. Simple probability demands that the remarkable arrangement of the universe and the awesome complexity of the human body couldn't have occurred by chance in the process of evolution. Our reason and faith tell us that divine order was divinely created.

Faith is believing without seeing. None of us, except perhaps those who have had the near-death experience, has seen God, nevertheless, we believe he exists. We reason with our mind, but some beliefs seem to be instinctive or intuitive. When we see the wonder of a newborn baby, the beauty of a flower, the unsurpassed splendor of the heavens, the power of a storm or mighty ocean waves crashing to the shore, our intuition tells us there must be some supreme being who created all these things. We must almost instinctively acknowledge that somewhere there is something, much greater and more powerful than man, more certain than random chance!

IS THERE A RECORD?

Is there evidence other than the marvelous creation we see with our eyes or what we intuitively feel? Is there perhaps a written record about God and creation? The answer, of course, is yes! We generally call it scripture, any writing or book of a sacred or holy nature. We have the Bible, which includes the Torah, Old Testament and New Testament. There is the Koran, the Bhagavad Gita, The Tibetan Book of the Dead, The Tao Te K'ing, The Naj Hamadi, the Dead Sea Scrolls and other scriptures, some very ancient. They speak to such subjects as God, creation, life, death, heaven, hell, paradise and salvation.

But are they a reliable record? What is their authority? Aren't they just other books about ancient history? Isn't much of scripture just myth? Scripture most certainly includes history and, likely, myth as well. It also undoubtedly contains the word of God. It is up to us humans to use our minds and common sense to decide which is which. Let's examine the scripture called the Bible. Doesn't it contain stories that couldn't possibly be true, such as Jonah's spending three days in the belly of the whale, then being cast out on the beach, alive and well? Surely the whale's digestive juices would have caused great harm, if not death, to Jonah.

What of Noah and the Ark? The ark was to be 300 cubits (about 450 feet) in length, 75 feet wide and 45 feet high. It doesn't seem likely that Noah and his sons had either the shipbuilding expertise, manpower or time to construct such a vessel, specially one that required special compartmentalization and ramps in a three-story structure, needed to adequately house two of every known species of life. Think of the great animals such as the mastodon, rhinoceros, hippopotamus, water buffalo, polar bear and moose. What of the multitude of other smaller animals and kind within species, such as all the different kinds of snakes? What of the ostrich and all other birds, as well as the insects? It would have been absolutely impossible to house two of every species in such a small configuration as the ark.

What about the matter of food and water for the animals? They were to be in the ark for a very long period of time. Scriptures say Noah, his family and the animals were in the ark for seven days before it started to rain. Then it rained for forty days. After the rain stopped, the "waters prevailed upon the earth for an hundred and fifty days." It took another three months for the waters to recede and another two weeks for Noah to determine that the waters had abated from off the earth.

That would make it about 300 days that they were confined in the ark. That would require a tremendous amount of food. Some of it would have to have been harvested from the animal's original locales. There would have been the need for a large supply of extra animals as meat for the carnivores. Noah would have had to store large amounts of water, as the ark had but one window and one door, which were to be sealed during the deluge, making it impossible to get their drinking water from that source. How did he dispose of the enormous amount of animal waste that would have been created?

Then there are the logistics of gathering the animals from around the world. For example, how did Noah get the Siberian tiger and the polar bear from the far northern regions, the penguin from Antarctica and the ostrich from Australia? How did he determine that he had both a male and female of all the birds and insects?

Where did all that rain come from? God could certainly create more water from his endless source of energy. But he already had established the natural laws of evaporation from the seas and condensation upon the land that brings the rain. As he is immutable, and would not change those laws, it would have been impossible for it to rain enough to cover the earth to a level above the mountains. Continuous rainfall simply would recycle the water from the seas to the land to return again to the sea, never significantly altering the level of the seas. Even if God did decide to change those natural laws, rain would have had to fall at a rate of about 700 feet (not inches) per day to cover the highest mountain! Such a prolonged deluge surely would have pounded and destroyed the ark. How could all that water recede in three months and where did it recede to?

Even if we were to grant that many of the great animals, such as the dinosaurs and mastodons, already had become extinct and God assisted Noah by miraculously transporting the animals from all over the world to Noah's location in the Middle East, and simply created all that water as he created the universe, the logistical impossibility of the rest of the operation, renders the story of Noah and the Ark nothing more than myth.

Further, it is unlikely that our wonderfully compassionate, perfect-in-justice God would destroy all of mankind, except for Noah and his family, in such a terrible manner, or in any way at all. Scripture says God did it because the world was full of corruption and violence, except for Noah and his family. But what of the babies and little children? How can a newborn baby be corrupt and *violent*? It would certainly be unjust for God to destroy them, especially as he says in other parts of the scripture that he places great value on the little children and they are not to be harmed.

Despite these stories and other inaccuracies, the Bible does have credibility. We know it is the biggest selling book in history. It has been accepted by hundreds of millions of people as containing God's word. Despite man's intrusive interference, the Bible's central message remains intact and absolutely trustworthy. It provides us with God's word that shows us how we are to live in this life so as to be right with God and achieve eternal life. Rulers have tried to destroy the Bible. Nations have burned it. Governments have declared it illegal, still it persists. The truths of the Bible are as timeless as they are marvelous. Consider just the one saying, "Do unto others as you would have them do unto you."[2] Think of the tremendous impact of that precept if we obeyed God and lived according to it. What a wonderful world this would be!

Intuitive belief, as well as the logic of our mind, tells us that murder, lying, rape and robbery are wrong and that love, kindness and truth are right. That same intuition and reason tells us which words of the Bible are from God and which are of men. We instinctively know that greed, vengeance, killing of people for their land and smashing babies against the rocks are *not* God's ways, but those of man. We know that showing love, goodness, kindness, caring, compassion and forgiveness to one another, as instructed by the Bible, *are* truths.

That the effects of living by those truths are good cannot be denied. That message of the Bible can be relied upon implicitly. The Bible does have reliability, authority and credibility. For the reasonable person, it confirms the existence of God. So it is with the other scriptures of the world.

THE NEAR-DEATH EXPERIENCE

We need to examine one more area that provides us with reasonable evidence of God's existence. Although it has existed for centuries, it is only in the last two decades that its study has come to prominence. It is the phenomenon of the "near-death experience."

It is a happening that has provided a great deal of controversy. Extensive research by medical and psychological investigators has resulted in both supporters and critics of the purported encounter with death, an after-life and God. I was among the skeptics. Emotionally, I would have liked to embrace the message of the "experiencers," for who would not want to have "first-hand" evidence of the existence of God and the certainty of an after-life. But intellectually, I had my doubts about people returning from the dead, having met God and experiencing the "ecstatic" joy of dying.

Yet, the idea of it all was highly intriguing, and so I pursued it. After about a two-year period of research--reading all the NDE (near-death experience) literature, attending seminars and talking personally to experiencers--I became convinced of the validity of these encounters.

The experiencers believe in the *reality* of what occurred to them. They refute completely any other explanation such as hallucination, dreaming, fantasy, influence of drugs, medication, oxygen deprivation, extra-sensory perception, and the like. More and more medical people, who in the past have tended to ignore or disbelieve these stories, are now coming to believe that these happenings are actuality rather than otherwise. Almost anyone who talks to a true experiencer cannot but believe in the validity of what happened to that person.

Researchers found physicians and psychiatrists who, having experienced an NDE, attest to the actuality of the happening. These people are trained and capable of distinguishing dream, fantasy or hallucination from reality. Doctor Melvin Morse, M.D., pediatrician and NDE investigator, and his research team, proved that a person actually needs to die or be near death to have a near-death experience. This finding silenced many skeptics who had said that these events were just hallucinations that any seriously ill patient could have. Doctor Morse went to great lengths to show that "hallucinations resulting from a variety of drugs, psychological phenomena, or physiological stress cannot mimic the powerful experiences of the NDE."[3]

Doctor Raymond A. Moody, Jr., M.D., Ph.D., and one of the early pioneers in NDE exploration, has said, "If anyone were to research the topic with an open mind he would be convinced of the reality of the near-death experience."[4] In Chapter Fourteen, The Experiencers, I'll provide extensive and more detailed evidence in support of the NDE's authenticity.

Meanwhile, imagine, if you will, a life in which there is no fear of death, life that is serene because death is not a termination of the self, but rather simply a passage from a "here" that is filled with strife, frustration, pain, sorrow, hate and other cares of the world, to a "there" where love is all-encompassing; where joy and love of knowledge are all important.

With the realization of such a future awaiting us, the small concerns of the world cease to be important. In fact, every care and concern becomes a small concern which will be resolved in time, thus allowing a concentration on the things that are truly important: Love of humanity and pursuit of knowing for the betterment of mankind.

People who undergo near-death experiences--that is, a condition that teeters on the brink of permanent death of the physical body--have returned from that precarious state to report phenomena that are so startling as to present incredible implications.

They have reported being transported out of their body to a point above their corporeal remains, flying up a tunnel of brilliant light, to the presence of beings who emanate light and love. They are then escorted to the presence of a one Being who seems the epitome of all knowledge and love. They are shown every instant of their lives, good or bad, and are made aware of the fact that love of others and pursuit of knowledge for the betterment of this life and eternal life are the two most important things one can do in a lifetime. Then, for a variety reasons, they are returned to this life to continue what is deemed unfinished. They often return with that wonderful sense of complete serenity and a loving spirit.

Hallucination, hoax, mass conspiracy or religious hysteria? How can diverse people of different ages (sometimes children who have no preconceived notion of afterlife), language groups, nationalities, religious affiliation (or lack of it, as some are atheists), all have such consistently similar experiences independently of each other?

It is as if thousands were all to go to a country independently of one another and return to tell you of their journey. No two tales would be exactly alike, but could you, would you doubt the existence of the country just because no two tales matched exactly or because you had no personal knowledge of it, had not seen it and had not been there? Can you see love? No. But do you doubt that it exists? Of course not.

The lives of these experiencers undergo a drastic change. Materialism loses its importance in their lives. They become more spiritual, searching for a right relationship with God and fellow human beings. Almost unanimously they have no more fear of death and express the conviction that there is an afterlife and that *God does exist*.

Critics say that, even so, the near-death experience and the message of the experiencers does not constitute absolute scientific proof of life after death or the existence of God. Technically they would be correct; however, any reasonable person would have to admit that these experiences present very convincing evidence of a life that continues beyond this earthly one as well as the existence of a supreme being. They certainly reinforce that belief already held by most of us and provide food for thought to the doubter! Through the senses of the experiencers, God is almost certainly giving us a glimpse of such wonders as an ethereal world that exists, his ineffable love and the joy of being in his presence.

We will never "scientifically" prove that there is a God. But what is so sacrosanct about scientific proof? Because we can't examine the evidence under a microscope or prove it mathematically or scientifically, we refute it or ignore it. How foolish to do so! We cannot examine the feeling of love but we certainly know it exists. We can't see gravity, completely examine it or fully understand it, but we are aware of its force and accept it.

To limit our beliefs to only what can be proved objectively is indeed narrow-minded. To paraphrase Shakespeare in "Hamlet", there are more things in heaven and earth than we can dream of. The world, and life, are much more than we can see and prove in the laboratory. Carl Gustav Jung, psychiatrist and psychologist, has said, "We should not pretend to understand the world only by intellect; we apprehend it just as much by feeling."

Besides it is possible that science has about run its course. Although there are refinements to be made, little of significance may be left to discover that can benefit humankind. Further, a good case could be made that science has adversely shaped us into a materialistic world--a consumer culture in which we strive to gain "things"--thus suppressing our spirituality, that is, enlightenment as to our purpose in life, our true nature, the nature of God and the relationship between God and man. Although science has improved the lot of humankind through convenience, it has certainly caused us considerable grief through such things as the invention of gun powder and weapons. Science has not promoted peace and harmony among humankind, but often strife and discord.

Bryan Appleyard, in his work UNDERSTANDING THE PRESENT: Science and the Soul of Man, shows that "Though science has advanced our understanding of the universe and provided us with the toys and weapons of modern civilization, it has failed to answer the ultimate questions: Who am I? Does life have a purpose? Is there a God? What lies beyond death?"[5]

He argues that "science has changed the world, but not the human condition; that many scientific questions have been answered, but the solution to life's problems still elude us."[5] A better understanding of spiritual matters can answer all of those questions, solve life's problems and change the world for the better! It is time for spirituality to flourish--there is a great deal about it to discover.

Through our "hearts" and minds we need to expand our beliefs, never assuming that we have the ultimate truth, but always searching for knowledge and relying more on the wisdom of the heart--our inner or higher self. Poet George Santayana put it well when he wrote, "O World, thou choosest not the better part! It is not wisdom to be only wise, And on the inward vision close the eyes, But it is wisdom to believe the heart." Unfortunately, we seldom listen to our heart. We are often even hard of hearing when it comes to accepting that which is experienced by our conscious mind.

When we see the wonder and beauty of the universe, the multitude of scriptures that speak of God and hear the extraordinary message of the experiencers, our mind and heart tell us that God does indeed exist. We should believe it! If we can conclude that God exists, then what is he really like? What is the nature of God?

Chapter Ten

THE NATURE OF GOD

What *is* God like? Can we really know? Is he a crowned, white-haired, white-bearded, old-looking gentleman sitting on a golden throne somewhere in heaven, as he is often pictured in religious stories? Is he an omnipotent, most-sovereign monarch who rules the universe from on high? Is he surrounded by seraphim and cherubim continually worshipping him, and the angels of heaven singing their never-ending song "Hail to the Chief," as the scriptures imply? Or is he a spirit, as the scripture also says, who can manifest himself in many ways? Is he really omnipotent, omniscient and omnipresent? We can understand that he is all-powerful and all-wise, but how can he be everywhere at the same time?

Is he really a God of vengeance, anger and wrath, as some religions often teach? Or is he a God of love, kindness and mercy? Or can he be both? Are we to believe that all those events of blood, violence and massacre in the Old Testament were either perpetrated by God himself, or by the Israelites because God commanded them to do so? The Christian theologians generally say yes, those are the inspired and infallible words of God. The explanation is that God is just; those people were wicked and deserved to be punished and so God destroyed them, either by the swords of men, or by his own hand.

Did God himself really destroy the Pharaoh and his soldiers in the Red Sea as they were pursuing Moses and the Israelites who were fleeing Egypt, as the Bible records? Is it possible that

God told Joshua to go into Ai, a city of 12,000 inhabitants, and "Kill every man woman and child, but you can keep the cattle and the spoils?" Or that he told Moses to kill all the Midianite males but could keep the virgins? Were the babies and little children in Ai also wicked and deserving of being slaughtered? Is it possible that God *would* condone all that killing. The Church would say yes, because of the sins of their fathers. What *absolute nonsense*!

The Church goes to great lengths to try to explain these terrible atrocities. Christian dogma cites Adam and Eve in the garden of Eden. How, through the "fall"--that is, because of Adam's and Eve's disobedience to God--they became sinners and, subsequently, all their progeny are innately sinful from birth. Hence, all children are sinners, as well as having the sins of their fathers visited upon them. But, in establishing such doctrine, the Church completely ignores God's word in the scripture, which says, "The son shall not bear the iniquity of the father."[1]

The Christian Church also ignores the word of the one they call Lord and Master, Jesus Christ. He said, "Anyone who has seen me has seen the Father."[2] St. Paul, whose writings are the foundation of much of Christian doctrine, also expresses the same likeness between God and Christ when he speaks of the "Glorious gospel of Christ who is the *image* of God."[3] As an *important* aside, it should be noted that *we* also are the image of God, being "made in his likeness." Those two statements by Christ and Paul make it clear that our recognition of Christ, his life and his qualities, is a recognition of God.

Christ was kind, patient and forgiving. He neither killed nor harmed anyone. Some say that isn't so, that Christ was not exactly a "peacenik," citing his whipping and driving the money changers from the temple. When one examines that story, it appears likely that it never took place. The sales in the temple were taxed by the government, an important source of revenue. Government guards were posted at the temple. It is

The Nature of God

not likely that they would allow a lone person to disrupt the business in the temple.

Christ said, "Not only are we not to kill, but we should not get angry with one another without cause, or we shall be in danger of judgment." He healed the sick, had compassion on the multitudes and fed them. He cared for people and comforted them. He truly loved his neighbor as himself and forgave others. He said that God puts great store by the children, and woe to them that harm the little ones! Therefore, that is what God is like. He is loving, good and compassionate beyond our understanding. How then could God in any way be responsible for those evils portrayed by the Old Testament? *He could not be and was not responsible!*

A wise man once said that it appears that man has made God in man's image. We have most certainly done that, making God a person with human visage and even implying that he has human frailties such as our often-displayed tendency toward anger, vengeance and violence. That is what our forefathers in the Old Testament surely indulged in. They were cruel and vengeful. They plundered the goods of their enemies and massacred them. So, to excuse themselves, their leaders said, "Our God is a vengeful God, he has destroyed our enemies, or God commanded us to do this." And so it was recorded. Those massacres of men, women and little children indeed may have occurred, but certainly not by or at the command of God!

God does not change; he does not alter the rules as the game of life goes along. Surely his omniscience would preclude establishing rules that needed to be altered at some later date. He is constant and immutable, as most religions teach. God gave his people the Ten Commandments, one of which is "Thou shall not kill." How, then, could God, who is unchanging, do an about-face and tell his people to kill their enemies? How is it possible to justify that Old Testament violence, supposedly at the behest of God, with God's instructions, given in later scripture, that we are to love our enemies, do good to them that persecute us, return evil with good, turn the other cheek, and don't worry about those who can kill the body but not the soul? We cannot make that justification and, therefore, *must* conclude that the Old Testament characterization of God as angry and vengeful is the *errant word of man*.

The commandment "Thou shall not kill" has never been qualified by God. There are those who would disagree, quoting the proverb, "He who lives by the sword, shall die by the sword." Obviously, that is an untruth, for we know there are those who lived by the sword but did not perish that way, some even dying peacefully in their bed. It was undoubtedly formulated by men as justification for killing each other. That proverb is often used to support the death penalty. But we should ignore it because it contradicts an unqualified commandment from our immutable God that we are not to kill, which is then reaffirmed by Christ in the New Testament.

Throughout time, religion and men have distorted God's word and gone to great lengths in order to justify killing. We have seen that St. Paul said God put all governments in power and their ordinances are to be obeyed without question. That and other scripture, of similar nature, is often used by religious fundamentalists to support the death penalty for criminals, as well as to justify war.

Martin Luther, who was sometimes referred to as a "second Paul," took the same position as St. Paul, with even more explicit statements of how God is responsible for wars, killing and governments. He said, "For the very fact that the sword has been instituted by God to punish the evil and protect the good and preserve peace is proof, powerful and sufficient, that fighting and slaying and the other things war-times and martial law bring with them, have been instituted by God. What else is war than the punishment of wrong and evil? Why does anyone go to war, except because he desires peace and obedience? Although slaying and robbing do not seem to be a work of love; therefore, a simple man thinks it not Christian to do, yet in truth even this is a work of love. By way of illustration, a good physician, when a disease is so bad and so great that he has to cut off a hand, foot, ear, eye, or let it decay, does so, in order to save the body."[4]

That's rather faulty thinking, wouldn't you say? Even in his own time, the untruth of his logic was clearly evident. No matter how one twists it, robbing can *never* be a work of love. Slaying can be an act of desperation or self-defense or even self-righteousness, but *never* an act of love! When one kills in service to one's country, or in defense of one's loved ones, such as an intruder in one's home, it can be an act of self-defense or survival or vengeance, but *never* love. Killing for any reason *cannot* be an act of love!

To compare slaying and robbing to a physician who cuts off a decayed limb to save the rest of the body, as Luther does, is a poor, if not completely illogical, analogy. More often than not, in war, it is not the corrupted flesh that is killed, but rather the whole and clean. Look at the Persian Gulf War. The Iraqi leaders were the unjust and they're still alive, well and in power. The Iraqi people, the old men, the women and the children, and many soldiers who were forced, against their wishes, to fight, were the good and just. Tens of thousands of the good were killed and maimed. And now because of the terrible destruction the "good guys" (governments) perpetrated on Iraq's infrastructure, hundreds of thousands more of the just and good, the children, are dying from starvation and disease. What horrible injustice brought about by a supposedly "just war." What a terrible desecration of God's creation! Surely, it's blasphemous to say that God instituted this!

Look at the horror of the Civil War in this country--Father killing son, son killing father, brother killing brother, and Christians killing other Christians. Surely, you can see how absurdly wrong Luther was when he said, "What else is war than punishment of wrong and evil? Why does anyone go to war except that he desires peace and obedience?" Neither peace nor real obedience were threatened in the case of the Civil War. And neither side was more or less wicked than the other. What disrespect for God Luther showed when he said that war, killing and robbing can be acts of love and are instituted by God!

Taken in, along with other false perceptions of God, is the mistaken notion that God is in control of this world and causes all things to happen, both good and bad; that he is responsible for all governments, wars, murder, famine and all misery that occur to mankind on earth. Or that he allows these things to happen perhaps as a lesson, perchance as punishment or for some reason unknown to us. None of that is so. *God is not in control of this world.* You can be sure that if he were, things would be peaceful and orderly.

God created this earthly paradise for us and put *us* in charge. He gave *man control of the earth.* He said *we* are to have "dominion over all the earth."[5] *We* are to "subdue it."[6] Yes, man rules the earth, and **that** is why all the distress, injustice and tragedies occur. That is "why bad things happen to good people." They are the results of man's failure to listen to God and his prophets, or perhaps even his desire to follow *false* prophets. He gave us all the rules and guidelines we need to live in peace and harmony, making this world a paradise, but we refuse to accept them, obey them and live by them. Instead, we give governments power, such as the power to kill, and follow their ordinances even when they contradict God's instructions. We have organized ourselves into divisive religious sects establishing doctrine that causes suspicion, discord and even hatred, violence and death. We have "trampled the laws of God" for the sake of false religious beliefs and tradition.

We have based the misconception of God being in control of our world on the errant writings of such *men* as St. Paul and

Martin Luther, meanwhile ignoring the *fact* that God has told us in the scripture that *we* are in control of this earth! It is surely God who makes the "world go round" and God who is the force that gives life to the earth and its inhabitants, but *mankind is the caretaker. We* are in charge and *we are responsible*! Through false, man-made religious doctrine, we have made God what he is not and blocked perception of what he really is.

If God is not a person with humanoid countenance, then of what form is he? We need to think of God in terms of spirit rather than possessing human form and attributes. God cannot be classified by gender, but is simply spirit. The scriptures clearly tell us that, "God is a spirit and in spirit shall ye worship him."[7] Spirit is defined as a supernatural being, the breath of life that animates or gives life to all organisms. God is a living entity, the supreme primal being, in spirit form, who is the origin of all that is. He is the ordering force of everything that exists. He is a never-ending source of energy from which the universe flowed and continues to do so!

He forms the stars and planets and places them in their galaxies and orbits. He is the force of gravity and the dynamism that keeps the earth at a constant speed of rotation. Scripture says, "It is only the spirit that gives life."[8] God, the spirit, is the force that gives life from seed, plant as well as animal. It is most certainly true that, "Only God can make a tree," as Joyce Kilmer has surmised in his poem, <u>Trees</u>. God is the life force that guides growth of all plant and animal life into the *innumerable* and varied forms that exist in this world. What imagination God has! What beauty God creates!

Most of us believe that God is the creator of the universe and all living things in the universe, but give little thought as to *how* he creates. Of course, that's understandable, as we are so little able to envision the way in which a universe, containing millions of galaxies, was created, or even how our relatively small world was made? However, through an understanding of quantum physics and awareness of the basic building blocks of all life and material, we can get a glimpse of the process of creation.

A quantum is the basic building block or smallest unit of anything. At the quantum level, *matter comes into being out of something that is not matter.* Physicists know that matter, such as a molecule, can come into existence from thought or intelligence. For example, neuro-peptides in the human body spring into existence when we think certain thoughts.

When we see a block of cement or steel, we think and speak of them as solid and motionless. But through an understanding of quantum physics, we know that isn't so. They are made up of atoms that are constantly in motion, thereby representing energy. As we know that thought is energy, we can reasonably conclude that matter, such as the basic building block, is the expression of intelligence, thought and energy.

We humans can create matter, such as neuro-peptides, by thought. Surely, that is how God creates matter. Remember, we are made in his image. And, as God is all-intelligent and *all-powerful*, then it is reasonable to believe that he created the universe by intelligent thought and his endless source of energy. Then we can also understand why he is omnipresent, for his energy, his thought, his intelligence, his being, his spirit is present in every atom of everything that exists. The universe is a pyhsical manifestation of God. That also explains why he is omniscient, for being present everywhere, he is aware of all things. Just as scripture says that "not one sparrow shall fall to the ground without God's knowledge."

Note that the quantum concept of how God creates is supported by Taoist scripture. "Not visible to the sight," which correlates with God as spirit. "It is inexhaustible," means God's energy is endless. "It (Tao/The Way/*God*) is the Mother of all things" and "It is the beginning of Heaven and Earth"[8] which surely shows that God creates all that is. Koranic scripture is also supportive of God's creative power by means of intelligence, thought and energy. "God only needs to say 'be,' and it comes into existence."

Spirit is thought of as an invisible force such as consciousness or essence. We think of it as the principle that animates the body, giving us life. The scripture declares that "God is spirit,"[9] and "only the spirit quickens (gives life)."[10] Therefore, we can conclude that it is God who gives life to humans. Is it not also reasonable to conclude that he is the creator of *all* matter? Although physicists acknowledge that matter, at the quantum level, comes into being out of *something* that is not matter, and that the *something* is intelligence and thought, they are reluctant to take that last step and identify the *something*, the *intelligence*, as God. *There is nothing else that it could be!*

Quantum physicists also accept the concept that the universe is "nonlocal." That is, all objects and things in the universe, such as people, animals, trees, the earth, the atmosphere, the planets and stars are not separate entities, but are all an integral part of the whole. It is a theory, postulated by physicist John Bell, that "all objects and events in the cosmos are interconnected and respond to one another's change of state."[11] British physicist David Bohm speculates, from a scientific viewpoint, that there is an "invisible field that holds all of reality together, a field that possesses the property of knowing what is happening everywhere at once."[12] As we believe that God is the creator, then it is certainly logical to conclude that the "interconnectedness," the "invisible field" and the "something" from which matter springs into existence, is simply God the spirit, the intelligence, the thought and the energy that have created all that is and holds it together in perfect order and harmony!

Surely that concept of creation of the universe is more reasonable and credible than believing the universe emerged from a *speck of nothingness* as the scientists have postulated with their theory of the Big Bang. When we observe the orderliness of the universe with all the natural laws that govern its order, it would seem logical to believe that some *intelligence* designed and created it. It is certainly more believable than the concept that all that "primordial soup" somehow *formed itself* into the orderly systems and galaxies that make up the cosmos. The universe may have begun with a "Big Bang" as the scientists have *theorized*. But it was God that was the "spark," the "unfathomable way" in which the universe emerged. He is the energy source of the hot dense primordial soup of elementary particles, whence all of the universe has come.

When the scripture says that God is spirit, it also says, in "spirit shall you *worship* him."[13] What does it mean to worship God in spirit? Are we to bend the knee and bow the head to this God-king in heaven, aggrandizing his name, extolling his virtues and continually giving him praise and compliment? Does our repetitive pious prayer please God? Is God really pleased with that kind of worship? It is not very likely!

Worship means to give honor, respect, high regard, love and obedience. To worship God, then, is to give him deep respect, reverence and love. To worship God is to obey him. As God is spirit, being present everywhere and in all things, then to *worship God in spirit* is to show respect, regard and love for *all of creation*. When we love our neighbor as our self, living in peace and harmony with one another, *as well as our environment,* we are honoring and showing reverence to God and only then is he pleased with our *worship!*

When we "feed the hungry, give drink to the thirsty, shelter the homeless, take care of the sick, visit those in prison" and generally take care of one another, then are we properly worshipping God, showing him love and respect. For God said, "When you do these things to one another you do them unto me."[14] The Christian Church teaches that those are the words of Christ speaking of himself as king and God. Scripture does attribute those words to Christ, but what we must remember is that Christ said on three occasions that he was not telling us his own words but what God had told him to say.

Because God is truly omnipresent, then we need to reexamine our perceptions of people, places and things. The lowly, homeless street urchin is just as holy and as much to be respected as any church or government official. Also scripture tells us that "God is no respecter of persons."[15] Status doesn't count with God; none of us is more or less important to him than another. Your home is as sacrosanct as any church; God is just as present in the shack in shantytown as in the greatest cathedral. Ancient relics have no more significance to God than modern things. God cannot be pleased when humans fight and kill one another over places and things that *they* designate as "holy." Surely human beings, made in God's image, are more precious to him than a place or a thing!

As God is spirit, present everywhere and in everything, then what is the true nature of this world that we live in?

Chapter Eleven

THE NATURE OF OUR WORLD

If we can accept that God, through his intelligence, thought and energy, created this world we live in and that he is therefore omnipresent--that is, present in all things that exist--then it is rational also to accept that everything in the universe is interconnected. Surely, it is a spiritual connection, with God the spirit--the *universal field of energy that constitutes all things*--as the medium for that link. We have seen that scientists Bell and Bohm have put forth theories of interconnectedness.[1] Most physicists, especially those in quantum physics, as well as other scientists, are now leaning toward that concept.

Mankind is indeed a part of God's entire creation, not separate but intrinsically joined to that whole creation. We are a portion of that complete totality just as each cell of our body is part of the entire body. As the state of health of our entire body depends upon the condition of its parts, so the state of the whole world depends on the condition of its inhabitants, including all plant and animal life as well as mineral matter. Just as harm to any part of the body affects the whole, so does harm to any part of creation affect the whole.

Quite often we do not see mankind as the cause of harm in the world, but look elsewhere, even to God, as the cause. When some tragedy or negative circumstance happened to you, did you say, "O God, why me?" Or, "Why have you done this to me, O God?" Most parents who have lost a child have said that in one form or another: "Why my child, O God? How could you let this happen to my poor innocent little girl?"

Have you ever been in a conversation with someone, perhaps an atheist, who asked you, "If there is a God and he is as powerful and as loving as you say, and if he is in control of all things, then why does he let all these bad things happen? Why the terrible wars and killing? Why famine and pestilence? Why the Holocaust? How could God let that happen to his 'chosen' people? If God so loves little children, why does he allow children to be born with Downs Syndrome or deformed limbs or other debilitating diseases?" Do you recall what you said?

Some of the stock answers often given are: "We simply don't know." Or, "It is God's will," or "God has a reason beyond our understanding." The Church has some nice pat answers: "God has never said we won't have trials and tribulations. God is testing you/us. Look at what happened to Job. God took everything away from him, his family, his wealth, his home, everything! But God later returned to Job even more than he had taken because Job had kept the faith. So, too, must we keep faith in God when bad things happen to us." Or, "We must accept the good with the bad because it is God's will." Ministers like to quote St. Paul, who said, "We can rejoice, too, when we run into problems and trials, for we know they are good for us--they help us to learn to be patient. And patience helps build trust in God."[2]

These are nice, theological-sounding answers, but they are foolish, and there is no truth in them because God has no part in them. How can anyone believe that it is God's will, his desire, that terrible things should happen to us. *All the affliction and sorrow that happens to mankind is of **his own doing***. Even the child who is born with deformity. Somewhere along the line, in the conception of that child, man did something to cause that disfigurement. The mother or father may have ingested some chemical or foreign substance, either intentionally or unintentionally, which then caused the deformity. Some distant ancestor in the line may have had his or her DNA altered, for the same reasons, showing up generations later as a deformity in the newborn child. Excepting, for example, a mother who deliberately uses drugs while she is pregnant, no individual should feel guilty for the birth of a deformed child. But, nevertheless, it is certainly the fault of mankind, not God!

Even in accidents in which no individual is considered at fault, the cause is still the doing of man in some way. What about the inhabitant of Africa who lives in proximity to wild animals and is maimed or killed by a wild beast? What of a small child who doesn't know what a rattlesnake is, stoops to examine it, is bitten and dies? How could man possibly be at fault? Yet he is because, out of disobedience to God, man is out of harmony with his surroundings, including all other animal life. And because of that lack of harmony, the behavior of the wild beast and snake over against man is hostile and harmful. If man were in *complete* harmony with his earth, as God expects us to be, then it may be that the behavior of those animals would be friendly and benign.

It is a hard concept to accept, yet the scriptures lead us to believe it is so. The Old Testament speaks of the "peaceable kingdom"[3] that is to come when we all shall live in peace and harmony in obedience to God's instructions, and when God's will is done on earth as in heaven. When the wolf and the lamb will lie down together, the cattle will be safe among the lions who will eat grass like the cows, the babies will crawl safely among poisonous snakes without harm and there will be no more harm in all of God's holy kingdom.

What of earthquakes, hurricanes, famine and pestilence? It is possible to acknowledge that man might be responsible for famine and pestilence because of his destruction of the environment, careless disposal of waste and other such actions. But how could man possibly be responsible for earthquakes and other devastating "natural phenomena?" Surely, they are the result of the way that God created this earth, aren't they? Perhaps not! After all, God created this earth to be a paradise for us and his will is to be done on earth as in heaven. Surely, such things as earthquakes, destructive storms, famine and disease do not exist in paradise and heaven. Besides, God has told us that nothing will hurt or destroy in his kingdom when we are full of the knowledge of God.

Could it be that God causes them to happen now as punishment for our wrongdoing and even the innocent, such as children, have to suffer for the sins of the whole? Then, when we learn to obey him and live in peace and harmony with one another and with our environment, God will cause them to cease? But God has perfect justice and is merciful and forgiving, and, therefore, he could not cause the innocent children to suffer. That leaves only mankind as the source of all earthly distress. Such a precept is almost impossible to accept, nevertheless, it is likely true.

The theory of interconnectedness that dictates that one part of creation responds to another's change is very significant and is the basis of how man causes all earthly distress, including earthquakes! If man were content, happy and at peace with himself, others and his environment, then his earth would be calm, at rest, and, literally, a paradise. When man lives otherwise in a state of anxiety, anger, hatred and violence, the world becomes a hell, as we have witnessed throughout the history of mankind.

In Genesis God says we are to *subdue* the earth. Subdue means to tame or overpower. Could it be then that we are to conquer and bring into subjection all forces of the world, including earthquakes, hurricanes, typhoons, tidal waves and winds? But mankind cannot do that until we are in tune with one another, living in peace and harmony according to the instructions that God has given us. We must also have a better understanding of the power of our minds.

The mind and thought are generally considered a field of energy that is active not only within our bodies, but can be projected and remain active beyond the body. A great deal of witnessed and documented psychic data supports this concept. Humans have been known to project and receive thoughts over great distances across continents and oceans. We know that humans project energy and what is known as *aura*. Most of us have sensed these energies that emanate from others. We feel ill at ease in the presence of certain people, even though there has been no verbal or body-language exchange. On the other hand, there are those people in whose presence we really feel comfortable under similar circumstances. Children and animals are particularly sensitive to those types of energies that people project.

We all have heard of the expression green thumb as applied to people who supposedly have good luck in growing plants. Others can use the same fertilizers, watering techniques and so forth, but don't have the same success. It is very probable that something more than physical care caused those with a green thumb to achieve greater success in their plant-growing endeavors. That something would involve mental emanations in a real love of what they are doing. Experiments have been done in which seeds and plants respond with increased growth to positive thought, love and even prayer. It also has been shown that plants respond positively to music.

Scientists have studied individuals who, through what is called psychokinesis, can move, bend and break objects with the power of their minds. Uri Geller is a well-known Israeli psychic who can bend objects, such as metal rods, at will, through the power of his mind. Scientists have found and studied hundreds of people with similar abilities. City College of New York conducted experiments with psychic Ingo Swann who, simply by thought, was able to raise the temperature of a graphite block inside a vacuum at the opposite end of a room.[4]

There are other illustrations of this flow of energy from humans. Kirlian photography, a lensless technique developed by Russian scientists, has photographed the aura of humans. The Massachusetts Institute of Technology has measured electromagnetic energy flowing from the human body.[4] It is possible that man is the source of all natural earthly distress, generated by his mental activity. It is also likely that he has the equivalent ability to calm, and to cause that adverse natural phenomenon to end by eliminating stressful mental activity as well by employing use of good, positive, calm and loving thoughts.

The scriptures, as well, tell us that we can change these things if we choose to. Perhaps you remember the biblical story of Jonah, the whale and Nineveh. The people of Nineveh were exceedingly wicked and violent. They and their city were to be destroyed because of it. We don't know the manner in which that destruction was to occur. So God sent Jonah to warn them. After his refusal and supposed adventure with the whale, Jonah finally did warn the people of Nineveh. They paid heed to the word of God sent through Jonah, modified their behavior, turning from their evil and violent ways, and were spared.

It is commonly accepted that *God* was going to destroy them, but when he saw that they had ceased their wrongdoing, he spared them. The scriptures say, "And God saw their works, that they turned from their evil way; and God repented of the evil that he had said he would do unto them, and he did not."[5]

Can we see the inconsistency there? God was going to do evil to the people of Nineveh? He was going to return evil with evil? That is not possible! Elsewhere in the scripture God says we are not to kill, we are to love our enemies, and requite evil with good. Could God do any less? It might be argued that

The Nature of Our World   143

because the people were so wicked, they deserved to die. But the entire population of Nineveh? All 120,000 of them? Certainly every one of them was not so heinously evil that they deserved the death sentence. Even we human beings are very lenient when it comes to applying the death penalty for wrongdoing. And what of the innocent children and babies? Knowing that God is perfect in love, mercy and forgiveness, it would be absolutely impossible for him to kill those little ones.

What of God's commandment that "Thou shalt not kill?" He forbids killing. But it is okay for *him* to do so? Surely not! Then there is God's admonition to us, given through Christ, that we are to forgive others seven times seventy for their sins. Christ did not mean literally that we are to forgive another's wrongdoing 490 times. It was a metaphor meaning there should be no limit to forgiveness. That would certainly have to apply to the people of Nineveh. They were to be forgiven, not killed.

Given all these factors, we can only conclude that whatever manner of destruction was to happen to Nineveh, it was not to be the doing of God! It is also a logical conclusion that if the cessation of their wicked and violent behavior and thoughts turned aside or averted the destructive force, then the wicked and violent thoughts and actions were the source of that destructive force.

If one person can bend metal with the energy of his mind and another raise the temperature of a graphite block by the same means, could not the violent energy projected by most of the 120,000 minds in Nineveh cause distortion to the earth, the sea or the air, resulting in some natural disaster that would destroy Nineveh? Then, when they repented, ceasing their evil thoughts, with violent energy no longer emanating from their minds, the sea or earth or sky was calmed and the disaster avoided?

This concept is certainly more conceivable than believing that God could sentence to death and himself carry out the killing of 120,000 people, including little children and babies!

If the saving of Nineveh from destruction by some natural disaster was the result of human behavioral change by thousands of people, then millions of people, by their good behavior and loving, kind thoughts, might save the world from catastrophe, *subduing* even the storms and earthquakes! Perhaps Nineveh is just another biblical myth and, then again, maybe not. We need to keep our minds open, for without that openness there would be little understanding and little progress for humankind--scientific, social or spiritual.

Given the recent increase in violence by "nature," it would appear that the amount of frenzied and violent energy emanating from millions of human minds is on the increase over-powering the benign thought and behavior. Geologists have reported a significant increase in worldwide seismic activity. A Russian researcher warned that the Koryakskaya Volcano on the Kamchatka Peninsula could explode any time, causing a disaster as catastrophic as the eruption of Vesuvius in 79 A.D. In 1996 damage estimates from the worst flooding in memory across the far western United States reached more than $2 billion in California alone. At least 76 people were killed and more than 42,000 left homeless from floods and landslides in Brazil as storms raged across the area for more than five days.[6]

Strange weather patterns were being experienced around the world. Bitter cold swept across South Africa, with temperatures plunging to 15 degrees--a record cold in a normally temperate country. On the other end of the scale, unusually high temperatures were experienced in India with record temperatures of 120 degrees causing hundreds of deaths. A week of torrential rainfall in eastern Cuba caused flooding that killed at least nine people and damaged thousands of homes as well as a great part of the sugar crop. The climate in Kenya changed from a withering drought to unusually heavy rain, causing erosion, flooding and destruction of tons of food and relief supplies that were destined for Somalia. In Vietnam, whirlwinds lashed the countryside, destroying over 600 homes and 5000 acres of rice paddies. In South Africa, baboons went on the rampage attacking motorists with showers of stones.[7]

Are these just samples of things to come unless mankind gets its act together? Certainly, these types of occurrences are happening to us all the time, and have throughout history; however, their frequency and intensity seem to be increasing. According to scripture there "shall be great tribulation, such as was not seen since the beginning of the world... For nation shall rise against nation and kingdom against kingdom; and there shall be earthquakes in divers places, and there shall be famines and troubles: these are the beginnings of sorrows."[8] If what is happening in the world today is indeed just the beginning of sorrows, then put your imagination to work and visualize the state of the world when these problems are multiplied two or fourfold! There will be "great travail and anguish... men's hearts will fail them; there shall be great distress upon the earth!"[9] Apparently and unfortunately, some of these things are necessary for man to learn. Christ says these things "need be." It seems that it is going to take a very large "two-by-four" to bring man's attention to the fact that he is doing something wrong and must change his ways!

I know it seems a faaaaar stretch to think that humankind could be responsible for earthquakes. Nevertheless, given the evidence, I believe that it somewhat reasonably postulates the ultimate mind power that humankind is capable of. Just a little over 100 years ago it would have been considered insane to think that the mind of man could be responsible for the reality of a fifty ton metal machine that could fly through the air at 600 miles an hour. The idea that the earth was round was once the thought of crazy people. Some people were put to death when they put forth the idea that earth wasn't the center of the universe.

We have the evidence that man can do amazing things with thought power emanating from the mind--for example, Uri Geller bending metal with the energy of his mind, psychic Ingo

Swann raising the temperature of an encased graphite block with mind-thought, the magnificent things that humankind creates with the thoughts of the mind and our ability to either cause illness or heal ourselves by the power of the mind

If a single individual can do such things by projecting thought energy, imagine the effect that could or would be generated by many minds! The collective power of thought energy from millions of minds would be *awesome*! Isn't it conceivable then that tens of millions of people who are projecting random waves of frustrated, angry and violent energy could have an adverse effect on weather or even the Earth's crust and tectonic plates, *of which they are an interconnected part*?

Even that idea of the interconnectedness of all things in the universe was a strange notion just a couple of generations ago. Now it is beginning to be accepted by scientists. Visionary Vaclav Havel believes in it as well as the idea of the earth as a mega-organism. Highly respected scientist James Lovelock, in his work GAIA, puts forth the theory that Gaia (Mother Earth) is a living, super-organism, and that man is a dynamic part of that entity. He even speculates that the human collective intelligence may constitute a Gaian nervous system.

If that is so, then the idea of man causing earthquakes with the bad vibes of his mind isn't that far out at all. Then, if we consider physicist John Bell's theory that "all objects and events in the cosmos are interconnected and respond to one another's change of state," and factor in scriptural prophesy that "God's will is to be done on *earth* as in heaven"--certainly no quakes in heaven--and factor in the prophesy that when the peaceable kingdom comes there will be "no more harm in all the earth," then the premise of man being responsible for the climatic and geological stability of the earth seems even more reasonable.

Sure it's difficult to accept that mankind is responsible for all the natural disasters that occur on this earth. But shouldn't we keep an open mind to that possibility? Certainly the disasters don't just happen by themselves. There has to be some force that causes them. It wouldn't be correct to say that it's just nature, for God is the force behind nature. It is simply not reasonable to attribute them to God, whom we believe has perfect love and justice. It is neither loving nor just to make innocent people suffer. If we eliminate God and "nature" as the cause, it leaves only man. We should keep our minds open to that possibility and then examine what we might do about it. Exploration and research might be appropriate, such as experimenting with millions of minds coordinated in peaceful mind-wave emanation bringing about a change in human behavior as well as that of "nature."

It could be a monumental but not impossible task. Such attempts have been tried before. Groups with thousands of members have undertaken peaceful mind emanation programs to reduce crime in major cities, including Washington, D.C. Although they have claimed some success, it has obviously been minimal. The reason for lack of any substantial change should be obvious: they were vastly outnumbered. Also, such actions have to be carried out with the *sincere belief* that they will work.

BLESSING AND PRAYER

There is another misconception about the nature of our world--that God alters world conditions and events through his blessing and in answer to prayer. "God bless you." What does that mean? Or "God go with you?" They are generally thought of as requesting of God the special bestowal of divine favor on a particular person or that he personally look out for and protect a person. Does God really do that? I do not believe so.

A great misunderstanding exists as to the nature of prayer and God's blessings. We tend to think that God blesses some more than others, and we don't understand why. When good fortune comes to a good, religiously devout person, we're inclined to think that God blessed him with that good fortune because of that devoutness. If evil happens to an evil person we think that God saw to it that he got what he deserved. But when evil comes to a good person, we can't comprehend how God could have let that happen. Likewise when a perceived Godless individual is blessed with riches and the "good life," we have trouble understanding the seeming injustice of it.

It would seem that either God has to be biased toward some of us or he is impartial. It surely has to be the latter. He does not interfere in our well-being or our ill-fortune. Being omnipotent he could easily do that, controlling all of our actions, making everything right. But then we would not have free will and would not be made in his image. According to scripture, "God gives his sunlight to both the evil and the good, and sends rain on the just and on the unjust as well."[10] That is a quality of our world; it is "user friendly" to *all equally*. God blesses everyone, both the good and the bad, in like manner. He gives us all the material needs as well as the mental and spiritual attributes necessary for us to live comfortable, peaceful and harmonious lives. It is *we* who determine the quality of that life and the circumstances around us, or others determine those things for us. *God is not involved.*

But what about prayer? Doesn't God directly intervene in our lives by answering prayer? Millions pray to God, asking him to bring about some change in their own or other's lives. We frequently ask him to intercede in the affairs of the world, bringing an end to war and other atrocities that continually occur. Then, when that change or circumstance comes about, it is believed that God was somehow directly responsible. If it doesn't happen we rationalize God's seeming refusal to answer in various ways: we aren't worthy or what we asked for wasn't good for us. Or he will answer in his own good time, meanwhile testing our faith or perhaps molding and tempering our character by tribulation. Or the catch-all phrase, "God's ways are not our ways," is sometimes used.

Consider the times we called on God for something in our time of need and didn't seem to get an answer. Most of us know a situation in which a devout person has had to endure difficulties and suffering although many prayers had been offered to God to relieve the situation. How often have prayers gone out to God to stop wars and do something about the senseless slaughter, or to intervene on the behalf of children who are in perilous situations only to see the carnage and killing continue or the child suffer and even meet with an untimely and unpleasant death? How can we possibly believe that God, who is perfect in love, mercy and justice, could refuse to answer, for any reason, a prayer to relieve the terrible suffering of the children of the world? According to our concept of prayer, he has refused, regardless of the rationalization!

The most common perception is of an omniscient, omnipotent God sitting in heaven, listening to the millions of prayers that are uttered by a few billion people, hearing them all, perhaps categorizing them according to their urgency and validity, deciding which ones he is going to answer, based on we know not what, and then "pushing the right buttons" to bring about a solution to the problem. Or some believe that God answers prayer by sending angels to resolve the issue. That is all a misconception.

Prayer *is* answered, but not in the way we think. Our not understanding our own nature and underestimating the *power of our minds* has resulted in this misconception. It is man *himself*, with the help of God, who brings about change by prayer. The key as to how that is done is given to us in scripture. We are told that whatever we ask for in prayer, **believing**, we will receive it.[11] It is something **we** do, the **believing** *with the mind*, that is the primary factor in bringing about results. The thoughts of our powerful mind not only shape our character and behavior but also the circumstances around us to include the bringing to fruition of the things we ask for in prayer.

Belief in prayer is like the placebo effect in medicine. Doctors are puzzled as to why people who are unknowingly given a "sugar" pill, and told that it will help or cure their problem, quite frequently show improvement and are sometimes even cured of their ailment. The answer should be obvious. It is the patient's *belief* that he will get well that heals. Likewise, it is *belief* expressed by our *powerful mind* that brings results from prayer.

James Allen, in his book AS A MAN THINKETH, makes the connection when he says, "The divinity that shapes our ends, is in ourselves, it is our very self. Our wishes and prayers are only gratified and answered when they harmonize with our thoughts and actions."[12] The thoughts of our mind in prayer shape our actions, which, in turn, solidify into circumstances. That is how prayer is answered concerning desires for our own welfare. Our prayers aren't answered, and we don't receive what we ask for, for the same reason. While we are praying for something, we are at the same time continually frustrating its accomplishment by thoughts and desires that do not harmonize with what we are aspiring to, the most common being a lack of sincere *belief* that we will receive it.

Consider the Lord's Prayer, in which millions continually pray for God's will to be done *"on earth* as in heaven." That prayer is not being answered because there is no *belief* involved. In the first place, the prayer is a practice in rote; it is most often mindless repetition. Secondly, almost no one really believes that the way things are in heaven, with peace, joy and happiness prevailing, will happen on earth. Rather, they believe conditions on earth will always be turbulent and continue to get worse.

Other factors involved in answered prayer are the soul and interconnectedness. That is where the help of God comes in. Our mind, body and soul are intertwined, constituting the totality of our being. Also, the mind and soul are part of the cosmic consciousness, the total field of energy that constitutes everything in the universe. Therefore, all aspects of our being are interconnected with every other being as well as every thing. That is how prayer to change "things" occurs. It is how prayer for other people works. The connection is from the thoughts of our mind, through the cosmic consciousness, to the energy, mind and soul that make up other things and people. The soul, the field of energy given from God, can be called upon, by prayer, to aid us in restoring health, growing spiritually, achieving our desires and helping others.

We need to pray properly for it to work. For example, when praying for healing, prayers often take the route of asking God to intervene, then sitting back and waiting for God to take action and the results to occur. That kind of intervention isn't going to be forthcoming. The prayer should be for the healing to take place accompanied by the ***belief*** that it will. It is that way of praying, enhanced by continuous and collective use, that will bring results.

Some researchers believe that prayer for others is effective because our minds are non-local--extend beyond our bodies--and are interconnected in some way. But they do not make the jump to say it is done through a universal mind or cosmic consciousness. They think it is too unscientific, preferring to believe that the prayer connection is made through electromagnetic morphic fields of the mind. Of course, that's pretty unscientific, also.

But if we can accept that all of creation is one interconnected, vast field of energy; that we have a mind and a soul that are intertwined yet separate entities of energy; that there is a God, and that he is the creator by reason of his omnipotence and "endless source of energy;" then it would seem logical to conclude that the connection is through the universal mind. Further, scriptural testimony that all things are possible *with the help of God* would lead us to believe that prayer is not accomplished by man alone from one extended mind to another, but through that <u>cosmic consciousness</u>, a universal field of energy created by God.

Controlled research has been performed on both things and people, to provide reasonable evidence of that connection. Two groups of plants in different locations but growing under identical conditions were used in one test. One group was prayed for to the effect that they would thrive and grow rapidly, as well as having thoughts of love directed at them. The other was not. At the end of the test period the group that received the benefit of prayer was taller, fuller and healthier.

Doctor Dean Ornish, in his book REVERSING HEART DISEASE, cites research done by Dr. Randy Byrd at San Francisco General Hospital. It was a "Study of 393 patients who were admitted to the coronary care unit during a ten-month period. He arranged for people to pray for 192 of the patients, but not for the 201 others. These two groups were comparable in terms of age and disease severity.

"Doctor Byrd recruited people from around the country to pray for each of the 192 patients. He asked each person to pray every day in whatever form he or she wished. Each patient in the experimental group received daily prayers from five to seven people, although these patients were unaware of this.

"He found that the prayed-for patients suffered fewer complications in three areas: First, only three required antibiotics, compared to sixteen in the control group. Second, only six had pulmonary edema (fluid in the lungs), compared to eighteen in the control group. Finally, none of the prayed-for patients required intubation, while twelve of the others did."[13]

Doctor Ornish commented that, while this study is small, it suggests that we may be more interconnected than we often realize. Other studies of prayer for things and people show similar findings. Extensive research is currently being conducted, which is already yielding like results.

We have greatly underestimated the power of our minds. We have not understood the tremendous impact and influence that the thoughts of our minds can have upon our lives, the lives of others and our environment.

In addition to understanding our true nature, the nature of God and the nature of this world we live in, there is a hurdle, a great barrier, that must be overcome before humankind can achieve true spiritual growth, peace and harmony.

Chapter Twelve

RELIGION THE GREAT BARRIER

We would do well to consider the consequences that denominational religion has brought to the human race through its man-made doctrine. Religion is usually considered beneficial but is often otherwise. It has been the source of great enmity and violence. It is a major factor in dividing the human race, when it should be uniting us with one another and with God.

Most religious leaders would say they believe in freedom of religion and often express tolerance toward other religions and beliefs. They probably do, sort of. However, if one were to question or express disbelief of their religious doctrine, one would likely find himself not welcome in their midst. It is interesting to note that in Saudi Arabia on the road to Mecca, as you near the city, there is a road that branches off with a sign that says Infidel Bypass. All non-Muslims are infidels (unbelievers) and are not allowed in Mecca.

More seriously, religious leaders damn other people to hell. Most would deny it, but, in fact, they do! When they teach and preach that everyone must believe as they do to be saved, they are proclaiming that those who do not are not saved. They are condemning to eternal hell anyone who is not of their religious persuasion. They do it in absolute contradiction of God who unequivocally tells us in the scriptures that we are not to condemn others.

Attempts to impose religious beliefs through evangelism and holy war only intensify the discord. And even more derelict is the failure of the religions to follow God's basic instruction to teach love, kindness, mercy and forgiveness as the way to peace, harmony and *righteousness with him*. The source of all this alienation and failure to teach God's truths is flawed religious doctrine--dogma created by men. The religions of the world are by no means evil. They have accomplished much good, albeit at the same time hampering mankind's spiritual development by intertwining false, man-made doctrine with God's truths.

The great commandments that God has given to all the religions of the world are to acknowledge him, love him, and love and care for one another. Almost all religions hold to those tenets. Then they make the mistake of adding man-made doctrine and laws, or interpreting the basic laws and instructions of God to meet their own requirements or beliefs. They require us to follow some great prophet or religious figure such as Christ, Muhammad or Buddha if we are to be saved.

They declare their religion as the only true one, which must then be accepted and believed in totally if one is to achieve "paradise" or "heaven." Then they have the audacity to proclaim that their *loving* God damns everyone else to hell! How illogical! What narrow-mindedness! What disrespect for God!

The basic dogma of most religious faiths is the same. We have seen that Judaism requires the Jew to be in a right relationship with his fellow men in order to be right with God.[1] Likewise the Muslim must want for his brother what he wants for himself if he really believes in Allah.[2] And the Christian must love his neighbor as himself.[3]

Surely, our neighbor, our brother, our fellow man means *all* human beings. But unfortunately, to many Jews it often means only another Jew and, likewise, with the Muslim and Christian. When we look at what is happening in the Mideast, we can see clearly that this is so. To see the hatred that exists between Jews and Arabs and the indifference and intolerance of Christians toward others, we can only conclude that, judged by their own religious doctrine, a great number of them are *not* believers and certainly are *not* in a right relationship with God.

There are about 950 million Christians in the world today. Most Muslims believe every one of those *infidels* is damned to hell. There are just over one billion Muslims in the world. A vast majority of Christians believe each and every one of those *heathens* is going to go to hell. God has perfect, *unconditional* love and therefore cannot damn anyone.

The religions indeed believe that God is perfect in love and *justice*, as well as being a compassionate and forgiving God. How then is it possible for God to condemn, to eternal hell, a child or anyone else who has never heard of, never been taught about, nor understood a Christ or Muhammad or Moses or Buddha? That would surely be unjust!

It should give any reasonable, thinking person cause to wonder that such a compassionate God could condemn so many people to hell because of their religious beliefs. There has to be an inescapable, logical conclusion that all religions cannot be right, which should also give cause to wonder about the validity of their beliefs.

We even become violent and kill each other over religious beliefs. Look at the two great religions Islam and Christianity. History records that the armies of Islam, in the seventh century, spread their belief by aggressive war. Even their fellow tribes were put to the sword if they refused to pledge their allegiance to Muhammad. After Muhammad's death, Islamic armies attacked Syria, India, Africa, Mongolia and Spain in an effort to "force salvation upon the world."

Then, for almost two hundred years, in the twelfth and thirteenth centuries, the European Christians mounted eight major crusades in their "holy wars" to repossess Palestine and the Holy Lands from the Muslims, which then became, in part, crusades to gain riches and power, and assert religious control over a people. That sort of strife has continued throughout history and even exists today. A recent report showed that, of the 42 armed conflicts that were occurring at the time the report was conducted, over two-thirds were fueled by religion.[4] These hostilities are happening because the religions of the world have ignored God's command that we are to love one another--even our *enemies*, showing mercy and forgiveness. **Peace among the nations and people of the world can never be achieved until the barriers of false religious dogma are removed.**

Religion is not only a major factor in keeping the human race separated, it is also a significant barrier to our spiritual growth. Every Sunday, in thousands of Christian churches throughout the world, hundreds of millions of people are conditioned to think that they are by nature sinful and unclean; poor miserable sinners. Their minds are programmed with, and their memories have stored the concepts that it is human to err and that they will continue to sin for the rest of their mortal life. As they think, so are they! In that manner, the Christian Church has unwittingly kept mankind in bondage to sin.

Our ability to grow spiritually and improve our relationships with one another is stifled, even thwarted, by much of the religious teaching of the world. We are sometimes taught that it is our nature to sin and create all the hell that often plagues humanity. Those teachings surely demean and suppress the abilities of God's and man's magnificent co-creation: the human being. Such doctrine impedes growth and must be changed, for it represents a formidable barrier to that evolutionary thrust toward a higher level of human consciousness and oneness with one another and with God.

Religion often promotes much of the guilt and low self-esteem so prevalent in the human race. Christianity, especially, depicts man as a groveling, poor, miserable sinner who can do nothing by himself to change that condition. We have been pictured as beings who "don't know how to do good but are rotten through and through" as St. Paul tells us. Or that there is no goodness in man, only "evil and darkness in the hearts of men" as Martin Luther has declared.

We are made to feel guilty if we don't belong to a Christian church, if we don't attend regularly, if we don't participate in church activities, if we don't give enough financial support to the church, and if we don't evangelize and bring others into the organized church setting.

We are constantly reminded that we are *by nature* sinful and unclean beings, sometimes being told that we are totally corrupt, with no redeeming factors. As one Christian said to me, "It has always been a downer for me to go to church each Sunday to confess, to be told and even sometimes sing that I am such a rotten human being when I feel that I'm not that kind of person at all."

We know how the implanting of thoughts and concepts in our minds, especially with repetition and emphasis, brings those things to fruition in our lives. That continual programming of millions of church-goers with the idea that they are poor, miserable sinners who will remain so until the day they die is that ultimate, societal, self-fulfilling prophecy.

Denominational religions' claim that *only* their scripture is true and infallible further contributes to the divisiveness among us. We will be exploring the scriptures of Christianity and Islam, providing evidence that neither is immune to fallacy and that the inflexible dogma often selectively derived from their scripture sets the stage for much of the alienation and distrust that exists among humankind.

THE SCRIPTURES--THE BIBLE

The Christian theologians argued for several centuries over what writings were to be included in the Bible. Obviously then, man-made interpretations were involved. With the New Testament, the guideline as to context was whether the writings contained the apostles' teachings. That is more fallacy--interpretation by man again coming to the fore. Without going into a lot of detail it is enough to say that politics were as prevalent then as they are today. Some of the Church fathers wanted to include writings that were done earlier than those that now make up the New Testament. Others wanted to limit the New Testament to the four gospels, the Pauline epistles and a few others which finally became the New Testament.

Today's Christian theologians claim that God inspired these men to make the right selection. They make the same claim for the decisions and dogma that was formulated by men at the Augsburg Confession, the Council of Trent and other ecclesiastical conferences. When we see that the conferees at the Augsburg Confession wrote that Emperor Charles V was *Most Mighty* and *Invincible*, as well as formulating the doctrine that babies are born wicked and lustful, the claim that God inspired those men has to be suspect.

That all of the Bible has been influenced by God is part of Christian confession. Christians believe that God in some way directed and guided the writings, that they can be relied upon implicitly without question and that there are no mistakes in the Bible; it is a perfect book. *All* of the Bible is certainly not flawless.

We have noted the terrible violence supposedly blessed by or at the behest of God--the smashing of babies by soldiers, the slaughter of humans and keeping the spoils and the killing of men while saving the virgins for themselves. Those *cannot* be the inspired and guided writings of a loving God, but are surely the words of men.

Do Christians really believe that Christ said, "He that doesn't hate his father and mother cannot be my disciple?"[5] On two occasions Christ commanded that we love one another. Clearly there is a contradiction there. A young man asked Christ what he should do to have eternal life. Christ said he should "keep the commandments; refrain from murder and adultery, don't steal or bear false witness, honor your father and mother, and love your neighbor as yourself." The young man replied that "he had done so all his life." Christ then told him,

"You lack one thing, go and sell all you have and give it to the poor."[6] Fundamentalist Christians believe we must accept every detail of the Bible literally. Therefore we can only conclude that if they don't hate their father and mother and haven't sold all they own and given it to the poor, they aren't really Christians and followers of Christ.

We have already noted the inaccurate accounts of the number of men or angels that were present at Christ's tomb on Easter Sunday. Matthew and Mark said there was one. Luke and John said there were two. One minister, in trying to explain this discrepancy to me, said, "It is a fact that different moments in the story are being described." That isn't a fact at all! When we closely examine these stories, it is clear that the moment in the story was the exact same one in the different versions. It was the moment when the two Marys went to the tomb to anoint Christ's body at sunrise on Easter morning. It was the very moment they entered the tomb!

We also have previously noted the apparent discrepancy in the stories about Christ's ascension to heaven. The Christian theologians say there isn't a discrepancy, but that isn't so. According to Acts, it was forty days after Easter and that is the date observed by the Church. But Luke clearly shows that the ascension took place the day after Christ's resurrection and may even have been the same day, Easter Sunday.

Luke's account is as follows: The two Marys had gone to the sepulcher on Sunday, the day of resurrection. Not finding Christ there they went directly and told the apostles, who didn't believe them. Peter even went to see for himself. The *same day* two of the apostles went to Emmaus, about seven miles away. Jesus appeared to them, talked with them, and after a meal late in the day he vanished. The *same hour* they went back to Jerusalem to tell the others. They could cover that distance in about three hours or less, so were probably back in Jerusalem by early evening. While they were speaking to the disciples,

Jesus appeared to them all. He showed them his wounds, ate with them, opened their minds to the scripture and then led them out as far as Bethany, blessed them and was carried up into heaven. All of that could have occurred even before midnight on Sunday, but surely no later than the next day.

Even Mark implies in Chapter 16 that Christ appeared to the disciples in Jerusalem on Sunday evening as they sat at meat, upbraiding them for their unbelief and telling them to go and teach the gospel. After he had spoken to them, he was received up into heaven. Those are very clear contradictions of the Ascension version in Acts.

These discrepancies aren't important at all. They only show that the Bible contains the errant and fallible word of man. A number of open-minded, clear thinking theologians and religious leaders have acknowledged that this is so. We must always keep this in mind when we decide for ourselves what is right and wrong. The Bible can be considered inspired and infallible in that it also contains God's words, which achieve the purpose of giving us the instructions we need to grow spiritually, live in peace and harmony with one another and obtain eternal life.

A great deal of contradiction exists in the New Testament teachings, especially between St. Paul and the words of God as given through Christ in the four gospels of Matthew, Mark, Luke and John. The Church puts much store in the writings of St. Paul. In fact, when closely examined, it is clear that most of Christian doctrine is based on the writings of Paul. This is unfortunate, because St. Paul is inconsistent, unreliable and errant in his writings.

Should we give credence to Paul's statement to the effect that it's okay to marry, but "I wish everyone could get along without marrying just as I do."[7] What of his declarations that,

Religion the Great Barrier 163

"instinct tells us that women's heads should be covered when they pray in public"[8] and "nature itself teach that, if a man has long hair, it's a shame to him?"[9]

God has said we should go forth and multiply. If no one married, as Paul would prefer, we would be violating God's commandment, and the human race would be extinct in about a hundred years--unless a man and woman lived together and had children without the benefit of marriage, which Paul says is forbidden. Do you think that God gives a hoot whether a woman wears a hat in church, or a man has long hair? If, as many ministers believe, those are the inspired and infallible words of God, why do they allow those "shameful" pictures of a long-haired Christ in the church, and why do they allow women to come to church without hats?

About marriage and divorce, Paul says, "If the husband or wife who isn't a Christian is eager to leave, it is permitted."[10] How many pastors do you suppose give that counsel to couples who come to them in such a situation? They should, because that is God's word, according to Paul and according to Christian doctrine of biblical infallibility.

St. Paul also wrote that women should be "silent in church meetings for they are subordinate to men"[11]. He says, "That is a commandment from the Lord himself. But if anyone disagrees--well, we will leave him in his ignorance."[12] So you see, Paul is telling all the ministers who allow women to serve on church councils, or boards, and even to teach Sunday school, that they are disobeying a command from God and are ignorant on the matter of a woman's place in church affairs.

We have seen how, in Romans 13, Paul said that *all* governments are put in power by God; that anyone who resists an ordinance of government is resisting God and shall be *damned*.[13] Any intellectually honest person knows those words are absolutely false and therefore could not have been inspired by God!

He also said that rulers are "ministers of God, not a terror to good but to evil."[14] Do you believe that this is the infallible word of God? Do you believe that rulers like Hitler and Stalin were *ministers* of God? What of the terror they inflicted upon mankind? Was all that an illusion? Was the Holocaust for the good of mankind? According to St. Paul, it was.

St. Paul said, "Don't you know, we Christians are going to judge and govern the world?"[15] Even Christ said he didn't come into the world to judge it.[16] Paul wrote that the world's end would come during his lifetime.[17] Why would God inspire Paul to write what we *know* are untruths?

St. Paul shows considerable confusion when it comes to salvation and obedience to God's laws. Paul says we can do nothing to earn our salvation; we are saved by faith without the works of the law lest any man shall boast. He says we can't be saved by the works of the law because we can't keep the law. Then he turns around and says in Romans 13 that in loving others we are obeying *all* of God's laws, fulfilling *all* of his requirements. He says all Ten Commandments are wrapped up in this one--to love your neighbor as yourself, which satisfies *all* of God's requirements.[18] He says that this is the only law we need and that we have an obligation to live that way.

Anyone with an open mind, who wishes to, can clearly see that a great deal of Paul's writings are unreliable, outright wrong and could not possibly have been inspired by God. It is obvious that they are his own ideas. He even told us so when he said, "Here I want to add some of my own suggestions. They are not direct commands from the Lord, but they *seem* right to me."[19] That statement alone renders invalid the Church's claim that all of the Bible is inspired by God. Most certainly, St. Paul had some good things to say to us and some of his errors aren't important at all. But if we can't trust his judgment in small things, how can we trust him in the important matters such as salvation?

Religion the Great Barrier 165

Some religious scholars and teachers say such rules and instructions as those of Paul's were meant for another time or culture; as time passes, the laws change, or are no longer valid. Who then determines what laws are to be retained and which are no longer valid? By that logic man can change or disregard scriptural law and guidance as he wishes, or as cultural change dictates. Then the scriptures eventually become meaningless.

God's word is in the Bible. It provides us with his wonderful truths, his instructions for harmonious living, and how we are to be righteous with him. But the Bible also provides us with the imperfect, divisive and even completely erroneous words of man that foster false doctrine and misunderstanding of God, as well as discord among mankind.

Among the theologians are many intellects, evidenced by the enormous volume of religious doctrine and philosophy that they have generated. They have debated over everything from the very serious to the absolutely ridiculous, such as the number of "angels that can dance on the head of a pin." They have reasoned so much that they have totally confused the world as to what is scripturally correct concerning religion. Most certainly, scriptural writings were governed by or changed in the early years of Christianity to reflect personal views of the writers and the Church hierarchy.

Doctor L. David Moore, in his book THE CHRISTIAN CONSPIRACY, documents how early Church leaders "conspired"--not deceitfully, but uniting in a purpose--to establish doctrine that supported their beliefs, which then altered the teachings of Christ.[20] Episcopal priest, Father John W. Groff, Jr., said of Moore's work, "As you have so aptly described, those who made up the hierarchy of the early Church were both autocratic and authoritarian and thus unfailingly established doctrines which invested their office and themselves with absolute power over the baptized both in this life and the life to come. It continues today!"[20]

Still, we can say that the integrity of the Bible remains intact. Its message is powerful and has stood the test of time. It shows us how we can literally enjoy heaven on earth. It reveals the words of eternal life. That "word will never pass away."[21] We need to use logic, intelligence and common sense in examining that word. Common sense involves sound practical judgment and listening to the "heart." When common sense is added to intellect, it produces wisdom. Use your wisdom to search the scriptures and see for yourself what is right. Don't blindly accept everything you have been taught. Don't limit yourself to Christian scripture, but search all the holy writings of the world. You will find God's truths in all of them. It is important that you let your thinking be guided by the fundamental basis of almost all religions--a proper relationship with God and your fellow man.

THE SCRIPTURES--THE KORAN

Just as biblical scripture is fallible and Christian doctrine on the matter is errant, so are Koranic scripture and Islamic teaching. Muslims believe that *every* sentence, word and even *every* syllable of the Koran is accurate, as dictated to Muhammad by Gabriel. When one honestly and open-mindedly examines the Koran, it is obvious that this cannot be so. For example, we have seen that Surah 23:94 says "Requite evil with good." Yet Surah 42:35 says, "Let evil be rewarded with like evil." In the context in which these statements are given, their meaning is as stated. Obviously, both cannot be right. The Koran says it was *all* given to Muhammad in *a* (one) night. It would be *impossible* for Muhammad, an ordinary man, as Muslims believe, to assimilate and remember all that material in that time period. Also, according to history and Islamic teaching, it was given to Muhammad over a period of years.

The Koran was verbally given to Muhammad by the angel Gabriel. Muhammad then supposedly memorized it *exactly* and, in turn, gave it to others who were called "rememberancers." They also memorized it in detail, and without error, as Muhammad gave it to them. They in turn passed it on to still others who wrote it down. This took place over a forty-year period. Knowing the fallibility of man's mind and the unreliability of the memory, it is not realistic to believe, after forty years, and the sifting through so many intermediaries, that the revelations given to Muhammad were the same as those finally compiled in the Koran. History records that there were different versions, with decisions having to be made as to the selection of the final one; the second caliph after Muhammad having established the last and official version. Obviously, fallible human influence has been recorded in the Koran.

The Koran attributes some very strange and unbelievable things to Allah. For example, Surah 2:64 says, "You have heard of those of you that broke the Sabbath. We said to them: 'You shall be changed into detested apes.' We made their fate an example to their own generation and to those who followed them." Apes are not detested; they are also God's creatures and not despised at all. Where is there a record of any person ever being turned into an ape, so that it is set as an example for future generations? Can any reasonable person believe a loving and forgiving Allah would turn anyone into an ape just because he did not observe the Sabbath?

In Surahs 3:118 and 4:415, the Koran forbids believers (Muslims) from making friends with any but their own people. Surah 5:51 is more specific, saying, "Believers, take neither Jews nor Christians for your friends. They are friends with one another. Whoever of you seeks their friendship shall become one of their number." Who can believe that Allah, who desires and even commands that we live in peace and harmony, would issue such divisive instructions? Attesting to the errancy of this scripture is the statement saying that Jews and Christians are friends with one another. We know that they are not always friends, but often are greatly at odds with one another, especially over religious matters, and sometimes are even enemies. Some are friends, while others hate one another. Fortunately, all Muslims do not live by this code, but rather extend the hand of friendship to others, and very few, if any, change their religious affiliation because of it.

Just as in the Bible, the Koran is replete with references to harsh punishment, violence and killing, supposedly perpetrated by or commanded by Allah. The Koran also contains an overwhelming number of references to the wonderfully compassionate and forgiving Allah. Surely you can see the inconsistency--if not the impossible contradiction--in these statements. The inconsistency is readily apparent when we look at specific paragraphs, as well as the entire context of this matter.

Surah 5:39 says, "As for the man or woman who is guilty of theft, cut off their hands to punish them for their crimes. That is the punishment enjoined by Allah. Allah is mighty and wise. But whoever repents after committing evil, and mends his ways, shall be pardoned by Allah. Allah is forgiving and merciful." This is a *merciful* and *forgiving* Allah? It is not likely that a wise Allah commanded such cruel punishment. Does that apply to all thievery? Think of the incredible extenuating circumstances that might be involved. What if a man stole a loaf of bread because he was hungry, or to feed his starving children? Man's fallible judgment also can become involved. Who determines that there was theft? What about false or vengeful witnesses? What about faulty witnesses who thought they saw theft, but were in error? What about mistaken identity? It happens even today. If a thief mends his ways and repents, Allah will forgive and pardon him. Meanwhile he has lost his hand, making it difficult to earn a living or support his family. It simply is not possible for a wise, loving, compassionate and forgiving Allah to have issued such imprecise, cruel and unjust instructions for the crime of theft.

Surah 5:34 says, "Those that make war against Allah and His apostle (Muhammad) and spread disorder in the land shall be put to death or crucified or have their hands and feet cut off on alternate sides or banished from the country." Who decides the nature of making war against Allah or spreading disorder? The same flaws apply here as for the instructions for theft. Allah, who has perfect wisdom, compassion and love, would never provide man with such imperfect commands as these.

In Surah 5:9 Muslims are told to "Slay the *idolaters* wherever you find them. Arrest them, besiege them and lie in ambush for them everywhere." Surah 9:4 says, "Proclaim a woeful punishment to the unbelievers, except those *idolaters* who have honored their treaties with you in every detail and aided none against you. With these keep faith, until their treaties have run their term." This is saying that if Muhammad had a treaty with his enemies, the unbelievers, the idolaters, on secular matters, they would be exempt from punishment and death, but if no treaty existed it was okay to kill them. It is also saying that when the treaty ran out, he no longer had to keep faith with them and they could be punished. Those cannot be the instructions of a wise, just and honorable Allah.

Surah 17:31 instructs "You shall not kill any man who Allah has forbidden you to kill, except for a just cause. If a man is slain unjustly, his heir shall be entitled to satisfaction. But let him not carry his vengeance too far, for his victim in turn will be assisted and avenged." It is inconceivable that an all-wise Allah could have given Muhammad such contradictory, undefined and irresponsible instructions.

Allah is saying in that first sentence, that, although he has *forbidden* you to kill a man, it is all right to do so for a just cause. That doesn't make sense. When killing is condoned for a just cause, it opens the proverbial can of worms. Fallible man soon starts determining what is just. Then all kinds of errors and injustices occur. Who decides the point beyond which justice may not be carried? This kind of guidance leads to "blood feuds" that escalate and go on forever. It also means we have the right to take *justice* and revenge into our own hands. Surah 17:31 is not the word of an Allah perfect in wisdom!

Those are most certainly the words of an imperfect and unwise man. Surah 6:151 also says that you shall not kill--for that is forbidden by Allah--except for a just cause. The word of Allah is most certainly in the Koran, but so is the faulty word of man. It is most likely that the words "you shall not kill--for that is forbidden by Allah" are the words of Allah, to which man then added the words "except for a just cause" to rationalize and justify killing.

The Koran and Muslims contradict themselves on the subject of believers and unbelievers. Muslims consider themselves believers and all non-Muslims to be unbelievers. The Koran generally classifies those who do not believe in Allah and his revelations as unbelievers and places most Jews and Christians in that category. The Koran identifies a believer as one who believes in God, angels, Judgment Day and the doing of good deeds. Almost all Jews and Christians believe in these things and therefore are believers.

Surah 5:65 says, "If the People of the Book accept the true faith and keep from evil, We will pardon them their sins and admit them to the gardens of delight. If they observe the Torah and the Gospel and what is revealed to them from their Lord, they shall enjoy abundance from above and beneath." This clearly says that Jews and Christians are believers and can gain heaven if they observe their own scriptures. They are not required to be Muslim, follow Muhammad or accept the Koran and Islam as their religion. The Koran and Muslims are in error as to the nature of belief.

Surah 9:11 says, "Allah has purchased from the faithful their lives and worldly goods and in return has promised the Garden. They will fight for the cause of God, slay and be slain. Such is the promise which He has made them in the Torah, the Gospel and the Koran." There is no such promise in the Gospel! It does say that those who are killed in the service of God will receive their reward. But it says nothing about being rewarded for killing others in the service of God. The Koran is clearly in error.

Those who kill in the name of God--for example, blowing themselves up and taking others with them in acts of terrorism--will be greatly surprised when they leave this mortal life. Instead of finding themselves being rewarded in paradise, as they were falsely led to believe would happen, they will suffer anguish in the next life, understanding, seeing and feeling the cruelty and suffering they inflicted upon others. Allah *does not* condone killing under any circumstance.

Surah 8:36 says, "Tell the unbelievers that if they mend their ways their past shall be forgiven, but if they persist in sin, let them reflect on the fate of their forefathers. Make war on them until idolatry shall cease and God's religion shall reign supreme." Many Muslims, particularly the fundamentalists, use that passage, and the one above about slaying and being slain for the cause of God, to justify the Jihad, or holy war, against the infidels or anyone else that they perceive to be the enemies of Islam.

It is very likely that, in some way, Allah's instructions to Muhammad on this matter have been misinterpreted. Allah wants the unbelievers to repent and come to believe. Making war on them--that is, physically attacking them and killing them--is not likely to erase idolatry and change the unbelievers' minds. It is more likely to make them angry and defiant. We know from human experience that force is not effective in changing a belief. Under the threat of force, people may verbally acknowledge that they have changed their beliefs, but what they believe in their hearts has not changed. You can't *force* religion on people as the Koran and Islamic teaching suggest.

Further, you obviously haven't changed a person's beliefs if you have killed him. When the Koran says to make war on the unbelievers and slay them wherever you find them, it does not intend that you should do so literally. It almost certainly has a figurative meaning, which suggests slaying their "unbelief."

To make war, do battle or even slay is not always a physical action, but can be done in an intangible way, such as mentally or spiritually. It can be done with words--*the pen is mightier than the sword*. To make war against or slay can simply mean to be in a state of opposition against something, struggling or striving vigorously to change it. It can be done by education, verbal persuasion, kindness, example, or love. To do battle or make war can mean a prolonged or generally peaceful conflict pursued to bring about change by such means as fighting against crime, corruption, injustice or *unbelief*. Surely that is what Muhammad meant when he spoke of the greater jihad or "holy war"--to make war against unbelief.

The Koran does contain the wonderful truths of God and codes for harmonious and fruitful living. It also contains the imperfect, divisive, and sometimes violent and cruel codes of man which foster antagonism and disunity in the human race. Just as with other scriptures, the Koran has been misinterpreted, distorted, ignored and added to by religious teachers and leaders for the sake of tradition and purpose of promoting their own agenda.

It is patently clear, for anyone who wishes to see, that Biblical and Koranic scripture are neither without error nor unfailing, but most certainly contain the unreliable words of men. For theologians and religious leaders to continue to insist that their scriptures are without error, in the face of absolute proof that they are not, is indicative of closed-mindedness, a lack of integrity and an unwillingness to seek and find the truth.

It is especially reprehensible because it has contributed greatly to disunity among the peoples of the world.

ISLAMIC DOCTRINE

An even greater contribution to discord in the human race is the equally false dogma spread by religious denominations that *their* way is the right and *only* way to know God and be saved. Christianity and Islam are especially guilty of this, striving for religious domination through Islamic revolution and Christian evangelism. The Koran says we are not to force our religious beliefs and laws on one another but rather vie with each other for good works. It has to be said that the Jews and other religious groups, such as the Hindus and Buddhists, are more obedient to Allah in that respect.

Muslims are responsible for the divisive doctrine of Muhammad as the only way to know God and achieve paradise; that Muhammad is the "true prophet," implying that the others such as Moses and Christ are not. They teach that earlier codes--the Torah and Gospel--were canceled by the advent of Muhammad, who gave the world a complete and flawless code of life. Few Jews or Christians will ever accept such doctrine. This type of dogma is extremely detrimental to the harmony and oneness that God desires for the human race.

Islamic leaders claim that Muhammad's message is for all people and all ages. If that is so, then consider the following. Surah 23:1 says, "Blessed are the believers who are humble in their prayer; who avoid profane talk, and give alms to the destitute; who restrain their carnal desires except with their wives and slave girls, for these are lawful to them, and do not transgress through lusting after other women." According to Muhammad's code of life, given in the Koran, Muslims can have up to four wives and as many slave girls as they wish to satisfy their carnal desires.

As Muhammad's message is for all peoples and all ages, then all men today, Muslim, Jew, Christian, Hindu, atheist or whoever, can also have four wives and unlimited slave girls to fulfill their passions and sexual appetites and it is okay with Allah. Our common sense tells us that this way of living is impractical and would wreak havoc in our societies and with the family structure. Surely Allah does not approve of slavery, but intends that all people be free.

Islam also teaches that the Koran presents a message that invites the whole human race to a view of reality. Is it reality to *stifle harmony* among people by forbidding friendship with others who do not hold your religious beliefs? Is it reality to besiege and arrest those who do not believe as you do? Is it reality to *force* religious beliefs on others? Is it reality to cut off the hand and foot of those who say anything against, or oppose, Allah and His instructions? Is it reality for a man to have four wives and as many slave girls as he wishes to satisfy his carnal desires? Anyone who thinks so is not facing reality! Considering that Muhammad was a good, kind, compassionate and godly man, it is not likely that such codes were expounded by him, but rather that these are the codes of others trying to justify their way of life.

Certainly, most Muslims do not have multiple spouses or slaves but treat their sole wife and other women with respect. And the ideology of Islam is wonderful. Islam means peace and obedience to God, which is what the world badly needs. For Muslims to teach and spread this philosophy to the world is admirable and could be acceptable to most people. The basics of Islam are right and good. Islam is indeed "a way of life, the bases of which lie rooted in Divine Revelation; a way of life which is permeated with God-consciousness and is oriented to doing God's will and actualizing good and righteousness in human life." Of those who believe in God, few would argue with this wisdom, especially as it also embodies the basic teaching of Judaism and Christianity, as well as other religions. This kind of Islamic thought is wonderful and welcome.

What is not welcome is Islamic teaching that all people, of all ages, must swear allegiance to and follow Muhammad if they are to know God and be saved. What cannot and never will be accepted by much of the world is the Islamic claim that the message of Muhammad, as reflected in the Koran, supersedes and cancels all previous scriptures and codes.

There are major differences in the teachings of Islam and Christianity that foster alienation. For example, Christ said he is the son of God. The Koran and Muslims strenuously object to that, saying "Allah forbid that He begat a son." Christ said he was crucified, even told his disciples to examine the healed wounds in his hands. The Koran unequivocally says he was not crucified. This is a very major disagreement that could never be resolved, for the crucifixion is the cornerstone of Christian belief.

The Koran makes divorce easy for a variety of reasons. Christ said the only grounds for divorce is adultery, although this has to be questioned. Christ forbids killing. Muhammad and the Koran say it is okay under certain circumstances. This is a very big discrepancy, for it opens the door to "justified" killing by fallible man and sets the stage for violence in the world.

We can find disagreements about prayer, what can be eaten, about being children of God and about the nature of friends and enemies. The Koran says Muslims are not to be friends with Jews and Christians. Christ says we are to be friendly to all people, showing love to everyone without exception. He even says we are to love our enemies and do good to those who persecute us. The Koran says to have nothing to do with your enemies and, in certain cases, to kill them.

There is a major inconsistency concerning God's love. Christ says God loves everyone unconditionally; he just doesn't love some of the things that they do. But he loves them all as his children, his creation, and wants everyone to believe in him, obey him and be saved. The Koran states that God doesn't love unbelievers, aggressors or sinners. He guides them, step by step, to ruin and hell.

The reality is that these discrepancies aren't of great importance. The real issue is what God requires of us to gain Paradise/Heaven. And in this there is no variation. The Koran, the Gospel and the Torah all state the same requirements for salvation: Love God, obey him, do good works, and love and care for our fellow human beings, showing them compassion and forgiveness. The contention is between those who have interpreted the scriptures. Past and present religious leaders of the world must bear the responsibility. The great tragedy is the ignoring of God's word and the formulating of false religious dogma to support religious beliefs.

All religions have value and wisdom. However, they all embrace man-made dogma that often causes confusion and fosters divisiveness among humankind. Why should we tolerate that? It is especially true of Christianity and Islam--both trying to dominate the world with their religion. Muslims are responsible for that devastating doctrine of Muhammad as the only way to know God and the abrogation of the Torah and Gospel by the advent of Muhammad and the Koran. Christianity has devised creeds making it essential to be a Christian if one is to get to heaven--creeds that have no basis in the teaching of Jesus Christ.

Chapter Thirteen

CHRISTIANITY GONE ASTRAY

The Christian Church has indeed strayed far from the teachings of Jesus Christ. Rather than being grounded in the true gospel of Christ, Christian doctrine is based almost solely on the "gospel" of St. Paul. When speaking of forgiveness and salvation, most Christian ministers will immediately go to the epistles of St. Paul for their references. Almost never will they quote what Jesus Christ has said in the four gospels of Matthew, Mark, Luke and John about being saved and achieving heaven. And for good reason, because the gospel, according to Christ, is diametrically opposed to the teachings of Paul and the Christian Church

Before we go further, it has to be said that references to the doctrine of the Christian Church, and its analysis herein, do not apply to all denominations of the Church. Obviously, there are varied beliefs within different groups. For instance, there are a large number of Christians who do not believe that Jesus Christ is the *only* path to God; that there are those other-than-Christians who will get to heaven.

St. Paul says we are powerless to earn our salvation; our salvation is not based on good works or anything we can do, but solely on what Christ has done. This is the heart and soul of the Christian doctrine of salvation. We are reconciled to God only through God's punishment of Christ on the cross for the sins of all mankind. Now God's anger at our disobedience is satisfied and he forgives and accepts us for the sake of Christ's suffering.

It is a concept that is really quite bizarre. Having placed in man's way the instrument--the forbidden fruit in the Garden of Eden--that made man a sinner and separated man from God, he decided to redeem mankind. Actually, according to Christian teaching, God had planned all of this from the beginning of time. Then when the "time was right," a few thousand years after Adam, and after millions had died in their sins and gone to hell, God himself came down from heaven in the form of man to act as savior and redeemer.

As the man, Jesus Christ, God lived a perfect life, then offered himself as an unblemished sacrifice to himself to appease his anger at humankind for their disobedience and sin. He then punished himself on the cross and in hell, taking upon himself all the sins of the world that ever were committed and will ever be committed.

Now, whoever accepts and believes this "doctrine" is redeemed and made righteous with God through *faith* in God's redemptive act. It doesn't matter if one continues to sin. In fact, according to Christian dogma, man will always continue to sin. Having once been angry at us, turning his back on us and damning us all to eternal hellfire for disobeying him and becoming sinful, God is now no longer mad at us for disobedience and *continued* sin as long as we believe he punished himself, or took all our sins upon himself, or punished an "innocent" person, Jesus Christ. Isn't that rather strange behavior on God's part? It reminds one of the parent of a disobedient child telling the child to get a switch and beat him or her because he had failed to teach and bring the child up properly. It is reminiscent of the ancient Indian tribes who sacrificed virgins to the gods to appease their anger.

The amazing thing is that Jesus Christ taught *none* of this. You can search Matthew, Mark, Luke and John where the gospel of Christ is recorded, which the Church acknowledges, and you will not find this doctrine of salvation there. It is dogma that defies logic, scripture and Jesus Christ. Logically, God, being perfect in all things, including justice, could not punish an innocent person, Jesus Christ, for the sins of others. It also would be an injustice of great magnitude to condemn to hell anyone who has not come to know Christ. Nor is it reasonable that God, who is also perfect in love, would punish humankind in hell for simple disobedience. Doesn't any open-minded Christian find it strange, even unbelievable, that our wonderful and loving God would do such a thing just because we aren't perfect?

Secondly, scripture belies the Church's claim that God, in the person of Christ, led a perfect life. He broke the fourth commandment. The Church interprets that Law to mean that we must obey our parents in all things. At the age of twelve Christ disobeyed his parents by remaining in Jerusalem instead of returning to Nazareth with them.[1] It could not be that he was being obedient to a higher authority, his heavenly Father, as the Church says. For, according to Church doctrine, as a human being, he was to be tempted by all things that we are tempted by, and still obey the law perfectly. Obviously, he did not. Therefore, Christ was not without sin and could not have been the unblemished sacrifice on the cross. He even said it was necessary for him to be baptized.

Christ said that he who believes and is baptized shall be saved. Baptized means to be spiritually cleansed--made right with God. When we *believe* and accept Christ's message from God that we are to show love, mercy and forgiveness to others and put it into practice, we are acceptable to God. It is not water, but that word of God that cleanses (baptizes). As Christ said to the disciples who had accepted his teachings, "Now you are clean through the word I have spoken to you."[2] There is nothing wrong with considering baptism as "symbolic" of cleansing; however, to dogmatise baptism as essential to salvation has no basis in the teachings of Christ. God does not send "unbaptized" babies, or anyone else, to hell!

Christ did say, "No man can convict me of sin."[3] That certainly sounds as if he were sinless. But, as we have seen that he did not keep all of the commandments and, in his own words, needed to be baptized, his statement has to have another meaning. It means he cannot be judged and convicted of sin because he obeyed God, showing love, mercy and forgiveness to all. Neither can *we* be convicted of sin when we do the same, living as Christ told us and showed us how to do.

Nor do the Gospels record that God forgives and accepts us for the sake of Christ's sacrifice, but rather that we are forgiven when we forgive others. Christ declares this concept of forgiveness in Matthew 18, when he tells the parable of the unforgiving servant. A king had forgiven the servant his debts to the king. Then the servant refused to forgive those who were indebted to him. Learning this, the king then punished the servant. Christ said, "Likewise shall my heavenly Father do also unto you, if ye from your hearts forgive not every one his brother their trespasses."[4]

The Christian theologians have declared that "You and I don't have to meet certain requirements in order to be eligible for forgiveness."[5] They base that on their belief that Christ, through his suffering on the cross, met all the requirements that God demands of us because we have sinned. We, therefore, need do nothing but believe this. But there in Matthew 18, out of the mouth of the one that the Church calls their Lord and Master, Jesus Christ, is an *absolute requirement that we must meet to be eligible for forgiveness.* We must forgive others if we want God to forgive us! Who is to be believed, the Christian theologians or Jesus Christ? Christ's words completely refute and invalidate Christian dogma concerning forgiveness of sins.

God does not forgive us so as to escape "hell." To speak of achieving "salvation" as a way of avoiding God's condemnation to hell is a misnomer, for God does not judge or condemn. The need is to be saved from ourselves--from the anguish we will experience in the afterlife when we understand the wrong we have done others. We judge ourselves. As the Koran says, "They shall testify against themselves." But when we forgive our fellow beings their trespasses then God will forgive ours and there will be no judging or anguish.

Another way in which our sins may be forgiven involves the wonderful concept of love, as in, *loving our neighbor.* Christ said when we love our neighbor as our self, we will live in heaven forever. Obviously then, our sins would have been forgiven. We are also told that if we have loved much, we will be forgiven much, but that those who have loved little will be forgiven little. Also there is the incident where Jesus was speaking of the woman of ill repute, "Her sins, which are many, are forgiven; for she loved much."[6]

We are also forgiven through repentance. Repentance means to be sorry for our past wrongdoing and to *cease* further trespasses. We are continually told throughout the scriptures to cease our wrongdoing and do what is right and good, and then we will be right with God. He tells us in Ezekiel 18 that, "If a wicked person turns away from all his sins and begins to obey my laws and do what is just and right, he shall surely live and not die. All his past sins will be forgotten and he shall live because of his own goodness."[7] Christ tells us to "go and sin no more."[8] He certainly wouldn't tell us to do that if we weren't capable of it.

In speaking to the hypocritical, self-righteous Pharisees Christ said, "Surely evil men and prostitutes will get into heaven before you do. For John the Baptist told you to repent and turn to God, and you wouldn't, while the evil men and prostitutes did."[9] It couldn't be any clearer. The evil men and prostitutes repented, expressed sorrow for past sins, ceased further wrongdoing, turned to God's ways, and therefore were cleansed, made righteous with God, and eligible for heaven.

Christ also said that we are to forgive one another seven times seventy.[10] We humans don't always forgive like that, but we certainly have the capability to do so if we wish. As God cannot be less forgiving than we humans, he must forgive us at least 490 times. Of course, Christ didn't literally mean that we are to forgive seven times seventy. Surely his intent was that our forgiveness should have no limit. Therefore, God's forgiveness of us has no limits. The entire scripture from beginning to end is full of the wonder of God's gracious forgiveness of man. Psalm 103 says God's mercy is from *everlasting to everlasting* to those who respect God. And forgiveness is not connected to Christ's sacrifice on the cross, certainly not in the Old Testament, and definitely not according to the gospel of Jesus Christ.

Further, according to Christ's own words, he could not have been God come to earth. *Never,* ***ever*** did he claim to be God, or equal with him. He emphatically denied it saying, "Hear O' Israel, the Lord *our* God is the *one* and *only* God."[11] He often referred to himself as the son of God. It should be noted that he designated us also as the sons of God when he called God *his* Father and *our* Father, *his* God and *our* God. He also said, "You shall worship the Lord God, and *him only shall you serve.*"[12] Christ said he "came *not to be served;*"[13] therefore, if we are to believe Christ, he could not be God. When Christ was called good Master, he replied, "There is none good but God."[14] If he were God and perfect, he certainly wouldn't object to being called good. Christ frequently expressed his role as a *messenger* from God with a message of salvation--"I am not teaching you my own thoughts but those of God who sent me."[15] One who is God and equal to God would never make such statements as those.

Nor did he ever claim to be the only way to God. When Christ said, "I am the way, the truth and the life; no man cometh to the Father but by me,"[16] he did not mean that we have to believe in him, as the sacrificial lamb who died on the cross for our sins, in order to get to heaven. Christ was giving his farewell sermon to his disciples. He told them he was going to the Father to prepare a place for them. He said, "Where I go you know and *the way you know*."[17] Thomas said, "Lord, we don't know where you're going and how can we know the way?"[18] Then Christ answered, "I am the way the truth and the life."[19] Christ had just told them they knew the way! So the question has to be asked, what was it about Christ that had *already* shown the disciples the way to the Father? What was it that he had said or done?

It couldn't possibly be the "way of the cross." That hadn't occurred yet. Christ had told them he was going to die and be resurrected, but they didn't understand what he was saying. The scriptures say, "They understood none of these things."[20] They could not have known about the "Atonement." That doctrine hadn't even been established yet. The early Christians, including the disciples, believed in salvation through obedience to God by keeping the law. It wasn't until later when St. Paul started preaching his own version of the "gospel," whereby salvation is achieved only through faith in the "deified" Christ's sacrifice and his payment for our sins, that the doctrine of the atonement began to emerge.

Christ had told the disciples that they knew the way and, as they knew nothing about the atonement via the cross, they could have known the way *only* through Christ's teachings up to this point. The way to the Father was through all he had preached to them and the people about salvation, gaining heaven and eternal life. It was through listening to his message and obeying it.

Salvation was to be achieved by loving your neighbor as yourself, doing good deeds, having mercy on one another, and forgiving each other, thus to attain eternal life. *Nowhere* in his gospel had he spoken to them about his paying for the sins of all mankind on the cross. It was just the opposite. He told them to turn from their sins and do what is lawful and good in order to be right with God.

When Christ said, "I am the way the truth and the life: no man cometh to the Father but by me," he was saying to us that the way I have told you and showed you by my example is the way to eternal life, and the instructions I have given you from God are the truth. He was saying that believing in his message of love and obeying God's instructions are the only way to the Father and eternal life. It is the same way to the Father that the Torah and the Koran teach.

St. Paul clearly was in error as to how we are made right with God. There was dissension between Paul and the leaders of the apostles, Peter, James and John about the gospel and what was to be taught. Theologians have noted it, and Paul speaks of it in Galatians 2, where he criticizes Peter for teaching obedience to the law. Not only was Paul out of step with the teachings of Christ recorded in Matthew, Mark, Luke and John, but he was also at odds with the instructions for being right with God as found in Ezekiel in the Old Testament and as found in Peter, James and I John in the New Testament. Unfortunately, Paul won out and the religious hierarchy developed the Christian doctrine from his faulty writings.

Paul did not know and had not seen Christ and was not privy to his direct words, as were Peter, James and John, of whom Christ said they were one with him and God because they had heard his message and obeyed it. The teachings of Peter, James and John fit precisely with Christ's gospel that the decisive factor in getting to heaven is to obey God and do good deeds.

Peter said to Cornelius, the Roman army officer, "I truly understand that God shows no partiality, but in every nation anyone who fears (respects) him and *does what is right is acceptable* to him."[21] James tells us that "You will be doing the right thing if you *obey the Law* of the Kingdom, which is found in the scripture: Love your neighbor as yourself."[22] He says further, "You see then, that it is by **his actions** *that a person is put right with God*, and not by his faith alone,"[23] and, "Do not deceive yourselves by just listening to his word (God's); instead, *put it into practice.*"[24] James has also declared that, "If you have been merciful, then God's mercy will win out over any judgment of you."[25]

In I John 2, we are told that, "If we obey God's commands, then we are sure we know him. If someone says that he knows him, but does not obey his commands, such a person is a liar and there is no truth in him. But whoever *obeys his word* is the one whose love for God has really been made perfect. This is how we can be sure that we are in union with God: whoever says that he remains in union with God should live just as Christ did."[26] In his second letter John says, "This love I speak of means that we *must live in obedience to God's commands*. The command, as you have heard from the beginning, is that you *must all live in love.*"[27]

Christ's teachings differ vastly from those of the Christian Church. Christ's teaching embodies *our* merit and what *we do* as the key to salvation and righteousness with God. In Matthew 16:27, Christ says, "For I, the son of Mankind, shall come with my angels in the glory of my Father and *judge each person according to his* **deeds.**" Think about that statement! Christians believe Christ is going to come again on Judgment Day and decide who among all mankind, both the living and the dead, is fit for heaven and who will go to hell. Christian dogma says he is going to make that decision based on acceptance or non-acceptance of himself as the sacrificial lamb who paid the price on the cross for our sins and that our own merit or good works will not enter into that decision. But we have just seen in Matthew 16:27 that Christ unequivocally said he is going to make that decision based on *our deeds,* what we have done in this lifetime!

We are told in at least a dozen different ways in the gospels how we are to achieve salvation and eternal life. They all involve what we do; showing love to one another, doing good deeds, obedience, changing our ways and how we live. None embrace faith alone without the works of the law, as St. Paul has declared. It is not faith in what Christ has done, but faith in what *Christ told us to do* that saves us.

Christ clearly told us that we can change our way of living and do what is right and good, and that it is necessary to do so to gain heaven. He said to follow his example and do the things he told us to do. He said that those who hear his voice shall rise again, those who have done good to eternal life and those who have continued in their wrongdoing to judgment. He said the "decisive factor in getting to heaven is to obey God."[28] Christ was asked what was necessary to live in heaven forever and he replied, "What do the scriptures say?" His questioner answered, "Love the lord God with all your heart and soul and mind and your neighbor as yourself." Christ said, "You have answered correctly. This do and you shall live."[29]

He *never* qualified that message. He didn't say we had to believe in him as the sacrificial lamb or that we had to *believe* he paid the price for all the sins of mankind. *He **never** equated his suffering and death on the cross with salvation.* But he clearly equated salvation with good deeds, being merciful and showing love to one another.

He also gave us some other good news. He told us and showed us how easy it is to do all those things he commanded.

Not out of gratitude because someone else took the rap for us, nor by striving to be perfect. We can't obey God and do what is good and right by being pious, turning inward and denying ourselves, nor by self-flagellation, the haven of the cowl, or by diligently trying to observe the law, as some have tried to do in the past and continue trying to do today. St. Paul, Martin Luther, John Wesley and the Pietists tried all those things, but they didn't succeed because they didn't listen to Christ, obey him or believe in what he told them.

We obey God and do all the things that Christ commanded us to do through that wonderful and simple expedient called LOVE! We obey God and do what is right and good by turning outward, giving of ourselves, serving others, being kind, living life fully and abundantly in an atmosphere of love and caring for our fellow human beings. Sin cannot exist in the presence of love; the caring, giving, merciful and compassionate love that Christ showed us and told us to show to one another. *And if we should fail, it doesn't matter, God will forgive us as long as we forgive others.*

Love is the *new* covenant God made with us through Jesus Christ. In the Torah, God gave the people the Ten Commandments--the Ark of the Covenant--as rules to live by. In the Gospel, Christ also told us we are to keep the law of the Commandments. The difference is that he gave us one new commandment that enables us to keep all the others.

In Matthew 22:36, a lawyer asked Christ, "Sir, what is the most important command in the laws of Moses?" Jesus replied, "Love the Lord your God with all your heart, soul and mind. This is the first and greatest commandment. The second most important is similar: Love your neighbor as you love yourself. All other commandments and all the demands of the prophets stem from these two laws and are fulfilled if you obey them. Keep only these two and you will find that you are obeying all the others."[30] In John 13:34 Christ said, "A new commandment I give you: That you love one another as I have loved you."

It is really quite amazing that the Church leaders and Christians put their trust and faith in the unreliable teachings of St. Paul and reject the words of the Sovereign God, Jesus Christ and the apostles Peter, James and John! Surely, Paul and the theologians intended no wrong and were sincere in their beliefs, as are the ecclesiastics of today. However, when we honestly analyze the evidence, it is quite clear that they got it wrong concerning human nature, salvation and the cross.

The cross does have a purpose but it has nothing to do with Christ's work as a savior. For, as Christ said, in praying to God, *before* he went to the cross, "I have glorified you on earth: I have *finished* the work, which you gave me to do."[31] He also said, "We must go on to other towns as well, and give my message to them too, for that is why I was sent."[32] His work was to bring us the message of obedience to God--practicing love, good works and forgiveness so as to get to heaven. The cross had another meaning.

The Old Testament had prophesied the coming of a Messiah who would set his people free. It even spoke of the cross as the way he would die. Christ said that he gave his life so that we would believe that he was that Messiah, "When you have killed the Messiah, then you will realize I am he."[33] To prove that Christ was the Messiah *is the purpose of the cross*. Then in accepting Christ as the promised Messiah sent by God, the people also would receive his word as from God, "You will realize that I have not been telling you my own ideas but have spoken what the Father has taught me."[34] Then in embracing his message, and obeying it, we would be set free from sin and gain eternal life, "You are truly my disciples if you *live* as I tell you to, and you will know the truth, and the truth will set you free."[35] "With all the earnestness I have, I say this--*no one who obeys me shall ever die!*"[36]

It is obedience to Christ's command from God to love one another, that sets us free from sin! We cannot be convicted of sin if we live as Christ told us and showed us how to do--

showing love and compassion to all. And if we slip along the way, it's okay--God's forgiveness is ours when we forgive others. As we learned from James, "If you have been merciful, then God's mercy will win out over any judgment of you."[37] Christ gave his life, on the cross, that we might believe he was the Messiah, sent from God with that message of love, which, if we obey, frees us from sin. That is how Christ ransomed us from sin.

Clearly, the theologians have not heard Christ's message. They did not hear him tell us that we are magnificent beings-- "the salt of the earth" and "the light of the world"--who can choose to do good--"loving our neighbor as ourselves"--letting our "light shine so as to make the world good," thus achieving heaven in the hereafter as well as here on earth. Instead they listened to St. Paul tell us that we are basically sinful--"rotten through and through"--whose nature it is to do wrong, often creating hell on earth.

But God hasn't given up on us. "A thousand years is as a day to God."[38] He is patiently waiting for humanity to work out its own spiritual development. He has given us the free will with which to do it. We have bungled it pretty badly so far. Although we are to do it on our own, it appears that God nudges us and sends us messages along the way. He has sent them through Adam, Buddha, Moses, Christ, Muhammad and others. Perhaps because we have failed to heed them and progressed so slowly, he is sending us another message--that he exists and what he expects of us--through tens of thousands of people who "died" and found themselves in some paradisiacal ethereal world. There they communicated with a Being of light, perhaps a manifestation of God himself, and were then returned to this world to convey a message, perhaps even to steer mankind away from the precipice of self-destruction.

Chapter Fourteen

THE EXPERIENCERS

"In the middle of one circle was a most beautiful being. It was neither a man nor a woman, but it was both. I have never, before or since, seen anything as beautiful, loving and perfectly pleasant as this being. An immense, radiant love poured from it. An incredible light shone through every single pore of its face. The colors of the lights were magnificent, vibrant and alive. The light radiated outward. It was a brilliant white superimposed with what I can only describe as a golden hue. I was filled with an intense feeling of joy and awe. I was consumed with an absolutely inexpressible amount of love. I had the overpowering feeling that I was in the presence of the source of my life and perhaps even my creator. In spite of the tremendous awe it inspired, I felt I knew this being extremely well. With all my heart I wanted to embrace and melt into it as if we were one."[1]

Another experiencer said, "I was aware...of my past life. It was like it was being recorded....There was the warmest, most wonderful love. Love all around me...I felt light-good-happy-joy-at ease. Forever-eternal love. Time meant nothing. Just being. Love. Pure love. Love. The Light was Yellow. It was in, around. and through everything....It is God made visible. In, around, and through everything. One who has not experienced it cannot know its feeling. One who has experienced it can never forget it, yearns for its perfection, and longs for the embodiment of It."[1]

Here are a few excerpts from the narratives of other experiencers: "It was really like a homecoming. It was beautiful, it was magnificent. And it was so warm."...."Oh, God, I'm dead, but I'm here! I'm me! And I started pouring out these enormous feelings of gratitude. My consciousness was filled with nothing but these feelings of gratitude because I still existed and yet I knew perfectly well that I had died"..."You are shown your life, and you do the judging. Had you done what you should do? It's the little things, maybe a hurt child that you helped, or just stopped to say hello to a shut-in. Those are the things that are important...You are judging yourself."[1]

Speaking of the life review, an experiencer said, "What occurred was every emotion I have ever felt in my life, I felt. And my eyes were showing me the basis of how that emotion affected my life. What my life had done so far to affect other people's lives using the feeling of pure love that was surrounding me as the point of comparison. And I had done a terrible job. God! I mean it. You know, I'd done a horrible job, using love as the point of comparison....Lookin' at yourself from the point of how much love you have spread to other people is devastatin'. You will never get over it. I am six years away from that day (of his NDE) and I am not over it yet."[1]

Extensive research reveals that those reports of journeys to another world, apparently a spiritual world, have been with us for ages. Carol Zaleski in her work, OTHER WORLD JOURNEYS, gives accounts of near-death encounters in medieval and modern times--from a soldier named Er, whose experience Plato detailed, to Carl Jung to all the NDEs that present day researchers have reported.[2] These reports now seem to be more frequent and, in our world of modern communication, the message is being spread throughout the world.

In the past, the stories told by the experiencers carried no credibility. They were usually dismissed as hallucinations, fantasy or the work of the devil. Even today they are sometimes labeled as such by critics and would-be debunkers. However, since 1975, when Dr. Raymond Moody, Jr. published his LIFE AFTER LIFE, the first book on the near-death experience, many other researchers have gathered a large amount of evidence that supports the reality of these experiences.

Doctor Melvin Morse, pediatrician, has conducted an extensive study of the near-death experience. In his book, CLOSER TO THE LIGHT, he relates the case of Katie, a nine year-old girl who died in a swimming pool accident. She experienced passing through a tunnel and meeting a guardian angel who helped her. She met relatives, a Being of Light and then was returned to life. During her NDE, Katie visited her home. "She saw her brother playing with a GI Joe, her sister combing the hair of a Barbie doll and her mother preparing a meal of roast chicken and rice. Later, when Katie mentioned this to her parents, she shocked them with her vivid details about the clothing they were wearing, their positions in the house, even the food her mother was cooking."[3]

Doctor Morse probed Katie's religious beliefs. He "wanted to see if she had been heavily indoctrinated with belief in guardian angels and tunnels to heaven. The answer from her mother was an emphatic *no*." Doctor Morse said his "deepest instinct told me that nothing in Katie's experience was 'taught' to her before the near drowning. Her experience was fresh, not recalled memory." He said that "Katie told her story in such a powerful and compelling way that he believed her implicitly."[3]

The term "near-death experience" was coined by Dr. Moody. It refers to people who have been pronounced clinically dead, having no heartbeat, nor respiration and, in some cases, a flat-line electroencephalogram. But, because of heroic efforts by medical personnel, and in many cases for reasons unknown to medicine, these people have returned to temporal life. They are now popularly known as "experiencers."

Calling these events "near-death experiences" could be considered somewhat of a misnomer, for the physical bodies, by our medical standards, did indeed die. Yet, because they are alive today, they obviously have not died. It is somewhat a matter of semantics. To be technically correct, they would have to be called "near-final-death-of-the-physical-body experiences." Even more correct would be to call them "resurrection experiences." Researchers and writers may have been reluctant to use such a term, for it would likely offend those who believe there has only been one true resurrection, that of Jesus Christ. They believe there will be no other resurrection until Judgment Day when all those in the grave will be "resurrected" as was Christ. Yet that is precisely what happened to these experiencers. The soul that sustains life in the physical body departed, leaving it in a state of death, but later returned to the body and gave it life again.

The clinically dead condition has lasted, in some cases, up to a known one hour. When the brain is deprived of oxygen, usually for five minutes or more, at room or body temperature, brain damage begins to occur. After an hour there would be extensive, irreversible damage to the brain. In some cases, C-scans showed massive swelling of the brain, however, when these people recovered, no damage had occurred and they were perfectly normal.

In describing that case of Katie, Doctor Morse said, "I stood over her lifeless body in the intensive care unit...A few hours earlier she had been found floating face down in a YMCA pool...An emergency CAT scan showed massive swelling of the brain...Three days later she made a full recovery."[3]

Doctor Morse also documents the case of an eleven year old boy who had a cardiac arrest, "He was without a heartbeat for at least twenty minutes. During this time, several cardiac medications were given, with no success. One of the nurses present remembers saying, 'I wish we didn't have to do this,' meaning that she thought the lifesaving attempts were useless.

"As a last resort, the physicians tried the cardioversion paddles again. They pressed the devices against his chest and pushed the buttons that sent electrical current jolting through his heart. Miraculously, the boy opened his eyes and said, 'That was weird. You sucked me back into my body.'"[3] He made a complete recovery.

Phyliss Atwater, researcher *and* experiencer, is unique in that she died three times and is still living today. Her encounters with death led her on a quest to find and question other experiencers. She located over two hundred other survivors. She said, "I often asked the question, 'How long were you dead?'" She said, "the average time 'out' was thought to be five minutes. Many were 'gone' longer, one for over an hour."[4] These people having made complete recoveries is scientific evidence that some supernatural force was at work and this evidence supports the validity of the experience.

During that period when they were clinically dead, these people encountered consistently similar experiences. The following sequence is a compilation of happenings that occur during the near-death experience, although all do not experience every one of these events. They often hear the doctor pronounce them dead. They find themselves out of their bodies, usually hovering above or nearby. Pain and physical distress are gone being replaced by a great sense of peace. They have another type of body, often described as a spiritual body, with unusual abilities.

Time and distance are irrelevant. They travel distances in an instant. They can pass through walls. During the sequence, most, but not all, pass through a long tunnel at very high speed entering into what has been described as a heaven-like place. Others come to meet them, usually deceased relatives or friends.

Communication is by thought rather than word. They encounter a Being of Light who radiates unconditional love, peace and joy. The Being shows them a sort of panoramic review of their life. They perceive it as taking place in seconds, yet it is inclusive of all things they have done, and they fully understand it. No judgment or condemnation is pronounced by the Being.

They are sometimes asked if they wish to return, or told that they must return. Most do not wish to because of the overwhelming peace and joy they are experiencing. But they find themselves reunited with their earthly, physical body sometimes suffering the pain they may have been experiencing just before death.

Doctor Kenneth Ring perhaps best articulates the meaning of the near-death experience, basing his conclusions on empirical research, medical data as well as the narratives of the experiencers. In his work, HEADING TOWARD OMEGA, he documents the events that occur to those who encounter death: "All pain and fear had vanished, warmth and comfort permeated my being and a feeling of solitude and peace surrounded me....I was floating in the air above my body. Not only was I floating, I could also fly at a terrific rate of speed....I thought it was some sort of tunnel and immediately entered into it and flew with an even greater sensation of the joy of flight....Friends and relatives came to help me and were very pleased to see me, exhibiting total love and acceptance....There was this most gorgeous living light; entering it was a wonderful, joyous feeling, an ecstatic experience....It was a great sense of freedom; it was like coming home. There are no words in the human language to adequately describe it."[5]

Doctor Ring relates one experiencer's encounter with the Being of Light: "Instantly my entire life was laid bare and open to this wonderful presence, 'GOD.' I felt inside my being his forgiveness for the things in my life I was ashamed of, as though they were not of great importance. I was asked--but there were no words; it was a straight mental instantaneous communication--'What had I done to benefit or advance the human race?' At the same time, all my life was presented instantly in front of me and I was shown or made to understand what counted. I am not going into this any further, but, believe me, what I had counted in life as unimportant was my salvation and what I thought was important was nil."[5]

Ring believes the lessons that the experiencers learn will help humankind evolve to a higher level of consciousness. For instance, experiencers have said, "We learn to share more love, to be more loving toward one another. To discover that the most important thing is human relationships and love and not material things. And to realize that every single thing that you do in your life is recorded. The little things that are recorded that you don't realize at the time are really important"...."One of the things that I discovered that is very important is patience toward other human beings and realizing that you yourself may be in that situation"...."I realized that consciousness is life. We will live in and through much, but this consciousness we know that is behind our personality will continue"...."And that death is not to be feared, because if death is anything, anything at all like what I experienced, it's gotta be the most wonderful thing to look forward to, absolutely the most wonderful thing."[5]

It is interesting to note that young children do not receive a life review. It is perhaps significant in that the Being does not find little children in need of a review because they are not considered deliberate sinners. That would fit in with the scriptural view of little children being innocent. Nor do all adults undergo a life review. Perhaps because they have met the criteria for nonjudgment such as having shown mercy or much love to others.

The out-of-the-body part of the near-death experience has been proven without doubt. When these events occur in a hospital emergency room, those who were resuscitated from their clinically dead condition were able to give elaborate, detailed accounts of the resuscitation procedures, equipment used, people present, their dress, and what was going on in other areas such as waiting rooms and halls outside the emergency room. These detailed accounts have been absolutely verified by doctors and nurses who were in attendance.

Doctor Morse documented the case of Jimmy, who "fell from a bridge when he was fishing and hit his head on a rock in the water below. The doctor's report says that Jimmy had stopped breathing and was without a pulse when a police officer pulled him from the deep water in which he had floated face down for at least five minutes. The policeman performed CPR for thirty minutes until the hospital helicopter arrived, but he reported that the boy was dead on the scene when they started the rush to the hospital.

"Two days later he was out of his coma. He described, to his physician, his entire rescue in vivid detail, including the name of the police officer who tried to resuscitate him, the length of time it took for the helicopter to arrive on the scene, and many of the lifesaving procedures used on him in the helicopter and at the hospital."[6]

Doctor Michael Sabom has done some fascinating work on out-of-body experiences, reporting the results in his book, RECOLLECTIONS OF DEATH. "Sabom asked twenty-five medically savvy patients to make educated guesses about what happens when a doctor tries to get the heart started again. He wanted to compare the knowledge of 'medically smart' patients with the out-of-body experiences of medically unsophisticated patients.

He found that twenty-three of the twenty-five in the control group made mistakes while none of the thirty-two near-death patients made mistakes in describing what went on in their own resuscitations."[7]

Doctor Moody reported that several doctors told him they were "utterly baffled about how patients with no medical knowledge could describe in such detail and so correctly the procedures used in resuscitation attempts, even though these events took place while the doctors knew the patients involved to be dead."⁸

If the out-of-body experience has been proven to be true, then it is likely that the rest of the near-death experience is also authentic. Further proof that the rest is also authentic is provided by the following event that occurs while the experiencer is in that "spiritual otherworld."

They encounter a relative such as a distant uncle, a great-grandparent, or a friend of another member of the family of whom they had no prior knowledge. That relative or friend identifies him or herself by name and relationship. Later when they tell living family members of the encounter, those family members confirm that such a person did indeed exist and that the experiencer was never told about and could not have had prior knowledge of that person.

Doctor Morse relates the experience of a young man named Cory who "told his mother that he had met an old high school boyfriend of hers who had been crippled in an automobile accident. She had never mentioned the man to Cory, not to hide her relationship, but simply because she had not seen him in many years. Cory said to his mother, 'don't worry, he said to tell you he can walk now.'"⁹

Although the near-death experience cannot be proven "scientifically," sufficient evidence exists that something very unusual has occurred to these people and that a lesson is to be learned from their encounters. It seems rather clear that God is sending us another message or reminder of his existence and what he expects of us.

What is the message that these modern day messengers bring us? There is absolutely no doubt in the minds of the experiencers that man has a soul, a spiritual self, that is released from the physical body when the body dies. From the proven out-of-body experience, it is apparent they are right. If we can conclude that the rest of the NDE is real, and it seems reasonable to do so, then we are being told there *is* a life hereafter in a paradise-like world different from this one we know. We come to understand that it is a spiritual world, the location of which we know not, but perhaps parallel to this physical world.

We are being told of the important things in this life. People come away from these encounters with the belief that love and knowledge, in that order, are most important, both in this life and the one to come. When they encounter the Being of Light they perceive the Being as having perfect understanding and perfect love, love that is unconditional. The Being asks, "What did you do for others because you loved them; how have you learned to love?" It further questions, "Are you able to love others in the same way?"[10] They take this to mean, "do they love others in the same unconditional way that the Being loves them."[10]

They also perceive that the Being of Light is not interested in theology, religious dogma, denomination, or even particularly what they believe. The thrust of their non-verbal conversation centers on the spiritual aspects of their life and their relationship with their fellow human beings.

We saw in the first chapter how NDE researcher Dr. Moody related the account of a man who had studied at a religious seminary before his NDE: "My doctor told me I had 'died' during the surgery. But I told him that I 'came to life.' I saw in that vision what a stuck-up ass I was with all that theory, looking down on everyone who wasn't a member of my denomination or didn't subscribe to the theological beliefs that I did.

"A lot of people I know are going to be surprised when they find out that the Lord isn't interested in theology. He seems to find some of it amusing, as a matter of fact, because he wasn't interested at all in anything about my denomination. He wanted to know what was in my heart, not my head."[11]

Ring reports of a woman in her mid-twenties who, after her NDE, told him, "Yes, I'm quite more religious than I was but I don't exactly believe in what the churches do. I don't like their methods. They're into scaring people. Everything they preach I don't feel is exactly true, so I have my own beliefs."[12] Another said to him, "I don't think it (church-based religion) has anything to do with what Jesus was about."[12]

Moody says, "People who undergo an NDE come out of it saying that religion concerns your ability to love--not doctrines and denominations. In short, they think that God is a much more magnanimous being than they previously thought, and that denominations don't count.

"A good example of this is an elderly woman in New Hampshire who had an NDE after a cardiac arrest. She had been a very religious and doctrine-abiding Lutheran since she was a child. But after the NDE, she loosened up and became a more joyous person. When members of her family asked her to account for the change in her personality, she said simply that she understood God after her episode and realized that he didn't care about church doctrine at all."[13]

Love seems to be the key to everything--not romantic, sentimental love, but caring and forgiving love. As one experiencer put it, "Love that is unmotivated, unequivocal, spontaneous, overflowing and shown to others regardless of their faults. The kind of love that makes me want to know if my neighbor is fed and clothed and makes me want to help him if he is not."[14]

Those who have the NDE undergo a spiritual awakening. They have a great desire to seek knowledge, particularly spiritual knowledge. What is their purpose in life; what is God's will for them; what is God's plan for mankind? They become much more avid readers.

They bring a message concerning the fruitlessness of materialism. Their materialistic views change drastically. Their lives are no longer possession-oriented. They in no way take a vow of poverty or disdain material things, but rather rearrange their priorities. The first priority now becomes spiritualism--

understanding and gaining a right relationship with God and their fellow man. They are less judgmental against others, and they always try to look for the good in everyone.

Their message is very much in accordance with the teaching of the scriptures. God exists and is spirit in nature. Doctor Ring reports the case of Janis: "I was raised Protestant...I gave it up in my early teens...I researched Catholicism. I found that was worse...Essentially, at the time of my accident, I was a ranting, raving atheist. There was no God...He was a figment of man's imagination...Now I know that there's a God. And that God is everything that exists, that's the essence of God...Everything that exists has the essence of God within it. I *know* there's a God now. I have no question."[14]

Their message that love and knowledge are the two most important things in this life is also very much in accordance with the scriptures. To show love to others is the dominant message of the gospel of Christ. Elsewhere scripture says, "And now abideth faith, hope and love, these three; but the greatest of these is love."[15] "Owe no man anything, but to love one another: for he that loveth another hath fulfilled the law."[16] "The greatest commandment is to love God with all your heart, soul and mind. The second is like the first: Love your neighbor as much as you love yourself."[17]

Concerning knowledge, the scripture says, "Knowledge is pleasant unto thy soul, apply your heart to understanding, cry after knowledge, ask for understanding, seek knowledge, happy is the man who gets wisdom and understanding and seek knowledge as you would seek hidden treasure, then you will understand the might of the Lord and find the knowledge of God." Clearly God puts great emphasis on the pursuit of knowledge about him. As scripture also says, "When the world is full of the knowledge of God then there will be no more harm in all his Kingdom."[18] Given the terrible violence and harm that is present in the world today, it would appear that the knowledge the religions offer as to the nature of God, is far from the truth.

The Bible tells us not to worry about or take pride in material things, but "Seek first the Kingdom of God and his righteousness"[19] and then the necessary material things will accrue to us. Scripture says, "Judge not that you not be judged."[20] All of that philosophy is very much in accord with the attitude and actions of the experiencers after their return from the "hereafter."

That latter admonition from God to judge not, and on which the experiencers place a lot of emphasis, is very important. It is a command from God that we all violate many times every day because we do not really understand its meaning. We judge when we criticize others. We do it constantly over many things. Stop and think of how often we criticize the people around us. We criticize how they dress, how they drive their car, how they perform their work, their looks, their tastes, and on and on. Judging others is a major factor that prevents harmony, peace and goodwill in our lives and throughout the world. When we judge others, it causes anger and animosity. It seldom brings about a resolution to the matter, but rather fosters resentment. It brings disruption and discord into our own lives. We often get angry and frustrated when others won't change their ways to suit us.

Instead of judging or criticizing, we should always look for the good in others, for it is there. We can help bring it out by showing love, patience and forgiveness toward others, rather than criticizing them for the things they do that irritate us or wrong us. It is part of our purpose in life to look for the good in others and through our own actions, help to manifest it in them. Each of us needs to do his part to change the world for the better. God has commanded us to do these things, and when we obey him, harmony and peace come into our lives and are promoted on earth. When we realize all these things, we come to understand God's wisdom in telling us not to judge others.

The experiencers understand this very well and practice God's adjuration. NDE researchers report that tolerance of, compassion for and acceptance of others as they are is a common result of the near-death experience. As one experiencer said, "Now I find that everyone that I meet I like...I very rarely meet someone I don't like. And that's because I accept them...I don't judge people."[21] Another said, "I try not to be biased, and not to judge people."[22]

You might ask about all the apparent criticism in this text; the criticism of the politicians, the theologians, the religions, government and the Church. How can that be reconciled with God's admonition not to judge? Surely we aren't to remain silent when we see obvious wrong being done. But then that requires man's fallible determination of what is right and wrong. Perhaps judging is different from criticism; judging having to do with condemnation and forgiveness in respect to sins and salvation. Perhaps we should not do it on a personal basis, but rather institutionally. There has to be some basis for rendering criticism of actions that seem wrong. After all, Christ was very judgmental of others. He was extremely critical of certain people, such as the self-righteous Pharisees. He called them some pretty strong names such as "hypocrites," "vipers" and an "evil generation." He called some "fools!"

The scriptures give us a clue as to how we are to reconcile this seeming conflict. Christ said, "Don't criticize, and then you won't be criticized. For others will treat you as you treat them. And why worry about a speck in the eye of a brother when you have a board in your own? Should you say, 'Friend, let me help you get that speck out of your eye,' when you can't even see because of the board in your own eye? Hypocrite! First get rid of the board. Then you can see to help your brother."[23] When we get our own "house in order," doing what is just and right, then we will see clearly what we should do and say about others. And any criticism should always be given in a kind, loving and tactful way without anger or bitterness.

Researchers into near-death experiences have been criticized for delving into that matter, even denounced by some of the clergy who say it is the work of Satan. The Bible says to "Beware of false teachers. You will know them by their fruits. You can detect them by the way they act, just as you can identify a tree by its fruit. You need never confuse grapevines with thorn bushes or figs with thistles. Yes, the way to identify a tree or person is by the kind of fruit produced."[24] Applying that standard then to those who have had the near-death experience and the message they bring from the spiritual world can leave no doubt that this phenomena is not the work of Satan but of God.

There can be no doubt where the experiencers fit in. Their own lives are changed for the better. They radiate energy, love, kindness and contentment. They have an "overwhelming, burning and consuming desire to do something for other people." Those whose lives are touched by these people are better off for it. The fruit they produce is love, kindness, confidence, compassion, patience and forgiveness.

There is one problem with the research that is being done in that field of NDEs. The researchers are in danger of doing to the message of the experiencers what the theologians have done to the truths contained in the scriptures of the world. The theologians have reasoned so much over the scriptures that they have lost sight of the scripture's basic message, thus causing great confusion among the people about the nature of God, their own nature, and what God expects of them. So it is with the researchers and the near-death experience. When one reads the NDE literature, it is obvious that some of it is written by psychiatrists and psychologists for like readers, with language that is not conducive to learning by the average reader.

One encounters such phrases as "amorphous structural-functional framework defined neither etically nor emically," "noumenon underlying phenomena," "primitive archetypal interpretation," "psychodynamical concepts," "neurobiological models," "veridical out-of-body perceptions" and other Freudian and Jungian-type language. Researchers speculate on the validity of the NDE and its similarity to experiences when the Sylvian fissure of the brain is electrically stimulated, or theorize about such things as the nature and complexities of the intangible astral world in which the experiencers find themselves. They argue about the type of society or culture that exists in that world. Is it a transcendent, Cockayne or Utopian one? There is discussion about the dimensional analysis of that world, derivative predictions and the nature and composition of the spiritual body.

Surely, all research is good, but care must be taken by the researchers not to minimize or even forget the basic message of the experience, which is that God exists, has unconditional love for *all* mankind, and is what he expects *us* to show to one another, in order to be one with him. That is the knowledge and understanding that researchers and NDE organizations should promote and teach to the world.

The evidence provided by the near-death experience is sufficiently valid for any reasonable person to conclude that man does have a soul, a spiritual self that does not die, but continues on to eternal life in a paradisiacal world where there is total love, joy and contentment. The evidence strongly suggests there is a powerful Being who sends the souls of the experiencers back into their earthly bodies for two reasons. First, the experiencers believe they have been returned to this mortal life to complete tasks which have been deemed unfinished, such as taking care of their children or straightening out their own life; secondly, to bring humanity another message of the assurance of God's existence, his love for us and what he expects of us.

The scripture provides support for the experiencer's claims that God exists, that there is an afterlife, and that we take on new spiritual bodies when our physical bodies die. Christ addressed the question of what happens to us after our physical body dies. He said, "God said to Moses, 'I am the God of Abraham, and I am the God of Isaac and I am the God of Jacob.'" God was telling Moses that those men, though dead for hundreds of years, were still very much alive, for he would not have said, "I *am* the God of those who don't exist!"[25] He also said that after we die and our "spirit rises to heaven, we neither marry nor are given in marriage; but are as the angels in heaven."[26] It is quite evident that when we die, we immediately take on our new spiritual bodies.

St. Paul was partly right when he said, "First then, we have these human bodies and later on God gives us spiritual heavenly bodies. I am telling you this strange and wonderful secret, we shall not all die, but we shall all be given new bodies. It will happen in a moment, in the twinkling of an eye, when the last trumpet has blown. All the Christians who have died will suddenly become alive, with new bodies that will never die and then we who are still alive shall suddenly have new bodies, too."[27]

But it will not happen all at once, at the sounding of the last trumpet, as Paul thought. It happens to each of us individually at the moment our physical body dies. What Christ said about Abraham, Isaac and Jacob shows that. They were alive and well in their new bodies at the time of Moses, hundreds of years after their "death." They still live today, not having to wait until some future date when the "last trumpet has blown." The testimony of the experiencers also gives evidence that this is so. It is not only Christians who receive new bodies, as Paul supposed. Certainly Abraham, Isaac and Jacob were not Christians. They knew nothing of Christ. They lived and died under the law of obedience and still got to heaven. Also we know that the experiencers come from all religious faiths.

Some are without a religious affiliation, yet they all received new spiritual bodies at the time of their physical death even though they were sent back into their old bodies.

Although the experiencers are told that love and knowledge are the two most important things in this life, as well as the one to come, they are not told everything that is going to happen in the next life. They encounter total peace, indescribable joy and the presence of a Being who radiates unconditional love, compassion and understanding. But they find a border beyond which they do not go. It is the border of not knowing completely what is going to happen to them in that new spiritual world. They are given glimpses of beautiful places or cities--perhaps the "mansions prepared for us." But some also encounter frightening NDEs where they witness people in great anguish, or even experience it themselves.

When we transition to the next life, we will know and understand many things. That is one message of the near-death experience. We will be made aware of all things we have ever done in this lifetime; that is the *life review* that many experiencers undergo. We will understand the good we have done, as well as the wrongdoing we have inflicted on our fellow human beings. We will be aware of the love we showed to others, as well as the hatred, indifference and cruelty. *That is the Judgment.* It will be of our own doing. This belief is common among those who have undergone the near-death experience. The Koran speaks of it in saying, "They will *testify against themselves.....*"[28] The *Day* of Judgment is the day that each of us dies! That is why scripture speaks of it as being like a thief in the night that comes upon us unexpectedly.

The "life review" that experiencers undergo could explain Christ's statement that he is going to "come with the angels and judge us according to our deeds." A "being" is present when they have the life review. Some experiencers identify that being as Jesus Christ and others perceive it as an angel or even God. Still, it is not Christ, an angel or God who is doing the judging, but we ourselves by witnessing and understanding all things we have done in this lifetime.

But if we have shown love and forgiveness to others, *no judgment* will occur. God has told us in the scriptures that if we have been merciful to others, his mercy will win out over any judgment of us--the life review will not take place. Scripture also tells us that if we have loved much we will be forgiven much. But if we have loved little, we will be forgiven little and punishment of some kind will follow. If we have been indifferent, unkind, cruel and vengeful to others, we will *feel* great guilt, remorse and anguish. That is the punishment, or hell, we will endure. There will be "weeping and gnashing of teeth."[29] One experiencer said that after her life review, in which she saw and re-experienced all the terrible things she had done in her lifetime, it was as close to experiencing "hell" as she could imagine. Can you imagine the incredible agony and sorrow that tyrants such as Hitler and Stalin must have experienced during their life review, watching and *feeling* the terrible cruelty they inflicted on their fellow human beings?

Therefore, it behooves each one of us to search for the knowledge that will enable us to wind up in the wondrous presence of our Creator. Understanding this will allow us to escape judgment and provide us the wisdom that will give us the confidence and surety that we will enjoy the presence of God forever.

The Torah, Gospel and the Koran, as well as other scriptures all contain this information. And, now, the "experiencers" bring us *reassurance* of that same knowledge, a message of love, mercy and forgiveness, the requisites for being right with God and achieving victory over death.

Chapter Fifteen

THE JOY OF DEATH

We treasure life highly and its enjoyments such as love, family, the beauty of nature, friends and food--they make life worth living. As death threatens to take away all these things, we look upon it with loathing, fear and even anger. Although about 85 percent of all people believe that this earthly life is not the end and that there is some kind of heaven where they expect to end up, there is still that unwillingness to consider death as anything but distasteful and so it is generally ignored. Even strong religious beliefs of an afterlife do little to assuage repugnance toward death.

Our perception of death, for too long, has simply been erroneous. It is thought of as the time when our life comes to an end and we go to a dark dank grave. It conjures up visions of the grim reaper, a black-hooded figure with a scythe, who cuts our very existence out from under us so we cease to exist. Or it is thought of as complete obliteration of our consciousness. It is often spoken of as going to sleep to awaken at some later time. Or it is decreed that we go to the grave to await the judgment day when we shall all come forth, at the sound of a trumpet, to be judged either fit to go to heaven or down into the fiery pits of hell.

Death is none of that! It is most certainly not the end! The evidence of this is overwhelming. Most people believe that we have some future beyond the cessation of this mortal life. We should not even think of it as death. It is the beginning of another stage of our being. Therefore, rather than call it death, it would be more appropriate to call it by another name such as *transition* or perhaps *graduation*. What happens to us at the time of the death of our physical body is no longer the "great unknown." We know a great deal about it. It is that knowledge that should be taught instead of the myths and false beliefs that are generally espoused today. We, our higher selves, do not go to the grave, but find ourselves in a heavenly other world. It is interesting to note that, in the ancient Aramaic language, the word for death means "not here; present elsewhere." We do not leave loved ones forever, but are reunited with those who have "died" before us and will be again with those to follow.

The evidence shows that death is not unpleasant, but rather a joyous experience. Scripture upholds that proposition of death as an exhilarating and blessed event. We learned from Christ that both he and the thief on the cross were going to be in *paradise* the same day that their physical bodies were to die. Also that, when we "die" we become as the angels in heaven. The Koran repeatedly speaks of the joys and pleasures of being in paradise after we leave this mortal life.

The testimony in the previous chapter, of those who have died and returned to tell us about it, clearly supports this premise. Another experiencer explained her encounter with death in this way, "This enormously bright light seemed almost to cradle me. I just seemed to exist in it and be part of it and be nurtured by it and the feeling just became more and more ecstatic and glorious and perfect. And everything about it was-- if you took the one thousand *best things that ever happened to you in your life and multiplied by a million*, maybe you could get close to this feeling."[1]

The scriptural evidence along with the testimony of the experiencers should give us incentive to examine and then discard the archaic, false beliefs about death that are generally held today. Even without that, we have had a great deal of knowledge available to us concerning death, yet that knowledge has been ignored or distorted by the philosophers, theologians, those who would profit from death and even our own imagination.

We know we cannot scientifically prove what happens to us at the time of death, however, a preponderance of evidence exists, some of it even supported scientifically, that death is not the end of life, but rather the simple shedding of this physical body and moving onward and upward to better things, to a higher level of consciousness. We have seen that experiencers, though clinically dead for at least a known one hour, with extensive damage to the brain having occurred, were returned to life in a normal condition. Surely that is scientific evidence that there is a spiritual force at work in the process of death and life after death.

Many strange things have been documented about dying people, especially those who die a lingering death as from terminal cancer. Quite often, just minutes or sometimes hours or even days before death, the patients find themselves without pain or discomfort. A sense of well-being prevails, and when death finally comes, their facial expressions reflect joy and serenity. I have personally witnessed that phenomenon in my work as a hospice volunteer.

Modern medicine knows a great deal about pain; what causes it, its symptoms and how it can be controlled, usually by substance application. It is all scientific fact. Patients, in cases like those above, find that the pain is gone without the use of medication. That is a proven fact, yet doctors don't know scientifically why it is gone. It has to be obvious that there is some other force that has brought it about.

Numerous cases have been documented of people who announce that they are going to die, that their time has come, even giving the day it is going to happen. They contact friends and relatives to say good-bye. It is not done in panic or anger, but with total acceptance and contentment. Their last days are spent in peace without pain or discomfort. We see this sort of thing time and time again, yet we ignore the obvious implication that death is not to be feared and that in some manner God has communicated this message to them.

Many terminally ill patients have pre-death visions in which they see and talk to others, usually relatives or friends who have died before. It is almost always attributed to hallucination, yet physical manifestations of those pre-death visions have been documented. Others have seen the person the dying patient was talking to. Others have seen physical objects in the room of the patient move, although they couldn't see the force that moved them.

Some true psychics can communicate with people who have "died" and *graduated* to the next life. They are often treated with disbelief, skepticism, even contempt, often by the theologians, although their remarkable talent has been proven beyond doubt.

A book called WE DON'T DIE tells the story of one such psychic, George Anderson. It was written by Joel Martin and Patricia Romanowski. Martin was a TV and radio producer and talk-show host, who, being a hard-nosed skeptic himself, set out to "expose" Anderson. He used controlled tests, even attempts to "set him up." The results never varied; Anderson's communication with the "deceased" was always accurate. He revealed information to survivors that could *only* have come from their loved ones who had died. Information was exchanged about matters that occurred *after* their "death." Messages were received that they were alive and well, messages of love and hope, messages of forgiveness to those who were accidentally responsible for their death and even forgiveness for murderers.

Joel Martin turned from a doubter to a believer, saying, "Understanding that death is not a termination but a transition, that as human beings we have capacities and abilities far beyond our imagination. We don't die. That making this discovery--and seeing its proof--has changed our lives eternally, goes without saying."[2]

The London Society for Psychical Research has, for over a hundred years, been gathering volumes of material on psychic phenomenon that provide reasonable evidence, that "death" is not the end, but simply a passage from here to there; that a supernatural force exists; that there is life hereafter; that death is not an unpleasant experience, but rather an incredibly joyous event and that our loved ones and friends who have gone before us are alive and well and will be there to greet us, even help us to make the transition from this life to the next.

But because we can't examine that phenomena under a microscope or even understand it completely, we refute or ignore it. We should not. As poet George Santayana said, "It is wisdom to believe the heart." Our "heart" tells us that there is more to our existence than this mortal life, and when it ends, our loving God and creator will take good care of us. Death is a spiritual matter that truly transcends religion. But it is a spiritual matter that we give little attention to. We shy away from it because we have, unfortunately, been conditioned all of our life to look forward to it with dread.

If we sought all the knowledge that is available about death, we would lose our fear of it and find ourselves more content and life less stressful. Perceiving that death is not something to be feared but welcomed and looked forward to with great anticipation also would greatly alter our outlook on, and behavior in, secular matters. For one thing we would cease the extraordinarily expensive and futile folly of transplanting organs so as to prolong this often less-than-wonderful life. Who would want to extend his mortal life knowing that an experience of awesome wonder and utter glory awaits us in the next life.

We would do away with the useless practice of preservative cryogenics, ostentatious funerals and the current way of grieving. Hospital procedures would change drastically; there would be no more "code blues" or human beings hooked up to elaborate life-sustaining devices. Materialism as a goal in life would fall to the wayside, as it has with the experiencers who understand the priorities involved in life and death. Spiritualism, with the goal of finding the right relationship with God and with one another, would come to the fore in our lives.

What if we looked at death as something good and as the ultimate goal to be achieved, rather than a bad experience and the end of life? What if we perceived death as one experiencer did: "As I reached the source of light I could see in. I cannot begin to describe in human terms the feeling I had at what I saw. It was a giant infinite world of calm, and love, and energy and beauty. It was as though human life was unimportant compared to this. And yet it urged the importance of life at the same time it *solicited death as a means to a **better**, different life.*"[3] If death is a wondrous and joyful event, and the evidence certainly supports this idea, then if someone were to kill us they would be doing us a favor, would they not? And an accidental death would be a blessing. That may seem bizarre, but *what if we had that perception of death?* Most of those who kill think of death as punishment. What if they were conditioned to think of death as reward? With the *threat* of death gone would there not be a profound change in the violence and killing that exists today?

When we deal with those who are known to be dying, we are more concerned with consoling them about having to leave this often less-than-pleasant life rather than giving them all the knowledge about death; that it is by far the best and most important event that will occur to them in this lifetime. We are often more concerned about the survivors and *their loss* rather than the *gain of the one who is dying*. Everything that we have been taught about death is wrong, even the grieving and mourning. To attend funerals and entertain thoughts of our loved one going to the grave and leaving us forever is simply a delusion, for the loved one is not there, but alive and well. How often have we read about or heard of a parent continuing to express great grief and anguish over a beautiful child who lies dead in the grave, gone before his or her time; not being able to enjoy life? The child is not there, but alive and well in the wondrous presence of its Creator. *God takes loving care of all his creation at the time of "death."*

As scripture tells us in speaking of our soul, our immortal self, we are "not slain when this its mortal frame is destroyed"....We are "eternal, universal, permanent, and unalterable; therefore, knowing it to be thus, thou *shouldst not grieve!*"[4]

Of course there should be sorrow and tears over the parting, but no more so than over any other *temporary* parting. And it should be softened and offset by the wondrous and glorious event that is taking place. It is not unlike a loved one graduating from college who then leaves the family to take up residence in some far place to go to work, perhaps get married, raise his own family, or generally pursue his own life. We celebrate their graduation, have a farewell party, and cry and hug them when we see them off at the airport, or send them on their way in their fully-packed automobile. We talk about when we will see them again.

So should it be with death. This life is a learning experience. When we die, it is simply a transition or graduation to another type of life. Some may graduate with honors, and some may have more learning to do. The "far-off place" we go to is beautiful, bright and wonderful. Total love that is unconditional and perfect understanding are found there. It is a place anyone would be reluctant to leave, even showing anger at having to leave, as some experiencers have related. We meet our friends and loved ones there. It is literally a reunion in paradise, where everyone is happy to see the other regardless of how the parting had been. We are completely whole in every respect.

Certainly there are differences from the college graduation simile. We can't write or call them on the telephone, although some have been known to communicate. We can't plan an airplane flight for the next meeting. And, of course, it isn't the same when a young child dies, having been taken from us so early in life. However, knowing that those who die, even the young children, are going to such a beautiful and glorious place where there is peace, joy and all-encompassing love, and that one day there will be a wonderful reunion, should be cause for celebration and tears of joy as well as sorrow at the parting.

We should change our way of doing things at funerals and in memory of those who have "died." Instead of expensive funerals and mausoleums, there should be a simple burial, or none at all in favor of cremation. To spend exorbitant amounts of money to inter a useless shell of a body, especially as the inhabitant is no longer there but safe elsewhere, is to be less than good and wise stewards of our resources. A much more appropriate use of those funds would be for the needy *living*. So also should it be with things such as eternal flames and life-long floral care of a grave.

Instead of a somber, tearful funeral service, a joyful wake would be much more fitting. A modest celebration with food, drink and music, suitable to the likes and beliefs of the family *and* the departed would be appropriate, along with tears and laughter. After all, it's an observance of joy and life, not death and despair.

Death and eternal life are greatly misunderstood. We never die; we live forever. We have, in the form of our soul, existed forever as part of the vast immeasurable energy of God. As one experiencer put it, "I was peace, I was love. I was brightness, it (the Being of Light) was part of me...You just know. You're all knowing--and everything is a part of you--it's--it's just so beautiful. It was eternity. It's like I *was always there* and I *will always be there*, and that my existence on earth was just a brief instance."[5]

Another said, "I became aware that it (the Being of light) was part of all living things and that at the same time all living things were part of it. I knew it was omnipotent, that it represented infinite divine love. It was as if my heart wanted to leap out of my body towards it. It was almost as though I had met my Maker."[5]

God is indeed our maker and when the body dies, we return to his presence in the spiritual world, retaining our individual identity but with a new spiritual body. Of course, we've always understood that our physical body dies. The scripture is clear about that when it says, "from dust you have come and to dust you shall return."[6] We know that the body does turn to dust in the grave, or is burned to ashes during cremation, or is consumed perhaps by other animals or the fish of the sea, should the ocean be our grave.

The Church falsely teaches that on Judgment Day the "graves will open and the dead come forth." They base it on St. Paul's statement, "All the Christians who have died will suddenly become alive, with new bodies that will never die and then we who are still alive shall suddenly have new bodies too. When this happens, then at last this scripture will come true--Death is swallowed up in victory."[7]

The Christian theologians also base this belief on Christ's words in John 5, where he says, "And I solemnly declare that the time is coming, in fact, *it is here*, when the dead shall hear my voice--the voice of the Son of God--and those who listen shall live......Don't be surprised! Indeed the time is coming when all the dead in their graves shall hear the voice of God's Son, and shall rise again--those who have *done good* to eternal life; and those who have *continued in evil*, to judgment."[8]

Do you see how conflicting that information is? How can the dead in the grave listen to the voice of Christ? How can all Christians in the grave come alive again when nothing of them is there? The bodies of those in the grave have turned to dust. How about Christians who have died at sea and been consumed by sea creatures? The cells of their body have been absorbed into the cells of the fish as food. An omnipotent God could surely reassemble the bodies of the dead if he chose to. But it doesn't seem likely, especially as we are told by the experiencers, and even Paul, that we will have *new* bodies. Neither are their souls there in the grave, having departed elsewhere at the time of their "death." Just as Christ told the thief on the cross next to him that he would be in paradise with him that very day, and as Christ said of Abraham, Isaac and Jacob, they were alive and well in heaven, although they had been "dead" for hundreds of years. He also said, when we die, we rise and become as the angels in heaven. And, of course, the near-death experience provides reasonable evidence that this is so.

Surely what Christ was saying in John 5 is that those who are dead in their sins, who are spiritually dead, separated from God, will rise again, be resurrected from that spiritual decay, be renewed and be eligible for eternal life in God's presence when they listen to him and do what is right and good. Remember, he said, "the time is *here*" when the dead would hear his voice and live. Right then and there it would happen. Obviously it couldn't have been the dead in their graves, for they would have come forth then. It could only have meant that those who were not saved but destined for spiritual death would achieve salvation and eternal life by listening to his message and obeying it.

"Victory over death" is not achieved when we become Christian, and when "sin no longer has power over us" as St. Paul taught. It is not when the graves open and the Christians come forth. Victory over death comes when we understand and accept the messages of Christ and the other prophets about what God expects of us, which is to show love, mercy and forgiveness to one another.

Surely God would not send anyone to suffer in hell for eternity, or even temporarily, because they didn't know about Christ. How do you *justify* such punishment, from a *perfect-in-*

justice God, for *simple disobedience* or because they haven't been *taught* about Christ? How is it possible to reconcile it with Christ's statement that, "Those who don't realize they are doing wrong will be punished little?"[9] Certainly being sent to hell isn't a small punishment! What of Christ's desire that *"none shall be lost but all might be saved?"* If only those who believe in Christ are saved, then literally billions will be lost and go to hell. How do we square such terrible punishment with God's compassionate and forgiving love for us?

The obvious answer is that God does not, indeed *cannot*, mete out such punishment. And if, either through our own stubbornness, ignorance, or negligence, or perhaps for reasons not of our own doing, we haven't learned what God expects from us in this lifetime, and therefore do not qualify for acceptance in his presence *eternally*, surely a merciful God would make available some course other than sending us to suffer in hell--an alternative such as reincarnation.

According to a Gallup poll, 38 million Americans believe in reincarnation. A tremendous amount of material that presents reasonable evidence in support of reincarnation can be found in the scriptures of the world. The New Testament of the Bible is supportive of rebirth when Christ speaks of John the Baptist as the reincarnation of Elijah.[10]

The early Christians believed in reincarnation for about five centuries until that belief was suppressed, and writings concerning it were destroyed, by the Church fathers because it was not compatible with Christian doctrine which requires acceptance of Christ as savior and redeemer so as to gain eternal life. Or, if we do not believe in Christ or have no knowledge of him, we are damned by God for our "innate" sin, and after death, our soul goes to hell to suffer eternally. Christianity makes no allowance for a second chance by means of reincarnation.

Editors Joseph Head and Sylvia Cranston in their book REINCARNATION: THE PHOENIX FIRE MYSTERY have done an incredible amount of research in bringing to the public knowledge about rebirth. The Rev. John Andrew Storey says about their work, "Such is the wealth of material contained in this book that the reader may well conclude that all the great thinkers of mankind have been reincarnationists, and indeed such a judgment would not be far from the truth."[11] Anyone who desires to know the truth about reincarnation would do well to read this work.

To deny reincarnation assails our sense of justice, which tells us that God would give a second chance to one who has never been taught the message of salvation. Reincarnation is an expression of God's mercy to those who have not learned in one lifetime the requisites necessary to be one with him forever. Eternal life means there is *no more death and rebirth*. It is as Christ says in John 20, "They which shall be accounted worthy to obtain that world (heaven), and the resurrection from the dead (spiritual death), neither marry, nor are given in marriage; neither can they **die anymore**; for they are equal unto the angels; and are the children of God, being the children of the resurrection." Surely God desires that all of humankind should experience heaven.

HEAVEN, HELL AND THE DEVIL

Heaven is thought of as the place to which we eventually ascend to if we are good or meet certain requisites, often as set forth by a religion. When we make that journey to heaven is also subject to various beliefs. Hell is usually thought of as the fiery pit or caverns we descend into after we die, because we have been bad or haven't accepted a religion's theological beliefs. These are narrow and erroneous concepts of heaven and hell.

It is also likely that the idea of the devil or Satan as a *person* or a *being* is errant. Satan is simply the *temptation that* **we** *generate through the wrongful thoughts and desires of the mind.* Satan is defined as the great adversary or enemy of man. Wrong thought certainly fits that description. Thoughts of worry, paranoia, greed, fear, anger, superstition, covetousness and negativity, to name a few, are indeed man's enemies, often creating a veritable hell for him.

Scripture also supports this concept of Satan. When Christ told his disciples that he was going to suffer at the hands of the elders and chief priests and die, Peter rebuked him, in effect telling Christ that it wasn't necessary to do that. Then Christ in turn scolded Peter, saying, "Get thee behind me, Satan."[12] Surely, Christ didn't think Peter was Satan, but only that Peter's *suggestion* that Christ didn't have to go through with his suffering and dying *represented temptation*. Christ was putting that tempting thought from his mind. According to scripture, Christ agonized over what he had to do.

Christ's temptation in the wilderness[13] is also supportive of that idea. Because the scripture records a conversation between Christ and the "devil" or "tempter," one might draw the conclusion that the devil was a person. But it is more likely that the entire story of Christ's temptation is simply an allegory, a form of communication frequently used in scripture to make a point. An allegory is defined as representation of an abstract or spiritual meaning through concrete or material forms; figurative treatment of one subject under the guise of another.

When we examine the story, one can easily see its abstract meaning through the use of material forms. The wilderness simply represented this materialistic world in which temptation often confronts us. Turning stones into bread represented materialism. That would seem quite clear from Christ's reply that, "we don't live by bread alone, but by the word of God."[14] The high-mountain scenario and the "devil's" offer to give Christ all the kingdoms of the world would be representative of power. And, of course, the devil (the tempter) represented temptation itself.

Even Christ's final words in the matter, "Get thee hence, Satan: for it is written, thou shall worship the Lord thy God, and him only shall you obey,"[15] could clearly have an abstract meaning. We are to put away the tempting thoughts of the mind that lead to wrongdoing and obey God and his instructions for right and just living.

To accept the story as reality is not very credible. It is not likely that Christ could turn stones into bread. That would violate God's natural laws. How was it possible for the devil to set Christ on the pinnacle, the pointed spire, of the temple? How did he transport Christ to the high mountain? No "exceedingly high mountains" can be found near Jerusalem, or, for that matter, anywhere in the world, from which Christ could see "all the kingdoms of the world, and the glory of them!"

Further, the teaching that Satan is an angel gone bad, fallen from God's grace, banned from his presence and who is continually battling with God for men's souls is illogical, if not absurd. My feeling is that no person or angel who has ever been in the presence of God and the total love and joy that exist there could ever do wrong or wish to leave that bliss. And certainly, "Satan" would be no match for the omnipotent God in a battle of any kind! The concept of the battle for man's soul is only within man himself. It is waged within the mind by the thoughts of right or wrong. No, it is not likely that there is such a person as the devil who makes his abode in a place called hell. More about hell later, but first let's examine the concept of heaven.

The New Testament tells us, "Heaven can be entered only through the narrow gate! The highway to hell is broad, and its gate is wide enough for all the multitudes who choose its easy way. But the gateway to life is small, and the road is narrow, and only a very few ever find it."[16]

Almost a billion Christians are living today who believe they are traveling that narrow road and are going to go through the narrow gate and get into heaven. That is certainly not a *very few*, even reckoned as a percentage of the population. And that's only those living today. What about all those who have died and all those yet to be born? How is it going to be possible for that great multitude to get through the narrow gate, especially as Christ said there will be only a *very few*.

If that passage is true, then a lot of Christians had better start worrying about who that handful, those very few, are going to be. They should also wonder about what's wrong with Christianity such that so very few are going to make it to heaven! The above scripture either has to be suspect, or has a hidden meaning, or a misunderstanding exists about the definition of heaven. It is probably a combination of all three. It surely could not be true literally, for then there would be little hope, but rather great despair for mankind.

To accept as apparent truth the idea that very few are going to enter the "gateway to life" does not correlate with other scripture, which tells us how easy it is to get to heaven. We need only to love our neighbor as ourselves, and we shall live in heaven forever. That's not hard to do. Christ says those who listen to his voice shall never die. We can do that, too. We need only to feed the hungry, "clothe the naked" and generally take care of others in need and then we shall inherit the kingdom of heaven. A great many do all of these things and will surely enter the gateway to life in heaven. The concept of few getting to heaven does not relate to Christ's statement and wish that all shall be saved. It doesn't even relate to the teaching of the Christian Church that we have only to believe in Christ as the sacrificial lamb in order to get to heaven. Billions have held this belief over the centuries. Surely then, that statement must have another meaning.

The scripture speaks of heaven both as a place and a condition or state of being. Genesis says God created the heaven and the earth and he called the firmament Heaven. Both the Old and New Testament tell of a new heaven and a new earth. And, of course, we are all aware of the reference to God the Father in Heaven. Similar references to heaven as a place can be found throughout the Bible.

But Christ speaks of it also as a state or condition. "The kingdom of heaven is like to a grain of mustard seed, which a man took, and sowed in his field: which is indeed the least of all seeds; but when it is grown, it is the greatest among the herbs, and becometh a tree, so that the birds of the air come and lodge in the branches thereof."[17] Further, Christ says, "The kingdom of heaven is like unto leaven, which a woman took, and hid in three measures of meal, till the whole was leavened."[18] Christ uses the kingdom of heaven and the kingdom of God interchangeably. He says we are to seek the kingdom of God first, and then the necessary material needs will accrue to us.[19] He tells us that we can't see the kingdom of God; it is neither here nor there, but is within us.[20] That would certainly imply that it is a condition rather than a place.

It would seem that the kingdom of God or the kingdom of heaven is something we can attain here on earth, a state of being that is highly prized and should be sought after. As it is like leaven that leavens the whole loaf, it would be a way of life that serves as an example such that when others see it, and the rewards thereof, they too choose that way of living.

Surely the kingdom of heaven is the way that God wishes us to live and what he has always intended for us. After all, he placed us in paradise. Who can deny the beauty and wonder of this world where man has not destroyed it? But because we have used our free will to make the wrong choices, we have made this earth something less than a paradise and in some respects, a veritable hell.

But it doesn't have to remain that way. We can change things. We can reverse the damage we have done, and with the help of God in his constant renewal of nature, find that paradise, that "kingdom prepared for us from the beginning."[21] To do so we have to listen to what God has been telling us *from the beginning,* which is to show love to our fellow human beings and live in peace and harmony, not only with one another but with *all of creation*. When we do that, then will we find and experience bliss, the joy of heaven, supreme happiness and the "peace that passeth all understanding." We *are* meant to enjoy life *fully*. Surely that is the heaven that Christ is speaking of when he says that the gate to it, the gateway to that life, is narrow. Indeed, few find it. At least, so far!

Scripture tells us that it is God's pleasure to give us the kingdom of heaven: that blissful life of happiness, joy and contentment. But we foolishly choose not to accept it, rather making the choice to travel the wide path that leads to "hell;" the path of hate, anger, violence, worry, condemnation, cruelty, vengeance, covetousness, promiscuity, greed, irresponsibility and indifference to the needs of our fellow human beings.

Although almost no one believes it anymore, Christian dogma places hell in the nether regions of the earth. The Church teaches that Christ, after his death on the cross, descended there and stayed for three days as part of the punishment he received for our sins. Christ did not descend into hell after he died. He said to the thief on the cross next to him, "Today, you shall be with me in paradise."[22] That fits beautifully with those who undergo the near-death experience, finding themselves in some paradise-like place *immediately* after the body dies. The Church completely ignores these words of Christ, arguing whether just his soul or both his body and soul made the descent into hell for those three days. Christ *never* said he was going to hell to be punished for the sins of all mankind.

Given that God has perfect love, it is not likely that he created such a *place* as hell, where he sends some people to suffer eternally. From a historical standpoint, hell was an old, Aramaic, idiomatic word used to describe mental torment signified by burning fires in the city dumps. Later the idea of torment by fire changed to "Gehenna of Fire," a place of extreme torment, and then in further biblical translations to "Hell," which biblical writers then undoubtedly associated with punishment and the devil.[23] Hell is assuredly none of those, but a condition or state of being, one that we bring upon ourselves or inflict on others. It is a state that we can experience either here in this lifetime or in the next.

We experience it when we fail to love and respect ourselves, abusing our bodies by irresponsibly ingesting substances that we *know* cause disease, suffering and death. Anyone who has watched a loved one or friend suffer and die from an overdose of drugs, or from lung cancer as a result of smoking for forty years, can testify to the hell that person went through. Anyone who has witnessed or perhaps even experienced the withdrawal from the abuse of alcohol knows well the hellish suffering that occurs.

We can create a mental hell for ourselves in our thoughts. By excessive, even unwarranted worry we can suffer great pangs of anxiety, causing harm to our mental well-being, sometimes resulting in physical debilitation as well. By our conditioned thoughts of anger, hatred, racism and discrimination we create discord often leading to violence, suffering and death.

We create a hell for ourselves and others when we do not love and respect nature, which is a manifestation of God, and by polluting and destroying the environment thereby causing disasters such as floods, dust bowls, starvation and death.

Just look at the hell mankind has produced by turning plowshares into swords, manufacturing massive amounts of weapons of destruction, hanging humanity, especially the children, on a "cross of iron," as Dwight Eisenhower once so aptly described the clouds of war. Do you think Hiroshima and Nagasaki, and their aftermath, weren't the epitome of hell, especially to those who lived there and survived? Think of all those babies and young children of Somalia, slowly and hellishly starving to death. Think of the hell that young boy in Somalia went through, aware that he was being buried alive. These things happened in Somalia because the "civilized" nations of the world provided the warring factions there with weapons enabling them to perpetrate that horror! What of those babies in Haiti, dying of disease and starvation because the "good guys" used their military power to blockade Haiti economically in the name of democracy?

All that hell we create for ourselves and others here on earth is due to one thing: disobedience to God and the instructions he has given us, which, if observed, would preclude all that suffering. Just observing his one command to love our neighbor as our self would do it. We have the complete ability to do it, if we were taught so, and that it is what God requires of us in order to attain the glorious bliss of heaven. But, instead, we are conditioned to believe that we cannot, that we are poor sinful beings whose nature it is to create all of this hell!

As to the hell in the afterlife, it, too, is a state of being and of our own doing. God could not sentence us to everlasting punishment in the pits of hell because we have been disobedient and judged unfit to be in his presence. The hell, the "weeping and gnashing of teeth," that the scriptures refer to is simply the anguish and remorse that we will feel and endure when we become fully aware of the harm and sorrow we have caused others, either deliberately or through our indifference to their needs.

As experiencers have said, "You are shown your life...and you do the judging. Had you done what you should? It's the little things...maybe a hurt child that you helped or just stopped to say hello to a shut-in. These are the things that are important...You are *judging yourself*."[24] One experiencer said, after witnessing her life review and all the things she had done to others, that the suffering and distress she felt was as close to hell as she could imagine.

The Being of Light, undoubtedly a manifestation of God, asks the questions, "What have you done to advance the human race?" "How have you loved others?" And you have to answer. If you can't answer satisfactorily, there may literally be *hell to pay*. You may have to pay with a state of mental agony. Some experiencers have encountered hellish conditions during their NDE. Some near-death experience researchers have speculated that what the experiencers see during their brief journey to that *other world* is based on the perceptions of the afterlife that they were taught and believed in during this lifetime. Or, in other words, the "visions experienced were projections from the mind of the participant; that mental images held in this lifetime determine what is met after death."[25]

It is more likely that all the visions experienced are a reality of the afterlife. In the hell-like conditions, the experiencer was witnessing the mental agony that some suffer when they understand and feel the distress and torment they have inflicted on others. Visions of gray zombie-like beings moaning and crying in great distress fits with the scriptural description that there will be "weeping and gnashing of teeth."

This condition could last a long time if one's deeds have been exceedingly wicked without showing remorse or repentance. Although the scriptures speak of some that will remain in that state forever, knowing that God is forgiving, it is not likely. Christ does speak of those who refuse to obey God, "And shall go away into *eternal* punishment."[26] If it is so, it will be those who are extremely cruel and evil, and knowing God's will, still refuse to believe and obey him.

Christ said, in speaking of blasphemy, that those who spoke against him can be forgiven, but those who blaspheme the Holy Spirit (God) will not be forgiven and are in danger of *eternal* damnation.[27] Do you see the contradiction here? They can't be forgiven, however, they are *only in danger of* damnation, not necessarily damned for certain. If they aren't forgiven or damned either, there would have to be an alternative, such as reincarnation. Or it could be an inaccurate reporting of what Christ actually said. Many experiencers feel that we will all be "home free" eventually, and that, as Christ implies elsewhere in the scripture, God wants everyone to be saved so that "not one is lost!"

There is a simple and easy way to escape *judgment* and any kind of hellish suffering. *Love, mercy and forgiveness are the way.* God has told us that if we have been merciful to others, his mercy will win out over any *judgment*. He has told us that if we have loved much, we will be forgiven much. We have been told that if we forgive others, God will forgive us. Obedience to and living by those words of God is the perfect formula for avoiding "hell" and achieving heaven, both in this life and the one to come.

Many people have a complete misconception as to what living by God's word means. They envision a life of strict piety or total commitment to religious obligations, perhaps joining a monastery, taking the cloth or becoming a missionary in some far-off land. It is often associated with a very restricted lifestyle which precludes the joys of living and requires a great deal of time on one's knees in church with hands folded. Nothing is further from the truth. Living by God's word results in the true joy of living.

These misconceived ideas can be a part of doing God's work, but they do not ensure that one will be *living* according to God's word. It is much more and, at the same time, more simple than that. God's work is doing good to others. We live by God's word when we show compassion and forgiveness to our fellow human beings. It is doing "random acts of kindness." It is the little things we do for others: a smile, a cheery good morning, a friendly wave, a kind word or a compliment. As one experiencer said, it is the little things that count. Living by

God's word is living in harmony with all of creation. It is using the environment wisely, not ravaging and destroying the earth out of greed and for profit. When we give of ourselves and do what is right and good, we will be living by God's word and will find that we are enjoying life to the fullest.

Heaven is a state of being that we can achieve and enjoy here in this lifetime, but it is also the place where we will *all* eventually find ourselves; a place where we will forever delight in the indescribable yet glorious presence of God. Hell is only a condition that we ourselves are responsible for, either here on earth or in the life to come. Although those who have not met the necessary requisites to escape judgment should be concerned about the mental anguish they may have to suffer, they should not fear death. That anguish will not endure forever. Or God, in his loving mercy, may offer a choice, such as further learning or service to others which may take place in the afterlife or by way of reincarnation. *We need to trust in the absolute love of God.*

An obvious question arises that needs to be asked and answered here. If there is nothing to fear from death and it is so joyous, why would we not all seek death, such as in suicide or reckless and dangerous living? Why would anyone who is ill or suffering from a disease, especially one that is terminal, wish to get well?

The scriptures tell us that we are not to kill, not to take life, which obviously would include our own. Experiencers, who have found themselves in that near-death encounter as the result of suicide, are told that they were wrong to do it. Yet God is kind and compassionate and will give those who take their life another chance in some manner. Nor is it likely that there will be any condemnation or judgment of those who have ended their life to prevent undue suffering. If they have lived a good life, the taking of their own life, out of despair, will be overlooked by God.

Life is a gift from God. It is not our prerogative to take it, either our own or another's. The experiencers understand that life is precious, that it is to be highly valued and protected. Our own common sense, as well as the wisdom of the "heart," tell us that this is so. We are given life to enjoy and learn. We should make the most of every moment of it. Although we should look forward to "death" with anticipation, we need to await that magnificent experience with contentment, understanding that our purpose in life is to enjoy it, do good and let our light shine making the world better.

All who have concerns about the death that is to come for themselves or a loved one, or are still in anguish and despair over a family member, especially a child, who has died, should search for knowledge about what happens at the time of "death." Put aside your preconceived beliefs about it. Read the literature on the near-death experience. There is a great deal of it, but it isn't necessary to read it all. Just a few of the books will give you sufficient insight that will change your views forever. Search the scriptures as well.

When you do so with an open mind and heart, then you will no longer fear death for yourself or a loved one. Your perspective about death for any human being, even the victims of murders and massacres that are happening around the world, will change. Instead of anger and despair at the loss of their lives you will feel sorrow at any suffering they may have incurred, but also relief knowing that they are being taken good care of by God. As to the perpetrators, your malice and hatred toward them will turn to pity and sorrow, and perhaps, even forgiveness. Even should someone have killed your loved one, you may find that your animosity, desire for vengeance, and inability to forgive has been assuaged. You will never think the same about death again.

If you have led a less than good life, you are likely to find that your new knowledge of death will change your lifestyle. Experiencers who have been drug users, alcoholics and criminals undergo a complete turnaround in their lives. Just reading about their experiences and gaining knowledge of life, death, and what God expects of you can alter your own life as well. Your new understanding will spark a desire for even greater knowledge that will lead you to a better life. It can lead you to a healthier life, even the healing of any infirmities you might have.

Chapter Sixteen

HEALTH, HEALING AND MEDICINE

This is the story of Jean, the daughter of longtime friends. It is a story of love, courage, faith and healing. Jean was in her twenties and nearing graduation from university when she was very seriously injured in an automobile accident. She had been hit broadside by a drunken driver and sustained extensive damage to her head and brain. She was in a coma for almost two months. One evening while her father was with her at the local hospital, the pastor came to visit and give support. Prior to leaving, he held Jean's hand and commenced to say the Lord's Prayer. Part way through the prayer, Jean began to move her lips, saying the prayer along with the pastor and her father. Jean then opened her eyes bringing tears of joy to her father and the pastor.

But the real miracle hadn't occurred--at least not yet. Considerable damage had occurred to Jean's brain on the side where the memory function takes place. She could remember very little. Her vocal cords were paralyzed. She could hardly speak. Her entire left side was also paralyzed. She could not use her left arm, nor could she walk.

The best brain surgeon in the West was consulted. His prognosis was not good. She was told she would never walk again. She would be confined to her wheelchair for the rest of her life. She could never finish college; she simply didn't have the necessary faculties for learning and remembering anymore.

But Jean and her family would not accept that prognosis. She started a hydrotherapy program. Daily, her father took her to a nearby pool for exercise. She began work with a psychiatrist who also was a hypnotherapist. He encouraged her in her goal to overcome her handicaps and taught her the techniques of self-hypnosis. She began to see progress, with improvement in her speech and motion of her left extremities. It was slow, hard work but she never gave up, nor did she entertain thoughts of failure. She *believed* and was *convinced* that she would regain her full faculties. And she did indeed overcome every one of her handicaps.

She has long since discarded her wheelchair. Today, Jean speaks normally and walks just like anyone else. She has regained the feeling in, and use of, the left side of her body. Through self-hypnosis, she has learned to transfer her memory function to another area of the brain. On occasion, she has small memory lapses, but they are rare. Jean finished college, and went on to work with handicapped children, teach sign language at the college level, and to conduct her own hypnotherapy practice.

She is a dynamic, warm, loving and caring person. She loves to help other people and takes great satisfaction in showing them how to overcome their problems through self-hypnosis. Hers is a marvelous story of success in overcoming adversity in healing of the body when the normal medical practices are helpless. She attributes her recovery to absolute belief that she would get well, the loving support of her parents and family, the power of the mind and the use of self-hypnosis in harnessing that power.

We all have power within ourselves that can heal, but few realize it or would accept such a philosophy. Most people would accept such disabilities as Jean's as irreversible, continuing to live out their lives in a handicapped state. It is much the same with terminal illness. When such a prognosis is offered, it is usually received with denial, or thoughts of death, and perhaps resignation to the fate that has been decreed. Little thought is given to recovery from the illness. Some do and fight it, often in every way known to medical science, but in the end they succumb. Some simply accept their circumstances, refusing to go through the often difficult trials of treatment such as chemotherapy, and in the end concede defeat in the battle for life. A very, very few beat the odds and recover, somehow having come up with the answer to miraculous healing.

Usually they chalk it up to their faith in the power of God to heal them, and call it a miracle. But they can't explain how God accomplished the healing, or why he chose to heal them and not others who also believe in God and his power to heal. In a sense, it is God who does the healing, but it is more accurate to say that the primary effort is by man.

The human body that consists of our physical self, the mind and the soul is, indeed, a self-healing organism. In the chapter on the Nature of Man, we touched on the healing processes of the body: how the intelligence in the body mobilizes its resources to effect, for example, the healing of a wound. The body can even mend a broken bone, if not too severe a fracture, without the help of medical procedures, or even without any effort of the mind. Even compound fractures, with assistance from doctors, are mended by the intelligence within. Medical practitioners acknowledge that they are not responsible for the healing; they only facilitate it.

But obviously, the ability of the body to heal itself has limits, succumbing to injuries such as massive wounds that destroy major organs. Almost always it yields to deadly diseases such as AIDS and amyotrophic lateral sclerosis, commonly known as Lou Gehrig's disease. More often than not it surrenders to cancer. But what of those instances of cancer and even AIDS where people have beaten the odds and continue to live long and healthy lives? What of the many miracle cures that have been documented? Why do certain people recover and others do not when the circumstances of the illness are basically the same? There is a very simple answer. Let's look at a few cases of "miraculous" recoveries, as well as some who didn't recover. Then we will analyze them all and find that answer.

Jackie Pflug was a passenger on Egypt Air Flight 648 when it was hijacked in 1985 and forced to land at Malta. She was chosen for execution by the hijackers, along with two other American passengers and two Israelis. As the gun that was pressed against her head exploded, she felt herself falling from the front aircraft exit to the tarmac where she lay for five hours in and out of consciousness, yet still aware that she needed to remain still and act dead. When the hijackers allowed a morgue detail to retrieve the five bodies, she knew she was going to survive.

The bullet had shattered the whole right side of her skull and the bone fragments damaged a large part of her brain. The doctors told her that, although her survival was a miracle, she would never be normal. They told her she would never be able to drive or work and would never be able to read above the third-grade level. She had lost most of her vision and severe epilepsy had destroyed her short-term memory. She could not tell time nor count money.

But, like Jean, she proved the doctors wrong. She literally willed herself to be healed. Prior to being shot, and after worrying for an hour about her possible fate, she said, "I just stopped struggling. I just closed my eyes and went into a place that was very safe. A place of non-worry, knowing that everything would be all right, no matter what happened. I started to pray and I asked God for my life, and I felt like it would be OK after that, whether I lived or whether I died, even though I'm not a religious person. We are not our bodies. We are spirits, and spirits move on."[1]

Later she said that her ability to will herself healed was connected to the "place of non-worry" into which she escaped before she was shot. She said that, through that experience, she felt that she was "taking God out of heaven and putting God inside me. Every morning, I get up and get myself quiet and get in touch with that power. I believe we can have heaven on earth by touching that power."[1]

Jack Colern, hospitalized and dying of AIDS, almost in an unconscious state, heard the doctors and nurses saying it was unlikely he would last through the night. But *he* didn't feel that way. "I had the unusual sense that I *was* going to make it; I was at peace." Not only did he make it, but today he lectures and shares his new spiritual and emotional strength with others. He says, "I am no longer afraid. Today, I don't just survive. My life is full of wonderful things. My sense of spirituality today is real simple, *let go and let God*. Once I let go I'm shown the way." He says the world is besieged with misery and destruction, but it doesn't have to be that way, even if you have a debilitating illness. "I don't want to be part of that, I want to be part of the solution."[2] He is indeed!

Bert, at age 70, was dying from severe coronary artery disease and diabetes. He was given, at the most, three months to live. A year and a half later, he was still alive. The doctors told his wife they didn't understand what was keeping him alive. But she knew and the hospice volunteer that worked with them knew. Bert and his wife soon would celebrate their 50th wedding anniversary. It was about a year and a half away from the time he received the news about his terminal illness. All during his illness they made big plans and talked a great deal about the coming event. All the children, grandchildren and many friends were coming. Although not able to express himself very well due to his illness, it was obvious that Bert enjoyed the big celebration. In a matter of days after their anniversary he died. It was clear to his wife and the hospice worker that Bert had literally willed himself to live so that he could celebrate his 50th anniversary.

John battled cancer for twelve years. In the early years it was in his lymph nodes in the neck area. He underwent both radiation treatment and chemotherapy, losing a lot of weight and all of his hair. He would wear a baseball cap most of the time. He was a devout Christian and had great faith in God. His attitude was amazingly positive; he was sure he would beat it. And he did. And got his hair back, too.

Some years later, cancer showed up again. Exploratory surgery showed it metastasized throughout his hip and lower spine. The prognosis was inoperable and terminal. But not to John. He made the decision that he would get well anyway. With treatment and complete conviction that he would recover, John is alive today, in good health, without any sign of cancer, and enjoying life in retirement.

Jerry also had cancer. He was riddled with it, in the lungs, stomach and liver. Although it was widespread, it was not so severe that his activities were curtailed. However, he was considered terminal and given about a year to live. He was a very negative person, took to his bed and simply resigned himself to his coming fate. He had little use for God or spirituality. In three months he was gone.

There are a few more cases that are appropriate to discuss which shed light on the answer of why some die and some recover from the same illness. They are from Deepak Chopra's book, QUANTUM HEALING.[3]

Chitra came to Dr. Chopra after removal of a breast due to a malignant tumor, which also had spread to the lungs. She had about a 10 percent chance of surviving for five years. She was concerned about dying, not for herself, but for her family, particularly her husband. Conventional therapy had done all it could for her, and she hoped that Dr. Chopra could help.

He started her on a new course of treatments involving Ayurvedic techniques. They consisted of a change in diet with special meals, use of medicinal herbs, oil massages, simple yoga exercises and meditation. It is a technique designed to bring the day-to-day existence into a deep state of rest and relaxation, the foundation for healing. She was very faithful in continuing the program and trusted that Dr. Chopra would make her well. After a year, x-rays showed no cancer cells at all, and there was mutual jubilation.

But that isn't the end of the story. Doubt began to creep in. Chitra began to entertain thoughts that the cancer would return. She was disturbed that her "miracle cure" was only a temporary stay of execution. She became extremely anxious, fearful and depressed. You can probably guess the rest. Cancer showed up again, this time in the brain, and in her extremely agitated and depressed state, she died rather quickly.

A man complaining of a painful chest cough was found to have a very large tumor between his lungs which, after biopsy, was diagnosed as oat-cell carcinoma, an extremely deadly and very fast-growing malignancy. The doctor told him he must have immediate surgery to remove the tumor and enter into radiation and chemotherapy treatment. But he refused treatment and left the office. The doctor lost track of him. Eight years later a man came to see him with an enlarged lymph node is his neck. Biopsy showed it also to be oat-cell carcinoma. The doctor soon realized it was the same man. When he asked the patient what he had done for the earlier chest tumor, he said he had done nothing--he had just decided he was not going to let himself die of cancer.

Laxman Govindass was a patient in a hospital in New Delhi. He was a peasant farmer whose drinking had gotten out of hand--an alcoholic with cirrhosis of the liver. His family had abandoned him, and he was deteriorating very rapidly, extremely emaciated and down to less than eighty pounds in weight. Doctor Chopra, taking his medical training at the hospital, had struck a rapport with him, visiting him frequently, just sitting with him to ease his loneliness and apprehension.

When it came time for Dr. Chopra to rotate to a village dispensary sixty miles away, he went in to say good-bye to Mr. Govindass and told him he would be back in about thirty days to visit him. The man said to him, "Now that you are leaving, I have nothing more to live for--I will die." Doctor Chopra replied, "Don't be silly, you can't die until I come back to see you again." He left thinking that he really wouldn't see him again because no one expected him to live more than a week.

A month later when he returned to the hospital he was greatly surprised to find the patient still alive, albeit little but skin and bones. When Dr. Chopra gently touched him, he opened his eyes and said, "You have come back. You said I could not die without seeing you again--now I see you." Then he closed his eyes and died!

A Boston fireman entered the emergency room of a suburban hospital complaining of sudden, sharp pains in the chest. The resident examined him and could find no evidence or irregularity in his heart function. He returned another time with the same complaint, and Dr. Chopra, as the senior physician, gave him a thorough examination, with the same results. He returned repeatedly, certain that he had a heart condition, but no test, including sophisticated cardiograms and angiograms, detected the slightest defect.

In the face of his extreme anxiety and its adverse affect on his work, he was recommended for disability retirement, but the fire department's medical examining board refused to approve it on the basis that there was no evidence of a heart condition. Two months later he showed up in the emergency room, on a stretcher, the victim of a massive heart attack. Within ten minutes of his coronary, which destroyed 90 percent of his heart muscle, he died.

Let's review one more case, and then we will analyze them. A woman of fifty came to Dr. Chopra complaining of severe abdominal pains and jaundice. Believing it to be gallstones, she was scheduled for surgery. But when the surgeons opened her up, they found a large malignant tumor that had spread to her liver and abdominal cavity. Judging the case inoperable, they closed the incision without further action.

After her daughter had pleaded with Dr. Chopra not to tell her mother the truth, he informed the older woman that the gallstones had been successfully removed, rationalizing that her family would break the news in time, and that in all likelihood she had only a few months to live. Eight months later he was astonished to see the same woman back in his office for a routine checkup. The examination showed no signs of jaundice, no pain and no cancer. Later she told Dr. Chopra, "When I was so sure I had cancer and it turned out to be just gallstones, I told myself I would never be sick another day in my life." Her cancer never returned, and Dr. Chopra writes, "The woman used no technique; she got well, it appears, through her deep-seated resolve, and that was good enough."

Perhaps you already see the common denominator in these cases of miraculous healing. There was a ***decision made by the mind*** to be healed: "She had *absolute belief* that she would get well." "She *willed herself* to be healed." "I *had the unusual sense* that I was going to make it." "He was *completely convinced* he would get well." "He had *absolute unwavering belief* he would get better." "He *just decided* he was not going to get cancer." "I *told myself* I would never get sick another day in my life." "Through her *deep-seated resolve,* she got well."

It is the same with the two cases in which Bert and Mr. Govindass lived well beyond the medical prognosis given for their condition. Bert literally *willed himself* to live until his 50th wedding anniversary. Mister Govindass *told himself and believed* that he could not die until he had seen Dr. Chopra again. But they also believed that when those specified times had passed, they would die, *and so they did.*

It also works in reverse. Through *decisions and thoughts of the* ***mind,*** we can literally bring on disease and cause death. The Boston fireman *was certain* he had a heart condition. Jerry *resigned himself* to his fate; he was a *very negative person.* For

Chitra, *doubt* began to creep in; she *became anxious, fearful and depressed.*

These are not isolated cases, they happen all the time. A man who had inoperable cancer was given a new drug that was reported to be effective in curing his type of cancer. His cancer disappeared. But later when he read a medical report that the new drug was not reliable in effecting cancer cures, doubt set in, his cancer returned and he soon died. The thoughts of our mind are very critical to the state of our health.

We have proof of that in the placebo effect. In scientific experiments, test groups may be given a placebo, a substance that has no medicinal value whatsoever. They are told that it has certain medical properties that will help or cure their problem. Subjects quite frequently show improvement and sometimes are even cured of their ailment. It seems logical that the *thought* of the mind and *belief* that the pill would help brought about the healing.

It is very likely that it is the placebo effect, the thought and belief of the mind, that is responsible for the results often realized from alternative methods such as faith healing and laying on of hands. The person *believes with his mind* that he will be healed. The reason that others are not healed is because they don't *really* believe; there is doubt. It is most probable that the same holds true for voodoo. For example, the sticking of pins through the heart of a doll resembling the victim, or invoking a hex, cannot, in itself, possibly cause harm if the target has no knowledge that it is being done. It is only when the victim becomes aware, *believes* that harm is possible and thoughts of fear and death are implanted in the mind, that those results may occur. It is also likely that substances like ground apricot pits, pulverized rhinoceros horn, bear gallbladder and other "health aids" work for *some* people because they *believe* these substances will help.

We simply do not understand the power of the mind. It is the dominant force, not only in shaping our behavior but also in determining the state of our health. It is the freedom and power that God has given us in the form of free will. The intelligence within us, our soul, knows how to maintain perfect health and how to heal if we are injured or incur a disease, but it *needs the cooperation* of our mind.

Sometimes the only cooperation it needs is for us to get out of the way with our negative and anxiety-ridden thoughts. That is why meditation is so effective in healing. The state of peace, relaxation and serenity that accompanies meditation lays the foundation for healing. It is why we sleep--so the body can restore itself. When our mind is at rest in a state of meditation, self-hypnosis or sleep, free of worry, frustration, anger and all thoughts of negativity, then the soul is free of those dominating forces and can go about its function of healing and restoring the body.

That is what is often referred to as 'letting go and letting God.' That is the way Jack Colern, hospitalized and dying with AIDS, was healed. As he said, "My spirituality is simple, *let go and let God*. When I let go, I am shown the way." Yet it is not God who directly does the healing, but God within us in the form of our soul, our spiritual self, that sustains life in our body and makes every effort to return it to normal when things go awry from disease and injury.

But, even better than "getting out of the way" by putting aside the negativity of the mind is the decision to cooperate fully with the soul, aiding in the healing by thinking good, happy, positive thoughts; by providing the body with proper nutrition and exercise; as well as making firm, confident decisions to recover from the disease or illness. Or, even more specifically, by use of the visualization technique; carrying in the mind the thought of being whole, healthy and cured.

Disease or illness is a disruption of the harmony between the mind, body and soul. The tendency of the soul is to maintain our body in perfect health. Our soul is that field of energy given to us by God. It has the intelligence to form and *perfect* our bodies from the moment of conception through birth and growth to adulthood. It is the force that sustains our life and knows how to heal. But it is still subordinate to the mind. Although it is unalterable and indestructible, its abilities can be overridden by the mind. With our minds we can literally *think* ourselves ill and even to death.

More often than not we do not respect our body, but abuse it both by the less-than-healthy thoughts we entertain, as well as the undecidedly unhealthy substances we take into our body, either intentionally or unknowingly. We cause harm to both our mental and physical self when we dwell on such thoughts as anger, hatred, frustration, impatience, worry, bitterness, paranoia, lust, covetousness and many others. We often ingest substances that are not the best for us, such as junk food, too much animal fat, excessive amounts of sugar, too much caffeine, tobacco smoke, immoderate quantities of alcohol, trans-fats, legal and illegal drugs, preservatives, pesticides, synthetic dyes and many pollutant-type chemicals that are spewed into the air that we breathe.

We have absolute proof that all those negative thoughts and harmful substances are generally detrimental to good health and often the cause of disease, yet we do little if anything to change our lifestyles to avoid them. And, of course, the food industry, the chemical manufacturers, the advertising media, the medical establishment and even government have not always acted responsibly nor been forthright in advising the public about the harmful affects.

The ulterior motive of profit often governs the production and promotion of the legal yet harmful products that are offered for consumption. A prime example is tobacco. Smoking is the greatest cause of preventable disease and death, increasing governmental health costs by about $22 billion annually in the United States alone. Over 420,000 Americans die each year from smoking-related illnesses. Tobacco is the cause of more death, debilitation and destruction than marijuana, opium, crack and cocaine combined.

What does that say about a government that makes narcotics production and use illegal while at the same time that same government subsidizes tobacco? It speaks loudly of politics. The tobacco industry is a multi-billion dollar business. It spends $4 billion annually just to promote its products while the government spends about $1 million in anti-smoking advertisements. The politicians in Washington have been cowed by the powerful tobacco lobby and the political leaders from the tobacco-producing states, often giving in to their opposition to anti-smoking measures in exchange for their support in other areas. Fortunately, this is beginning to change.

Certainly, tobacco farmers are not evil or anything of the sort. Growing tobacco is a long-standing and honorable tradition. But now that we have become aware of the harm that it causes, its production should be discontinued. Common sense would dictate that if we do not have the right to use marijuana, opium and cocaine because they are harmful to individuals in particular, and to society in general, then neither should we have the right to use tobacco, which is much more injurious and costly to both the individual and to society.

Land that is now used for the output of tobacco should be converted to the production of healthy products such as vegetables, fruits, grains and herbs. Their use is on the rise and will increase dramatically as we come to learn more about their nutritional value in maintaining good health and combating disease. With recent disclosures about the tobacco industry and the increased opposition to cigarette smoking, the handwriting is on the wall. The wise tobacco farmer will make the switch to other products.

The United States has spent $23 billion in the last few decades to find the cause of and a cure for cancer, but there has been very little progress. Meanwhile the incidence of cancer has increased. The problem is that medical research is looking in the wrong place and for difficult solutions when the answer is probably quite simple. The cause of cancer likely lies in environmental and food chain contamination, diet and the state of the mind. "According to the National Research Council, at least eighty percent of cancers are caused by identifiable factors that can be controlled. Thirty percent are attributed to tobacco, but an even greater number--thirty five to sixty percent--are caused by dietary factors."[4] Stress is a major factor in cancer as well as other diseases. Granted, control of all those causes can often be difficult, but *we do have the complete ability to do so*!

Studies show that if a parent or grandparent died of heart disease or ovarian cancer, for example, the offspring have a higher risk of dying from the same thing. In addition to the genetic or hereditary connection, more attention should be given to the possibility of a learned lifestyle correlation. One may be predisposed toward a disease that the parent died from because one often follows in the parent's footsteps when it comes to lifestyle and the types of food and drink one consumes. An inclination toward similar temperamental factors such as anger and worry is also a factor.

But even the genetic link can be altered by the power of the mind in cooperation with the ability of the soul to perfect the human body. Jordan Houghton was born with a defective gene that causes severe enzyme deficiency, most often resulting in death at an early age. It had already killed his brother, Beau, at 18 months of age. But scientists reported that "Jordan managed to heal himself, returning a flawed gene to normal. Somehow, at some unknown time, Jordan's body rewrote his genetic legacy and stopped his disease."[5] Jordan's beliefs, his positive attitude and love of music surely contributed to the healing. About a dozen examples of such natural gene fixes have been reported. Every one of us has the capability to heal ourself and maintain perfect health by deciding with our dominant mind, to cooperate fully with the life-sustaining and life-perfecting intelligence within us called the soul.

In the United States, there are over 20 million surgeries performed every year. Annually, about one million people die from heart disease, 150,000 die from strokes and 600,000 from cancer. About 75 million people are suffering from allergies at any given time. Arthritis affects, to some degree, about 75% of the elderly population. It has been estimated that 60 million baby boomers will have arthritis by the year 2020. Depression, diabetes, high blood pressure, vision problems, obesity, indigestion and many other ills plague our society, causing tens of millions of people considerable discomfort and a restricted, less-than-enjoyable lifestyle. *And it's all so unnecessary*! *Disease can be eliminated*! The elimination of disease is to be found in prevention. Prevention is to be found in responsibility. When we are irresponsible and disease overtakes us, then cure can be found in returning to responsibility and *belief* in the healing intelligence within us.

The medical establishment is starting to lose the battle for the health of mankind. *Disease is winning*! Illnesses such as heart disease, cancer, arthritis and AIDS are epidemic and ever-increasing in their rate of occurrence. We are spending billions upon billions of dollars on research in order to find a cure, but are little closer than we were at the start.

Heart bypass surgery has been touted as one of medicine's greatest achievements in fighting heart disease. But just how effective and safe is it? It is estimated that 50 percent of all bypass grafts clog up again after five years and 80 percent within seven years. There is risk of heart attack, stroke and death. Bypass surgery and angioplasty are only temporary restorative measures unless one changes his or her lifestyle by improving the diet and state of mind, for example.

Synthetic drugs and the scalpel are the standard "cure" for heart disease. Why should we use drugs and surgery as a cure when known, gentler and safer methods are available? Who would want to go through the expense and risk of heart bypass surgery, angioplasty and dangerous prescription drugs for cardiovascular disease when a non-surgical, safe, painless, inexpensive and even enjoyable procedure is available?

Rare is the doctor who would recommend the non-surgical way. And those with the disease can't ask for it because few know about it. Or, if they do ask their doctor, she would likely not approve of it despite the fact that the procedure is generally known to the medical profession. Nor would the AMA or the American Heart Association approve of it because they consider it untested, which isn't true. It has been tested both in Europe and this country.

Doctor Dean Ornish has *scientifically proven* that heart disease can be reversed without surgery. In his book, PROGRAM FOR REVERSING HEART DISEASE,[6] he reveals research and studies that show that diet and lifestyle not only prevent heart attacks, but actually have reversed the clogging of the arteries. His program involves healing of the heart emotionally and spiritually as well as physically. The Washington Post says, "There is emerging evidence that Ornish, with his non-invasive techniques, is accomplishing the same ends as are his scalpel-wielding colleagues."[6] The National Institute of Health says, "Dr. Ornish's program can lead to a better life as well as a longer one. It is the only program, scientifically validated, to begin reversing even severe coronary disease without using cholesterol-lowering drugs or surgery."[6]

Dr. William Roberts, Editor in Chief of the American Journal of Cardiology, says, "Dr. Ornish is on the right road and we need to get on it also."[6] Forty million people in this country have heart disease and that's only those who have been diagnosed. Sixty million have high blood pressure and 80 million have cholesterol levels that are too high. Over 1.5

million people suffer heart attacks in this country each year. Still, the primary treatment for all this misery continues to be surgery and drugs. Why isn't the medical establishment getting on with the non-surgical program for reversing heart disease, as Dr. Roberts suggested? That the use of bypass surgery, angioplasty and drug treatment for heart disease is a $15 billion-a-year business in this country undoubtedly has a lot to do with it!

Infection is becoming a serious problem with superstrains of drug-resistant bacteria emerging as a result of overuse of antibiotics. Until that problem is resolved, you can do your part by using natural products that have antibiotic capabilities. Usnea, Petasites Officinalis and Nasturtiums are plentiful, just to name a few. A combination of Echinacea and Goldenseal is quite effective. I've used it for sinus infection and it works. Natural antibiotics can also be found in gardencress, watercress, and horseradish. You can protect yourself and your children from disease by using vegetables and herbs with antibiotic capabilities in your everyday diet. Garlic, especially fresh garlic, is very effective. It not only adds a wonderful flavor to the food but is a potent deterrent of infection. You don't need anyone's approval to use these products, and therein lies the basis for disease prevention and good health.

Just as we are individually responsible for our behavior and salvation, so are we personally responsible for the state of our health. Unfortunately, most of us have been very irresponsible when it comes to the care and condition of our bodies. What we eat, drink and breathe in, as well as the state of our mind, is very important. Of the utmost importance is how we perceive the nature of our being. The latter can overcome deficiencies in the former. If we *believe* that we are self-healing organisms and that the soul has the ability to perfect and maintain our bodies in good health, with the cooperation of our mind, then a deficiency in the kind and amount of the food we eat, for example, need not cause us health problems.

For instance, look at the diet of some of the cultures around the world. Some of the Peruvian Indians who live at high altitudes live almost entirely on a corn diet. They eat fresh corn, corn mush, corn bread and even drink corn beer. They eat very little in the way of green vegetables or meat. Still, they are magnificent specimens with large lung capacities to compensate for the thinner air at higher altitudes. They have great endurance and are capable of running long distances with little effort.

By our nutritional standards, these people should be riddled with diseases such as scurvy, rickets, arthritis and osteoporosis due to diet malnutrition; yet they are not. It seems the only possible answer is that they believe, simply accept, that *what* they eat is all they *need* to eat. They *believe* they have the ability to exist and enjoy good health on what they eat. The lack of chemical pollutants in their daily environment is another positive factor. The soul, without their awareness to the contrary, does the rest.

So you see there is still that need for the cooperation of the dominant mind and the life-sustaining intelligence within us that is our soul. But we are often uncooperative, making bad decisions with our mind that tend to overwhelm the soul. We ingest harmful products that are not good for our body and do not have the understanding to call upon the intelligence within us that can offset their harmful effects. Or we eat, drink and breathe in harmful substances *knowing*, with our mind, that they are detrimental to our health, and so they become.

The best of all worlds is to consume and enjoy the things we know are good for us, avoiding what we know is harmful, and maintaining a state of mind that is free from stress. At the same time, we should hold the belief that we are truly, wonderfully made with the totality of our being able to sustain perfect health despite attack by antibiotic-resistance strains of bacteria or any other disease-causing organism.

This is the formula for enduring good health, healing, and even the cure for such diseases as cancer and AIDS. We prevent as well as *cure* disease by being *responsible* in what we ingest, in *maintaining a positive mental attitude* and **believing** in the ability of our life-perfecting soul and the power of the mind to assist.

In recovering from disease, a good and balanced nutritional program must also insure that a cleansing takes place at the start in order to eliminate all the toxic substances that have accumulated in the body. Our bodies are literally assaulted with toxins: poisonous metals such as lead and mercury; asbestos; chemically-laden paints and solvents; corrosives in air conditioning units; radiation; nitrates; radon; alcohol penetrants in colognes, perfumes and after-shave lotions; allergens; prescription drugs and over-the-counter medicines; numerous cleaning compounds found in every home; pesticides and herbicides; soaps; skin lotions; chemically altered substances such as trans-fats; chlorine; hair sprays and dyes; food additives; artificial coloring; artificial flavoring; auto exhaust; carbon monoxide; smoke; industrial pollutants, and many more.

These toxins are in the digestive system, the bowels, brain and blood stream. They are stored in the lymph nodes and body organs interfering with the normal functions of the body, deforming cells and causing disease. Is it any wonder that humankind is suffering from disease and ill health? ***It's the toxins folks***! It's the toxins that are making us sick and killing us! Research scientists say we don't have enough hard evidence to make such a judgment. Nonsense! We need to use our common sense and open our eyes to the empirical evidence. It is most certainly there.

Even the scientific evidence is present. A University of Toronto study reported that "bad reactions to prescription drugs were the U.S.'s fourth leading killer in 1994 with more than

100,000 dying from toxic reactions to medications that were administered properly, either before or after they were hospitalized. And more than 2 million suffered serious side effects."[7]

The Food and Drug Administration approves drugs and other substances after lengthy testing to determine if they are safe. But insufficient attention is given to the *cumulative* effect, which can become toxic, or the combination effect of taking a variety of drugs at the same time which can be deadly. If a specific substance shows no harmful effects, the FDA pronounces it as safe. It probably is when taken *individually*. But when we ingest multiple substances, along with the chemicals we breathe in and harmful foods that we eat, the cumulative effect, especially over time, can be lethal. Studies show that certain chemicals, when combined, increase up to tenfold in toxicity. Many of us know of people, especially the elderly, who are taking a half-dozen, and in some extreme cases as many as twenty, drugs at the same time. Many of these people just get sicker and sicker.

According to a recent study by Harvard Medical School's Dr. Steffi Woolhandler, and colleagues, about "25 percent of all Americans 65 or older are given prescriptions for drugs that they should almost never take; drugs that can produce amnesia and confusion, and others that cause serious side effects like heart problems or respiratory failure. Investigators said there is no need to prescribe these drugs to older people, either because safer alternatives are available or because the drugs are simply not needed."[8] *Most* of those people would be better off throwing their medications down the toilet, starting over with a medical doctor who also practices nutritional and holistic medicine and making sure that their system is cleansed of these synthetic, often toxic, drugs.

The cleansing can be done on a *fresh*-fruit, *fresh*-vegetable and *pure*-water diet. The fruits and chlorophyll-rich vegetables are very powerful detoxifying agents. This regimen should be accompanied by the use of special cleansing herbs for the blood, liver, kidneys and colon. But you need to be informed. You also must beware of remedies that do not do what their purveyors claim. A lifetime of accumulated toxins in the body cannot be eliminated overnight, or even in a few weeks, as some claim. It takes time and patience. An herbalist can be helpful. Do not fast; this only weakens the body.

When you are generally in good health, your body can tolerate a certain amount of toxic substances. But if you are ill and fighting diseases such as cancer or AIDS, your body and the healing intelligence within you can better accomplish the task of restoration to health without having to contend with all of those harmful substances.

If you feel uncomfortable trying to do this alone, then look for a medical doctor who also practices nutritional and holistic medicine. It is ideal to find a doctor who will work *with* you. Your input and desires need to be considered. Avoid any doctor who is not willing to listen to and try your suggestions, especially one who tells you that he knows best.

Then you need to make sure that your nutrition program excludes the many harmful products that are offered for consumption. Get most of your protein from plants such as nuts, beans and mushrooms. Protein deficiency is not a medical issue anywhere in the world. Eliminate refined sugar and white flour. Don't use products that contain artificial sweeteners. Keep the chlorine out of your body by using pure water, both to drink and shower with. In a steamy shower, you both inhale and absorb chlorine from the tap water. Filters are available that will eliminate the chlorine, as well as other impurities. Air filtering units are available that can eliminate most harmful particles and gases.

Some doctors who practice nutritional medicine believe, and studies are beginning to show, that hydrogenated fats (trans-fats) are very harmful. Margarine is a prime example. This can be a difficult problem as those fats are used in preparation of many products such as fast foods and most cookies and pastries. Although *some* food makers list hydrogenated vegetable oil under ingredients, they are not required to inform the public of the presence of these fats. Check labels and avoid products with hydrogenated oils as much as possible. For spreads, use margarine that has no hydrogenated oils or transfats.

Much of the supermarket-packaged food is processed, pasteurized or preserved, taking out nutritive value or adding substances that are not good for you. Avoid these foods whenever possible, choosing to use fresh foods when they are available. Use fresh-squeezed juices. Look for *certified* organically grown products. Farmers' markets offering these products are coming back and can be found in most cities. Even supermarkets are beginning to carry some organically grown produce.

Everyone should educate him or herself on the benefits of proper nutrition. A lot of material is available in the library that will help. Subscribe to publications such as a good vegetarian magazine and perhaps a reliable health newsletter. Many good books have been published on the subject. A new paradigm in health care is appearing with emphasis on proper nutrition and exercise as the way to prevent, as well as cure, illness. Albeit reluctantly, the government is beginning to recognize the importance of diet and lifestyle in fighting disease. The Surgeon General's office estimates that 66 percent of all deaths in this country are diet related.

In general, the medical establishment does not acknowledge the importance of a properly balanced diet--less animal fat and an abundance of fruits, vegetables and grains--in preventing as well as curing disease. Certainly many in the medical profession do so, but the vast and primary emphasis is on extensive and expensive testing, surgery, radiation and prescription drugs. That is not to say, of course, that most doctors are not sincere and dedicated. They are simply locked into the long-standing medical practices that are taught in the medical schools. Nutritional medicine is seldom a part of their training.

This is very unfortunate, for nutritional, holistic medicine is the better way. It's the way of the future. The medical establishment and the pharmaceutical industry would do well to recognize this and speed up the transformation that is already taking place. Certainly there have been some great triumphs in the field of medicine, such as conquering polio and small pox. Medical technology and pharmaceutics have done wonders in relieving human suffering due to illness. Still, we shouldn't have to wait until we get sick to start the doctoring, when we know how to *prevent* most illnesses? We do it through good nutrition, a healthy environment and a proper mental attitude.

We have to change our perceptions in this matter of our health, understanding that we are in charge of and responsible for the state of our health. We need to make the decisions as to how we are going to prevent disease and treat our illnesses and not leave it up to the medical establishment, the pharmaceutical industry or the government. You say we don't have the knowledge and expertise to do so? We do! We may not have the knowledge at our fingertips, but it's readily available and easily understood. And we certainly have the know-how to both make the decisions and carry out the treatment.

Maintaining good health is so simple; it's a shame we have ignored it for so long, choosing to suffer so much. The evidence is overwhelming that improper diets--not enough fruits, vegetables and grains; and using intemperate amounts of refined sugar, fried foods, fats, excessive alcohol, and too much animal fat--are hazardous to our health. It is common knowledge, yet we choose to stuff ourselves with cookies, candy, ice cream, donuts, French fries and hamburgers. Of course, we are egged on by the food industry and advertising media. Neither have the government or medical establishment, who are fully aware of that evidence, fulfilled their responsibility in this matter.

We are especially remiss in the matter of health when it comes to our children. For example, the overuse of antibiotics for children is dangerous. Earaches, ear infections and fluid in the middle ear are very common among children and the incidence is rising. It is very likely that the basic problem is diet related, as children start their junk food diets at an early age influenced by television and in turn influencing their parents. The standard treatment for those problems is antibiotics and surgery. Continued use of synthetic antibiotics results in building resistance to them to the point that they may no longer be effective, putting the children more and more at risk.

About 650,000 surgical procedures are done annually to relieve ear conditions, the most common being to pierce the ear drum and insert small tubes to drain middle-ear fluid. Recent studies show that most of these surgeries were not necessary; that if left alone the condition would have cleared by itself without negative repercussions.

"Cleared by itself," of course, meaning that the healing intelligence within the child handles the problem. Children usually don't get in the way of that healing with negativity of their minds. They are, for the most part, happy and content, not having yet learned about stress, although, in this day and age, stress is becoming more of a factor in the lives of our children. But they *do* hinder the healing by their less-than-proper diets.

Many parents are failing their children, not only by neglecting to teach and *show* them proper values and good behavior, but in the way that they feed them. Shamefully absent from their meals are fruits and vegetables. Notoriously present are all the wrong kinds of foods: sugar-laden cereals, whole milk and too many proteins and fats, such as are found in baloney and cheese sandwiches, hamburgers and hot dogs. Their liquid diet consists of a great deal of artificially colored and flavored water called soda pop when they should be given juices and nonfat milk as well as pure water. They are fed too many foods that contain pesticides, preservatives and synthetic substances.

Most diseases and illnesses can be treated naturally. God knew what he was doing when he made the blueprint for this body and our environment. "Nature" contains everything we need, both to stay healthy and cure disease. Within nature can be found the source of disease prevention. When we are irresponsible, bringing illness upon ourselves, or even if it should overtake us through no fault of our own, then nature also provides the natural medicine and remedies to assist the mind and soul in healing and restoring the body to perfect health.

We have already seen the importance of nutrition in reversing heart disease. The associated problem of high blood pressure, currently afflicting 60 million Americans, has a very simple, natural and effective solution: Reduce the fat in your diet, and eat lots of fruits, vegetables and *unpolished brown* rice. White rice has much of the nutritive value removed, thus losing its effectiveness in restoring elasticity to the blood vessels. Recent studies show that a dominant diet of fruits, vegetables and whole grains can significantly reduce blood pressure in as little as two to three weeks.

Standard treatment consists of drugs that lower blood pressure but do nothing to resolve the basic cause. Those drugs can have very unpleasant side-effects such as impotence, fatigue, depression and an irregular heartbeat. Why would anyone opt for such treatment when a better way is available naturally without any side-effects whatsoever?

Malignant melanoma, the most dangerous form of skin cancer, is on the rise, despite the fact that sunscreens are touted as a good preventative and used by many people. All this leads scientists to wonder how effective sun screens really are and whether they may inadvertently increase the risk of cancer and other disease by providing people with a false sense of security, as well as depriving them of the vitamin D benefits of the sun.

New research at the University of Texas in Houston suggests that "sunscreens can protect against sunburn, but not against melanoma," says the study's co-author, Margaret Kripke. "In addition, experts now speculate that the sun's ultraviolet A rays may be more harmful than once thought, rendering the many sunscreens that protect only against the burning ultraviolet B rays less effective than believed. Another factor may be the decrease in ozone concentration, the earth's 'sunscreen.' As a result, we're getting more radiation now than people did in the past."[9]

It is quite probable that another factor is involved in skin cancer, but it has been given little, if any, consideration. Why is it that some people who spend a great deal of time in the sun, over their entire lifetime, never develop skin cancer? The answer would seem to be that people are diverse; their chemical makeup is different, or some have stronger "immune systems." But what determines the chemical makeup of the body? It is the nutrients that we take into the body or the lack thereof that does so. Or body chemistry is altered by toxic substances that we ingest. Even though body chemistry can be genetic in nature, it can be altered by a change of diet. Although the sun and, perhaps, a reduction in the strength of the ozone layer may be contributing factors to skin cancer, it is more likely that faulty nutrition and ingestion of toxic chemicals are the primary cause. That melanoma is frequently showing up on parts of the body that are not exposed to the sun would lend support to this premise.

There is a basic rule of health: When we abuse the body there are *consequences* often showing up in the way of disease. These bodies that we possess are indeed wonderfully and respectfully made, but they are not invincible. We need to respect and take proper care of them. Then, should we incur illness or disease not of our making, we need to use remedies that are naturally provided for us rather than synthetic drugs and treatments that are often harmful. God, in his role of "mother nature," has provided us with a natural pharmacy without equal. But we need to educate ourselves in their use, as well as insisting that the medical profession and the pharmaceutical industry take advantage of that pharmacy.

To be fair, we can't put all the blame on the food industry, advertising, the medical field and the government when it comes to our health. Most of us know what's good and bad for us, but we're often weak-willed, lazy and irresponsible. We don't respect or appreciate our bodies. We welcome the fast food convenience and don't want to take the time to properly prepare the right foods.

Or we attempt to make sure we get proper nutrition by adding vitamins and nutritive supplements to our regular, often poor, diets. If you make sure you get a balanced diet, you don't need these supplements; although there are exceptions. For example, if you are suffering from a condition that requires more of a chemical or nutrient to correct than you would normally get from your regular diet, you should take a supplement until your condition has been alleviated.

Of course, we are conditioned to think that food needs fat, salt and sugar to taste good, and we are, therefore, often willing to take the risk. Or we live by the philosophy that it "won't happen to me." Except for the basic taste sensations of sweet and sour, bitter and salty, our tastes are cultivated and conditioned by the mind. We remember how we hated spinach and eggplant when we were young, yet somehow, when we got older, we began to like them. Baked eggplant Parmigiana is wonderful. Those who have gone on a low-salt diet out of medical necessity, and remained on it for some time, will tell you how unpleasant salted foods have become for them. Although now, the experts are telling us that salt is not the villain that they once thought it to be, and use of salt is not a factor in high blood pressure for most people. If, over a period of time, you gradually reduce your use of milk from whole milk to 2 percent, to 1 percent and then to nonfat, you will find that the nonfat milk tastes just as good, and that whole milk no longer tastes just right on your natural cereal or with your veggie sandwich.

Many believe that use of less meat and a vegetable-dominant diet deprives one of the joys of eating. Nothing is farther from the truth. Numerous and varied dishes can be prepared from nuts, grains, fruits and vegetables and they are absolutely delicious.

A veggie sandwich? Sure, they taste great. Use whole-grain breads without preservatives. Warm the slices very lightly in the microwave, but not too much, for they will turn to "cement." Toasted is great, too. Use low-fat mayo, mustard or lite butter. For the filling try any combination of romaine lettuce (it has the better nutritive value), a slice of vine-ripened tomato, sweet Oso or Vidalia onions, fresh avocado slices (avocado has gotten a bad rap; it's good for you, even helping to lower your cholesterol), fresh sliced mushrooms, red bell pepper (it has more nutritive value than the green, but green is okay if you prefer), mild green chili peppers, or anything else that your heart desires. Experiment and you will find some wonderful combinations. Then top it off with a low-fat cheese of your choosing. After you add the cheese, pop it in the toaster oven and call it a veggie melt. Some of the low-fat cheeses don't have much taste, so regular cheese is okay and won't hurt you as long as you don't use it habitually. Try soy cheese--some have great taste. Use different herbs and dressings as seasoning for your sandwiches until you find one, or a combination, that you really enjoy.

A variety of pasta dishes abounds. Pasta primavera (with broccoli, carrots and zucchini) topped with a marinara sauce and lightly sprinkled with Parmesan or Romano cheese is wonderful. The list of vegetarian foods seems endless: dozens of potato dishes, soups, salads, breads, pizzas, rice, nuts, stir fries, all kinds of beans and more. There are varied dressings for your salads that are low or even non-fat with zero cholesterol. Some are made with all-natural ingredients. Vinegar and oil are okay if you use a good oil like extra-virgin olive oil. We need oil in our diets, but the beneficial kind. Have you noticed that the Italians have such good complexions? They use olive oil and garlic liberally in their cooking, both of which are good for the skin.

You don't even have to give up your hamburgers and hot dogs. There are different burger and Frankfurter products on the market made from soy and other vegetable produce. They look like hamburger patties and frankfurters, with texture and taste being very similar. When you add the onion, lettuce, ketchup, mustard, pickle and chili, there is even less difference in the taste. Yes, chili! The burger-substitute product makes wonderful chili, as well as Sloppy Joes. Nor do you have to give up sweets. Use natural sweeteners like honey, molasses and *real* maple syrup. But keep your use of refined sugar to a minimum. A piece of cake, pie or candy once in a while isn't going to harm you.

Nor do you have to give up Fettucini Alfredo, chili Relleno, eggplant Parmigiana or Chinese food. The grams of fat in a small helping of those foods constitute approximately one's maximum suggested fat allowance for one day. Just don't eat any other fat for that day. Your body size and daily calorie intake may dictate no other fat for two days. When you fix such recipes at home you can lower the fat content to half or less, without losing significant taste, by using reduced-fat ingredients, a lesser amount of them and appropriate herbs to enhance the taste. Many restaurants are beginning to prepare such dishes with reduced-fat calories. Those kinds of dishes *occasionally* will not be detrimental to your health as long as your *regular* diet consists of plenty of fruits, vegetables and grains, and you keep a positive mental attitude about it.

Why would anyone not want to go on a nutritional program, knowing that you are not denying yourself the pleasures of eating and that you are going to be healthier, happier, more able to fend off disease and cure the illnesses that you already have? The beauty of such a program is that you will never have to be concerned about your weight; it will automatically take care of itself. Throw away your bathroom scales and calorie counter. Your grocery bill will be smaller. You will have fewer headaches, colds and backaches. Indigestion and constipation will disappear. Your over-the-counter medicine bill will be much smaller and likely nonexistent. Your breath will be fresher, and your need for deodorant will decrease. You will have more energy. It has done all those things and more for this author. I want to reemphasize that I have not had a cold, the flu or seen a doctor for illness in over five years. I attribute it to a good diet, positive thinking about my health and *belief* in my body as a self-healing entity. How we *think with our mind is very important.*

THE MIND CONNECTION

Equally important is the mental aspect of the healing program. We can generally live with a certain amount of stress in our lives, but if you are battling cancer or AIDS, it is *imperative* that you eliminate the stress in your life which comes from anger, hatred, worry and any other source. Granted, it isn't always easy, especially when you have to deal with people who are a source of anxiety. Certainly it's difficult not to worry if you *believe* that you are going to suffer and die, particularly if you entertain thoughts about the concepts of death that are prevalent in our society today. But it can be done; you can achieve peace of mind in *any* circumstance.

You can always remove yourself from a situation or location that causes stress; for example, a job. But this kind of drastic action normally isn't necessary. You can learn to eliminate the stress, whatever its source, by the power of your mind. It can be done through hypnosis or meditation and *changing your perceptions*.

We should really call it self-hypnosis, for it is actually accomplished by the individual and not another person. One uses learned techniques or follows instructions imparted by another. The concept of hypnotism is greatly misunderstood. It is often thought of as a trance-like condition in which you are unaware of what is happening to you. Self-hypnosis is simply a state of total relaxation of the body and mind. Your body is as thoroughly relaxed as in the sleep state. The mind is clear and at rest but completely aware, as in the fully-conscious state. Hypnosis is an altered state of consciousness in which your mind is free from outside distractions and highly receptive to thoughts and suggestions.

Another common misconception, even among most hypnotherapists themselves, is that during a hypnotic state the subconscious mind can be programmed. *It cannot*! As we have already discussed, in the chapter on the Nature of Man, the subconscious or soul is constant, unalterable and immovable. It is the *conscious mind* that is being programmed. We *know* that thoughts, happenings and ideas that are implanted in the memory of the mind, particularly with repetition or great emphasis, are very powerful in influencing our behavior. For example, we remember that certain actions bring unpleasant consequences and so we avoid them. On the other hand we recall with the mind that certain behavior results in pleasure and so our conduct is influenced accordingly. Just like Pavlov's dogs, we respond to a program with which we have been conditioned. It is the conscious mind that has been programmed, not the "subconscious." Clearly we respond with a decision of the mind. It is the values and beliefs that we have thought about with our mind, stored in the memory and held with deep conviction that control our behavior.

Hypnosis should be used as a means to relax and program the mind with beneficial thoughts while in that state of repose. A great number of books are available on hypnosis, including do-it-yourself manuals. You can use self-hypnosis to learn relaxation techniques, remembering that any thoughts you are entertaining while in that state constitute a programming of the *conscious* mind and memory, not the "subconscious."

Meditation is very much like hypnosis. To meditate is to engage in thought or contemplation, usually on a given subject, often in order to gain understanding or peace of mind. Or, meditation can take other forms, such as listening to music that you enjoy, walking on the beach, looking at the stars or lying in a meadow, smelling the fragrance of the flowers and feeling the soft breeze upon your face. Still, the purpose is to promote peace of mind, good health and mental well-being.

Another type of meditation does not involve thinking about a given subject, but rather is the absence of thought. It is called transcendental meditation. The idea is to transcend thought, sitting silently without thinking about anything whatsoever. The goal of transcendental meditation is to get in touch with your inner self, freeing your mind of all conscious thought and letting that inner self influence or "speak" to you. It is not easy to do, at least initially. Except when in the state of sleep, thoughts of some kind are always running through the mind. When you close your eyes and first try to empty the mind of all thought, within a matter of seconds, some thought will pop into your mind. Emptying the mind takes practice. Books that are helpful are available, as well as people who can teach you meditation.

Different postures can be assumed during meditation. A traditional one is sitting with legs folded and hands in the lap in the lotus position. But if one is not experienced with that posture, cramping will soon overtake the muscles, making meditation difficult if not impossible. Some believe that sitting erect and/or slightly swaying forward and backward is important. The ideal situation is to assume a position that is completely relaxing, such as sitting in an easy chair, so that no muscles are being used.

A <u>mantra</u>, some word that is continually repeated during meditation, is frequently used. Its continued use eliminates other thoughts. All these things work, but still require activity of the mind. One has to send thoughts to the muscles to remain in an erect posture or sway, as well as speak the mantra. Other techniques involve narrowing thought to the inhalation and exhalation of the breath or picturing blackness. As you see, they all require thought, so you need to decide which works best for you. When you become more experienced in the practice of meditation those techniques become pretty much automatic so that the mind is relatively free from thought.

To free the mind completely from conscious thought is very helpful in achieving peace of mind. But the greater benefit is to get in closer touch with the soul. When we get out of the way of the busy and often negative thoughts of the mind, then the inner or higher self, the soul, can go about its work of perfecting us both physically and spiritually. Meditation is an excellent way to ahcieve this.

Both self-hypnosis and meditation can be very instrumental in removing all forms of stress from the body and mind. Even when thrust back into a situation that is the cause of the stress, frequent use of hypnosis and meditation can help reduce its impact. Regular exercise is also very important in reducing and controlling stress. There is a last step that will literally eliminate stress from your life: CHANGE YOUR PERCEPTIONS! You need to change how you think about the stressful situation or the cause of the stress. "Get yourself new minds and hearts," as God has told us; as well, we need to remember that "as we think, so are we!"

For example, danger and challenge are stressful to most people, still there are those who thrive on them. It's all a matter of how they *think* about such activities. Whitewater rafting can be both challenging and dangerous, and to those who *think* of it that way, it is stressful. The veteran rafter finds it enjoyable, exhilarating and even relaxing because he *thinks* of it as such.

Driving an automobile in traffic can be a great source of trepidation and even downright hazardous to one's life and limb. Speeders, slowpokes, lane weavers, traffic tie-ups, confusing signs, honkers, drunken drivers, finger-givers, fist-shakers, rain, snow, sleet, heat and many other factors contribute to the tremendous stress that can be experienced. Although most of us consider ourselves good drivers who don't do these things, or aren't unduly influenced by them, we still often respond in kind. We honk, we curse and swear, fret, stew, shake the fist, shout, call other drivers names, won't let other drivers in and often drive too fast for road conditions, all of which drive our blood pressure sky high and are detrimental to both our physical and mental well-being.

None of these reactions on our part need occur if we just *change our perceptions.* It is possible to be calm, cool, relaxed and even enjoy driving under these conditions. The first thing we need to think about, understand and accept is that these kinds of reactions to bad drivers do not adversely affect them or change them. *The harm and change that occurs is to ourselves.* We become stressed, our blood pressure goes up, we get angry, feel unhappy, and our health and peace of mind suffer. Why would we do this to ourselves when it isn't necessary?

Through thought and power of the mind, we can simply tell ourselves that we are *not* going to jeopardize our well-being by allowing unsettling reactions to others. We *refuse* to react in that manner. Rather we can *choose* to stay calm, let the other driver in, ignore and avoid the reckless driver, and adjust our driving to the conditions. If traffic is backed up and we're going to be late, we simply tell ourselves that we can do nothing to change it, so there's no gain in getting upset. Relax, tune in to your favorite music, and enjoy it. Think about pleasant things, smile, laugh, sing and be courteous. Everyone of us can do it, but it takes time. Behavior that we have been conditioned to for so long is often difficult to change.

These basics of changing our perception and, thus, our behavior apply not only to driving, but to all of our relations with others; at home, in the office or wherever we are. Life can be wonderful! Why unnecessarily make it otherwise? Take charge; be in control! Show love, kindness and patience to others, perceiving that this is what God tells us is essential for achieving heaven on earth, as well as in the hereafter.

Can we truly eliminate all stress from our lives? What about drastic situations, such as losing one's job, bankruptcy, losing our home or divorce? Or perchance being face to face with violent death? How could anyone's anxiety level not be drastically elevated with a gun held to the head? The answer is "yes," we can eliminate stress and remain calm and unaffected in every one of those situations!

Again, the solution is to *change our perception!* No matter what confronts us, we have to *believe* that everything will be okay. For it will be! As one experiencer said, "I remember that I knew that everything, everywhere in the universe was OK, that the plan was perfect...I was just an infinite being in perfection. And love and safety and security and knowing that nothing could happen to you..."[10] God's plan *is* perfect, but because *man chooses* to do wrong, suffering often results. That is not okay. Still, in the end, everything will be! As the scriptures say, "Who can be against us if God is for us."[11] And he is indeed! Nothing can separate us from the love of God, no tribulation whatsoever! When we *think* like that, we can face *anything* that confronts us with serenity and composure.

Yes, even the gun to the head! Do you remember Jackie Pflug, who was aboard a hijacked airliner, scheduled for execution and shot in the head? Prior to being shot, and after worrying for an hour about her possible fate, she said, "I just stopped struggling. I just closed my eyes and went into a place that was very safe. A place of nonworry, knowing that everything would be all right no matter what happened....whether I lived or whether I died."

We all can live in that belief, *that everything will be all right, no matter what happens.* Everyone of us can find that *place of nonworry.* Jackie found it through prayer in her dire need. We, too, can find it when trouble confronts us. But we can have it right now by *changing our perception* of our own nature and the nature of God. We claim it by accepting that we are divine and immortal, as well as human and mortal and by believing that "we are spirits, and spirits move on," as Jackie Pflug says. It is ours by understanding that God is for us, and nothing can stand between us and his unconditional love; by understanding that all of us, without exception, will eventually be reunited with God.

We now have three of the four ingredients for good health and healing. One is to cleanse our bodies of the toxins that we have consumed with our food and the air that we breathe. Then make sure that we avoid, as much as possible, any further consumption of them. Two is to change our diet, eliminating or at least minimizing, the foods that we know are not the best for us, making sure that we eat primarily natural foods, without preservatives and preferably organically grown. Three is to get control of the stress in our lives, working toward the goal of complete serenity.

The medical establishment, researchers, the government and most of the rest of us are already aware of the above information, however, for varied reasons, choose not to avail ourselves of such a program or teach its benefits. That is so unfortunate, for we could eliminate so much suffering of the human race if we would do so. Yet, the handwriting is on the wall; the spiritual, nutritional and health revolution has already begun. Why not join in, get aboard and enjoy life?

Few are aware of the fourth factor. Or, society in general has failed to realize its significance, although its presence is known and its benefits proven. It is a factor that is very beneficial in preventing disease and sustaining good health, an element that is *absolutely essential* in curing life-threatening diseases. That factor is the power of the mind. It has been emphasized throughout this text. We *know* how the thoughts of our mind can affect our behavior. We even *know* that we can make ourselves ill or well by the thoughts that we hold in our mind. But those in the field of medicine haven't made the connection as to why this is so. They have failed to find the link because of false perceptions.

They have not perceived the human body as a true and efficient self-healing organism. Although it is acknowledged that healing ability is possessed by the body, it is widely believed that modern medicine, in the form of drugs, high-tech equipment and surgery, is absolutely essential in solving the health problems of mankind.

The greatest misconception concerns the total nature of man. Although most doctors and medical researchers probably believe in the soul, they aren't aware of its function in sustaining life and its ability to heal and perfect the body. Most unfortunate is the unawareness of the relationship between the mind and that healing intelligence within us called the soul. Even those few who promote mind/body and spiritual healing have not made the final connection--that the mind is dominant; that it is the free will that God has given us and that, when the mind is programmed with negative thoughts and ideas, negative results occur.

Thus, when a doctor makes a terminal prognosis and so informs a patient, he is pronouncing the death sentence. For when that thought is planted in the patient's mind and, usually after a short period of denial, he accepts the prognosis and *believes* he is going to die, **he will die**, just as surely as God made little green apples. The only time the "death sentence" can be commuted is when the *patient* changes the perception that he is terminal.

We have a great deal of evidence that all of that is so. Some of it has been presented at the beginning of this chapter in the cases of those who have recovered from terminal illnesses, as well as those who have not. It is only when the patient rejects the prognosis and *believes* he is going to get better, that terminal illnesses such as encountered with some cancers and AIDS, for example, can be overcome.

It is that *decision by the mind* that makes the difference. I want to reemphasize that the proof is in the results: "She had *absolute belief* that she would get well." "She *willed herself* to be healed." "I *had the unusual sense* that I was going to make it." "He was *completely convinced* he would get well." "He was *sure he would beat it*." "He had *absolute unwavering belief* he would get better." "He *just decided* he was not going to get cancer." "I *told myself* I would never get sick another day in my life." "Through her *deep-seated resolve,* she got well." And they all did!

In all of those cases, the individuals themselves, through the power of the mind, commuted their "death sentence." All of us in the totality of our being, our body, mind and soul, have the ability to heal ourselves of all disease. God has given this power and authority to us. After all, we are made in his likeness which would include the capability to heal. It is an endowment that we all possess. Of course, we must have possession of our mental faculties. When we do not, such as with certain mental diseases, then others must help, using modern medicines, nutritional medicine, prayer and *belief*.

The medical establishment should eliminate the prognosis of "terminal." Rather, patients should be advised that they have a life-threatening illness, but that it *need not be terminal*. If you *have* been diagnosed and pronounced terminal, you **must** totally reject it! You must get yourself a "new mind and new heart." A new mind that perceives your illness as only temporary and which can be overcome, a mind that understands that you are wonderfully and respectfully made, a self-healing organism, with the total capacity to heal itself. You must get a heart that *believes*, with deep conviction, that those abilities do constitute your true nature and that recovery from the disease is possible.

When you get all four of those healing and disease-preventing factors working for you, then you will be on the road to perfect health and recovery from any disease you may have incurred.

A new paradigm concerning health, healing and medicine is needed if we are to win the battle with disease that is rapidly overtaking and threatening mankind. We must improve the quality of our food supply, eliminating, or greatly reducing, synthetic chemicals that are used to grow and preserve it. We need to be aware that convenience is proving harmful to us, and we need to get back to preparation and use of natural foods. It is important that we get on with cleaning up our water and air supply. Progress has been pitifully slow. The World Water Council has estimated that at least "five million people die each year due to filthy drinking water, caused by massive amounts of pollutants, including sewage, industrial wastes and hazardous fertilizers being dumped into the world's lakes and rivers."[12]

The medical establishment must speed up the transition from drugs and surgery to natural and nutritional medicine, for it is the wave of the future; the true, natural and God-given solution to our health problems. All of us need to be aware of the importance that good nutrition and lifestyle play when it comes to the state of our health, and make changes as necessary.

Of the utmost importance is the need to change the perception of our own nature concerning disease prevention and the ability to heal. When we understand and accept the presence of an intelligence within us that is capable of sustaining and *perfecting* life, *with the cooperation* and assistance of the mind, then we can conquer disease, and illness will be a thing of the past. Then will we "die" only of old age. We could live to the age of 120, or perhaps even 969, as did Methuselah, and enjoy every minute of it. There is no need for mankind to suffer as we do from disease and illness. It is time to set aside all the false beliefs and ulterior motives that are present in our health care system and enjoy good health!

Chapter Seventeen

CONCLUSION

There is a great multitude of people waiting for the world to be destroyed in some Armageddon-like cataclysm. They believe it is coming, especially as they witness conditions waxing worse and worse, and they perceive mankind as descending into completely uncivilized behavior and depravity. Many believe it is relatively imminent. ***It isn't going to happen***! This world is going to continue until humanity learns to live in peace and harmony. Only then will some form of a new heaven and earth come into being. Scriptures tell us that all of God's laws *must* be fulfilled,[1] that his will *is to be done* on earth as in heaven,[2] that God's ways *will* reign supreme[3] and when (not "if") the world is full of the knowledge of the Lord, then there will be no more harm in all the earth.[4]

So let's not continue to suffer and let the deterioration of the world proceed. Let's get on with searching for knowledge of God and fulfilling his laws in order to return this world to the heavenly paradise that it was intended to be. We have the complete ability to do so. It's time to take charge of our lives and accept responsibility for our actions and the things that happen in this world. By false perceptions, especially of our own nature, we have let circumstances and the thoughts of our minds shape our lives and environment, to our detriment and sorrow.

James Allen, author of AS A MAN THINKETH, says it well: "Man is buffeted by circumstances so long as he believes himself to be the creature of outside conditions, but when he realizes that he is a creative power and that he may command the hidden soil and seeds of his being out of which circumstances grow, he then becomes the rightful master of himself.... Man, as the lord and master of thought, is the maker of himself, the shaper and author of his environment.... Man has but to right himself to find that the universe is right."[5]

Let us summarize how we have adversely shaped ourselves, our surroundings and what we must do to right them and, thusly, the world. Primarily through religious beliefs we have made the human being a poor, inadequate, mortal creature, with few redeeming qualities, whose destiny is to struggle through life, continually doing that which is wrong, and who can do little if anything of his own accord to change all that. We have been conditioned by others and our own thoughts to think in these terms and so it is what we have become. *As we think, so are we!* It is an image of mankind that must be *totally* rejected. We are better and much more than that.

We must accept what God tells us about ourselves: that we are made in his likeness, that we are wonderfully and respectfully made, that we are the salt of the earth and the light of the world, that we can bring forth good things from the goodness of our hearts, that we can turn from our wrongdoing and do what is right and good, and, even that we can be perfect.

We must perceive ourselves as magnificent, sentient beings who are masters of our own destiny who can control circumstances along the road that leads to it. We need to understand that *we* are responsible for our lives, our own good health, the condition of this world that God has given us to live in *and* our salvation. He has provided us everything that we need to make our habitat a paradise, live in bliss, and achieve heaven. He provided us with a soul that gives and sustains life. In accordance with God's blueprint and the free will he has given us, we create for ourselves a powerful, dominant, conscious mind with which we can control all aspects of this life as well as our destiny. In what we call Nature, God has supplied us with our food, shelter and everything else essential to our well-being. All he asks of us is that we show one another love.

But, in order to do that, we must change the perception of our nature from that of an error-prone, poor, sinful being to one who is *fully capable* of goodness and *fully capable* of letting our love show forth so as to make the world a better place. We must learn to love our neighbor as ourself. But first we need to discover how to love ourselves. How can we possibly do that if we continue to perceive ourselves as that sinful being whose nature it is to do wrong? How can we achieve self-love when we are bombarded with such concepts as being rotten, depraved beings with nothing but evil in our hearts? We must reject all such teachings by men and believe only God.

We must also believe him when he tells us that we are responsible for, and will be held to account for, our actions in this lifetime. So, let's start thinking of life that way, rather than blaming other people and events for our problems and the condition of the world. When we change our ways, taking responsibility and doing that which is right and good, then our lives and the world will change for the better.

Molli Nickell, author and publisher of Spirit Speaks magazine, said it beautifully: "The moment you begin to take conscious responsibility for your life, it will change dramatically. Owning your thoughts and deeds moves you into the status of being in charge of your own life as you create it and recreate it moment by moment. You'll discover self-empowerment which will lead to increased feelings of freedom. You'll become a happy creator, taking responsibility, making conscious choices, and being the awesome, powerful and joyful being you were always meant to be. Go for it!"[6]

But we have often been very irresponsible in our lives. Perhaps the greatest bane is the belief that materialism equates to happiness and success, and thus we strive to accumulate treasure and power. In doing so, all kinds of bad things happen to mankind and the world. Greed, corruption, selfishness and indifference raise their ugly heads. By-products are poverty, debt, crime, violence and war. Certainly this isn't true of all people. Gaining wealth, as long as it is used properly, is not wrong. Many use their material gains wisely, not storing up more than they can possibly use, providing jobs for others and helping those in need. But the predominant philosophy in the world is to "look out for number one; you can never be too rich; let the other guy fend for himself and do unto others before they can do unto you."

God has told us that the first priority is to seek his kingdom and his righteousness. God's kingdom is an earth that exists in peace and harmony. We think of war as inevitable. It is not! World peace is achievable. We simply have to change our perception, *believing* that it is attainable. Then we must take responsibility for what we have done in arming the world to the teeth, acknowledging that it was wrong and take steps to right that wrong.

We must change the perceptions that "might makes right" and provides security; that there will always be evil in the world and therefore we must be prepared to battle it with guns and explosives. Military might eventually results in insecurity. Love is a much better and more effective "weapon" against evil. We must listen to God, who has told us not to kill, rather than to governments and leaders who tell us that it's okay. If we believe God, then there is no need for weapons.

Nor do we need them to defend ourselves when we accept God's instructions that we are to turn the other cheek, love our enemies, and do good to those who persecute us. It's a hard philosophy to accept and live by, but God's wisdom is flawless. We certainly don't need weapons for the sport of killing animals. Sport is defined as activity requiring skill or physical prowess, of a *competitive* nature, as in racing, ball games and *hunting*. Sportsmanship is defined as *fair* and courteous conduct while engaged in a sport. Is it competitive and fair to blast innocent and helpless doves out of the sky with a shotgun? Is it sporting to blow away a defenseless deer with a high-powered rifle and a pinpoint-accurate telescope? We must adopt the mindset that commands that we change swords into plowshares; that realizes that only love can conquer hate.

In the interim, until we realize the abolition of armies and armament, the world's military establishment can use its resources for humanitarian relief. A very great need exists for such action. Funds currently being spent for the production of weapons of war, as well as space exploration, can be redirected into the manufacture of equipment and the use of manpower to ease the problems that confront mankind.

For example, water is plentiful in the world. It's just not accessible for various reasons. It's too salty, too much rain water runs back into the ocean, or it needs to be transported great distances. We can build catchment systems, water pipelines and waterways. Desalinization technology is here. It's expensive, but only a portion of the money that is spent on space exploration, "defense" and weapons of war would provide all the fresh water we need to turn much of the desert and drought-stricken area of the world into farmland and veritable green pastures, eliminating hunger as well as easing political turmoil. A major point of contention in the Middle East is the control of the limited water supply there. The Israelis have done a remarkable job of turning the desert into fertile and productive land. The same can be done for much of the other arid land in the Middle East, with the result that dispute, violence and war over territory there will greatly diminish, if not cease.

There are many other forms of "plowshares" that the military industrial complex can transition to for the benefit of mankind, without disrupting profits and employment. World peace is elusive, but not impossible. We only need to change our perceptions and actions will follow. And, after all, scripture tells us that, "Nation will not lift up sword against nation, neither will they learn war anymore."[7] Knowing that the peaceable kingdom *is* coming, why wait? Let's get on with it *now*!

We will never achieve harmony on earth until we change our perception of one another. Racism and discrimination are alive and well in the world. When we look at one another we see and think such thoughts as white, black, fat, thin, tall, short, beautiful, ugly, rich, poor, American, Jew, Arab and on and on. We think that way because we are conditioned all of our lives to do so by parents, educators, literature, religion, governments and media, and thus prejudice, intolerance and disunity come into being and thrive. Surely we have to be realistic, but when we classify people like that for the purpose of judging or criticizing them, which is commonly done, then it is wrong.

We need to deliberately change the way we think. When we look at a person we should see a being made in God's image, one who possesses the qualities of love, goodness and compassion even though they may be suppressed, one who is wonderfully and respectfully made and one who is to be respected and held in high regard, as God has told us to do. We should see *all* people as our neighbors to whom we are required by God to show love, kindness, caring, mercy and forgiveness. When we do so, then bigotry and injustice will have disappeared, and we will have found God's righteousness; we are right and acceptable to him.

We also have been incredibly irresponsible when it comes to our children. We have failed to bring them up in the nurture and admonition of the Lord; failed to teach them love and respect for others. It is not enough to *tell* them about love, respect, courtesy, kindness and all the values that are essential to a civilized and harmonious society. We must **set the example**. The model that children predominantly see today is one of disrespect, rudeness, impatience, anger, hatred and violence.

They are bombarded with that example from all sides: parents, peers, governments, literature, movies and especially television. No matter how much we *preach* values to them, it is the *example* from which they learn and which they then imitate. How can we expect children to be respectful and courteous when they see a parent who is rude to other drivers, shouting, cursing and using unfriendly gestures? How can they learn patience when they are treated with impatience? How can they learn to be kind when parents are unkind to them and each other? How can they learn love when they see so much hatred in the world?

The violence and sexual innuendo in books, magazines, movies and television are appalling. It is present even in children's books and videos. Those who produce that material are grossly irresponsible. The First Amendment gives us freedom of speech and expression, but does not give us license to teach such detrimental material to our children, which is surely what we are doing. That material is also bad for adults, for they too, are adversely influenced by it.

We rationalize by saying that parents can control what their children read and view. Or that adults don't have to buy the material and they know where the "Off" switch is. Producers of that material say they are providing only what the audiences want and demand. Many contend that it is not harmful, citing their experience with such material when they were children and that they turned out all right.

All of those premises are faulty. We are assailed by so much material that parents can't always control their children's access to it. Or the parents are not always in the position of being at home to regulate television viewing. They shouldn't have to put a lock box or "V" chip on the TV. Much of the material is insidious. The producers are not responding to what the audience wants, but what they have been *conditioned* to want by the tremendous volume and incessant flow of that kind of material, as well as the lack of good, decent nonviolent viewing matter. Radio is not innocent, either.

Also the programs and material of today are more violent, explicit and frequent than those of past generations. There can be little doubt that such material affects the behavior of the viewer. Children can become so negatively conditioned that they think it is normal behavior. Clearly they imitate what they see and read. There are many cases of crime and violence in which the perpetrator remarked that they had learned about it on television.

We don't seem to have grasped the concept that the continual programming and conditioning of the mind with the violence, sexual behavior, hatred and anger that is so prevalent on television can manifest those things in our actions. Is it any wonder that crime and violence among and by children is skyrocketing? It's time to take responsibility and clean up television and other forms of irresponsible media that are so adversely affecting us and our children. If they won't do it themselves, then we must do it for them through regulatory agencies and/or on an individual basis by other means, such as boycott.

We need to "empower" the children with good values, teaching them love, kindness, patience, politeness, caring and forgiveness *by example*. That *is* our responsibility. God holds us accountable. He has declared woe unto those who lead the little ones astray. Not woe that God is going to inflict, but that which is even now being experienced by society. We need to right ourselves, change our ways, and begin to raise our children properly.

We have been much less than responsible in sexual matters, such as indulgence and pregnancy at too early an age as well as promiscuity among adults. They all have caused harm both to the individual and society at large.

Sexual intercourse constitutes a very intimate and emotional experience. To enter into such a relationship when one is young and immature can be detrimental to one's well-being. Young people find it difficult enough to cope with the demands of life in getting an education, perhaps having to work, and dealing with peer and family relationships, without having to contend with a sexual relationship and concern about pregnancy and disease. Of course that can hold true for adults as well, especially those who are promiscuous in their sexual relationships. Promiscuity for both the young and adult is not only hazardous to one's health, but shows disrespect for one another, a deficiency in discipline and a lack of the caring kind of love that God expects of us.

Fortunately, some young people have good minds and are learning those things. Many are rejecting the advice of those adults and "experts" who say we are sexual beings whose nature it is to engage in sexual activity as soon as we are able; that children are going to do it anyway, so don't preach abstinence, but rather safe sex. A growing abstinence movement among teenagers reflects their wisdom.

To become pregnant either as a teenager or adult, when it is not desired, is most certainly careless and irresponsible behavior, regardless of the passion of the moment. To abort pregnancies further compounds the irresponsibility. If a society cannot agree on whether or not abortion is acceptable, surely most can agree that *unwanted* pregnancies are not and that steps should be taken, both collectively and personally, to prevent them, knowing that to abort them can be harmful both physiologically and psychologically.

To bring children into the world when they cannot be supported and provided for physically, economically and emotionally also shows a lack of responsibility. To oppose conception by means of birth control, on the basis of God's instructions to go forth and multiply, is illogical and irresponsible. Surely, we can do both, controlling conception, unwanted pregnancy and the number of offspring, at the same time that we propagate the species. What of celibacy? Would that not be disobedience to God's command to go forth and multiply?

How about homosexuality? Is it an abomination, or could it possibly be acceptable? Surely, it has been a major factor in the spread of AIDS. It would seem that it is not natural. By both biological and biblical standards, it is man and woman who constitute the basic relationship involving family and reproduction. Homosexual relationships cannot bring forth offspring.

What of the sexual act itself between members of the same sex? Although sex is an important and enjoyable part of living, it is not the most important thing in life. Why do we put so much importance on it when it comes to the relationships between those of the same gender? If we do not condemn oral and anal sex among heterosexuals, why should we between homosexuals? The answer, of course, is that *we should condemn no one*! Unconditional love will eventually sort it out. You can be sure that when anyone in such a relationship shows the kind of love that is kind and forgiving to their companion as well as to others, they are acceptable to God.

What of "living together" and having children out of wedlock? Although those lifestyles are becoming more common, such relationships are still frowned upon and even considered "sinful" by many, including most religious authorities. Is that really a sound and accurate assessment of those actions? What about Adam and Eve? Surely, God didn't hold a wedding ceremony for them and issue them a marriage certificate! Nor were their descendants, for many years, involved in such ceremonial procedures. The marriage ceremony and certificate are institutions of man. There is nothing wrong with that, but other aspects of marriage are more important.

There is much ado about the number of teenagers having children "out of wedlock." Wedlock should have little to do with it. If there was a marriage certificate, would that make it okay? Of course not! It is having children without the emotional and economic ability to care for them that is the problem. In our legalistic society, the marriage certificate does have importance when it comes to financial benefits, Social Security and inheritance, for example.

But the ceremony and certificate don't seem to have much, if any, value when it comes to marriage relationships, the children and staying together. If two can't get along or they aren't completely satisfied with the marriage, a common procedure is to forget about the children, get a divorce and try someone else. You can be sure that God is not pleased with marriage as it is perceived, instituted and practiced today. Of far greater importance to him is caring, courtesy, commitment and *respect* on the part of the participants. That is where the emphasis should be, rather than on ceremony and certificate.

All of this talk of irresponsibility is not to say that there aren't a great many people who do live good, decent and responsible lives. It is only to show the trend of irresponsibility and the misconceptions about responsible behavior that plague us.

Humanity has displayed a lack of good judgment and accountability in other areas. Much of the world has lived beyond its means, incurring excessive debt that threatens financial Armageddon. Politicians around the world have caused a high level of cynicism among the people, which has bred distrust and pessimism. Governments have fostered materialism through misguided priorities in spending and frequent indifference to the needs of the people of the world. The medical establishment has taken a wrong turn in the road that leads to good health and the prevention of disease, failing to recognize that God has naturally provided all that we need to achieve those goals. Although religion has provided comfort and guidance to a great many people, it has inadvertently divided mankind because leaders who have formulated religious doctrine have listened to other men rather than to God. All of those things must change and *will change*. We may as well get started.

We can resolve all the problems of the world if we wish to. World leaders, both secular and religious, must stand up and tell the people the *truth*, fulfilling their responsibility as leaders, regardless of political consequences. We need more secular leaders with vision like Vaclav Havel, the Czech President. In his recent address in Philadelphia on the 218th anniversary of our Declaration of Independence he declared that, "Only a new spiritual vision, cosmic in its dimension and global scope, can rescue civilization." Further he cites the notion that "Human beings are mysteriously connected to the universe" and that "The Earth is a mega-organism on which all of us depend."[8] Those concepts are not so mysterious, Mister Havel; their reality is unfolding before us.

All of us as individuals must do our part, generally sacrificing self-interest for the good of the whole. We must search for knowledge, always listening to the wisdom of the "heart," for it is the better part of knowledge. We need to understand and accept the **truth** that we have the complete ability, through the *power of our minds*, to right ourselves and, thusly, the world. Of the utmost importance is that we perceive love as the true panacea; love that is caring, kind, compassionate and forgiving! The kind of love that is the way to heaven--both in this life time and the one to come!

> *"The command, as you have heard from the beginning, is that you must all **live in love**."*[9]

REFERENCE INDEX
Most biblical references are from the Living Bible

Chapter One
The Dawning

1. John 14:6
2. Matthew 7:7
3. John 10:34
4. The Great Religions, Ross and Hills, Crest Books,
5. The Great Religions, Ross and Hills, Crest Books
6. Luke 10:27
7. Proverbs 23:7
8. As A Man Thinketh, James Allen, Running Press
9. Psalm 139:14
10. Genesis 1:27
11. The Light Beyond, Moody, Bantam Books, 1988

Chapter Two
Excommunication

1. Matthew 6:10
2. Matthew 16:27
3. Matthew 7:21-23
4. John 5:28-29
5. Augsburg Confession, Articles of Faith I, Book of Concord
6. Martin Luther biography, Here I Stand, Bainton, Abingdon Press
7. Matthew 7:16
8. Matthew 5;44
9. Matthew 13:33
10. Matthew 25:34-40
11. Matthew 16:27
12. Matthew 7:26-27

Chapter Three
Change
1. Here I Stand, Bainton, Abingdon Press
2. Matthew 5: 13
3. Matthew 5:14
4. Matthew 5:16
5. Matthew 12:35
6. Matthew 12:35
7. Genesis 6:9 King James
8. Genesis 6:9 Good News Bible
9. Matthew 5:48
10. Matthew 10:28
11. Koran Surah 6:59
12. I Corinthians 6:19
13. Luke 17:21
14. People for the Ethical Treatment of Animals
15. Das Kapital, Marx
16. Psalm 137:9

Chapter Four
Armageddon or a Golden Age
1. Matthew 28:20
2. Matthew 24:35
3. Matthew 24:7-8
4. Revelations 21:1
5. Isaiah 11:6-9

Chapter Five
Materialism and Spiritualism
1. Matthew 6:33
2. Philippians 3:19
3. Matthew 6:19,20
4. Luke 14:13,14
5. Ephesians 6:4

Chapter Six
Winds of Change?
1. Noetic Sciences Review #29, Winter 1993,
2. Institute of Noetic Science, Resource Guide

Chapter Seven
As We Think, So Are We
1. Proverbs 23:7
2. 60 Minutes Television Magazine
3. Matthew 12:35
4. Ezekiel 18:31
5. San Diego Union 8/27/93

Chapter Eight
The Nature of Man
1. Luke 23:43
2. Koran Surah 2:154
3. Koran Surah 6:61
4. Bhagavad-Gita Chapter 2:25-27
5. Reincarnation: The Phoenix Fire Mystery, Head and Cranston (The Tao Te K'ing)
6. Genesis 6
7. Genesis 4:4
8. Great Religions of the World, Ross & Hills, Crest Books
9. Psalm 51:5-13
10. Matthew 5:8
11. Romans 5:18-19
12. Matthew 9:13

Chapter Nine
Does God Really Exist?
1. Newsweek
2. Matthew 7:12
3. Closer To The Light, Morse, Villard Books, 1990
4. Reflections on Life After Life, Moody, Bantam Books
5. Understanding The Present, Appleyard, Doubleday, 1992

Chapter Ten
The Nature of God
1. Ezekiel 18:20
2. John 14:9
3. II Corinthians 4:4
4. Here I Stand, Bainton, Abingdon Press
5. Genesis 1:26
6. Genesis 1:28
7. John 4:24
8. John 6:63
9. John 4:24
10. John 6:63
11. Quantum Healing, Chopra, Bantam New Age
12. Quantum Healing, Chopra, Bantam New Age
13. John 4:24
14. Matthew 25:40
15. Acts 10:34

Chapter Eleven
The Nature of Our World
1. Quantum Healing, Chopra, Bantam New Age
2. Romans 5:3
3. Isaiah 11:6-9
4. We Are The Earthquake Generation, Jeffrey Goodman
5. Jonah 3:10
6. San Diego Union 5/25/94
7. San Diego Union 6/1/94
8. Luke 21:10-11
9. Luke 21:23
10. Matthew 5:45
11. Mark 11:24
12. As A Man Thinketh, Allen, Running Press
13. Reversing Heart Disease, Ornish, Ballantine Books

Chapter Twelve
Religion The Great Barrier
1. The Great Religions, Ross & Hills, Crest Books
2. The Great Religions, Ross & Hills, Crest Books
3. Luke 10:25-27
4. San Diego Union 8/28/93
5. Luke 14:26
6. Mark 10:21
7. I Corinthians 7:7,8
8. I Corinthians 11:6
9. I Corinthians 11:14
10. I Corinthians 7:15
11. I Corinthians 14:34
12. I Corinthians 14:37,38
13. Romans 13:1,2
14. Romans 13:4
15. I Corinthians 6:2
16. John 12:47
17. I Corinthians 7:29-31, 10:11
18. Romans 13:8-10
19. I Corinthians 7:25
20. The Christian Conspiracy, Moore, Pendulum Press
21. Matthew 24:35

Chapter Thirteen
Christianity Gone Astray
1. Luke 2:41-50
2. John 15:3
3. John 8:46
4. Matthew 18:23-35
5. Lutheran Witness/Church doctrine
6. Luke 7:47
7. Ezekiel 18:19-32
8. John 8:11
9. Matthew 21:31-32
10. Matthew 18:21-22

11. Mark 12:29
12. Matthew 4:10
13. Matthew 20:28, Mark 10:45
14. Matthew 19:17
15. John 7:16
16. John 14:6
17. John 14:4
18. John 14:5
19. John 14:6
20 Luke 9:44-45
21. Acts 10:34-35
22. James 2:8
23 James 2:24
24 James 1:21-25
25. James 2:13
26. I John 2:3-8
27. II John 1:5-6
28. Matthew 7:21
29. Luke 10:25-28
30. Matthew 22:37-40
31. John 17:4
32. Mark 1:38
33. John 8:28
34. John 8:28
35. John 8:31-32
36. John 8:51
37. James 2:13
38. II Peter 3:8

Chapter Fourteen
The Experiencers
1. Heading Toward Omega, Ring, Quill-Morrow 1984
2. Other World Journeys, Zaleski, Doubleday, 1992
3. Closer To The Light, Morse, Villard Books, 1990
4. Coming Back To Life, Atwater, Ballantine Books 1988
5. Heading Toward Omega, Ring, Quill-Morrow, 1984

6. Closer To The Light, Morse, Villard Books, 1990
7. Recollections of Death, Sabom
8. The Light Beyond, Moody, Bantam Books, 1988
9. Closer To The Light, Morse, Villard Books, 1990
10. Heading Toward Omega, Ring, Quill-Morrow 1984
11. The Light Beyond, Moody,, Bantam Books, 1988
12. Heading Toward Omega, Ring, Quill-Morrow, 1984
13. The Light Beyond, Moody, Bantam Books 1988
14. Heading Toward Omega, Ring, Quill-Morrow, 1984
15. I Corinthians 13:13
16. Romans 13:8
17. Matthew 22:36-40
18. Isaiah 11:6-9
19. Matthew 6:33
20. Matthew 7:1
21. Heading Toward Omega, Ring, Quill-Morrow, 1984
22. . Closer To The Light, Morse, Villard Books, 1990
23. Matthew 7:1-5
24. Matthew 7:15-20
25. Mark 12:26,27
26. Matthew 22:30
27. I Corinthians 15:50-52
28. The Koran
29. Matthew 8:12

Chapter Fifteen
The Joy of Death

1. Heading Toward Omega, Ring, Quill-Morrow, 1984
2. We Don't Die, Martin
3. Heading Toward Omega, Ring, Quill-Morrow, 1984
4. The Bhagavad Gita
5. Heading Toward Omega, Ring, Quill-Morrow, 1984
6. Genesis 3:19
7. I Corinthians 15:52-54
8. John 5:25-29
9. Luke 12:48

10. Matthew 17:11-13
11. Reincarnation: the Phoenix Fire Mystery, Head & Cranston, Point Loma Pub., Review
12. Mark 8:33
13. Matthew 4:1-10
14. Matthew 4:4
15. Matthew 4:10
16. Matthew 7:13,14
17. Mark 4:31,32
18. Matthew 13:33
19. Matthew 6:33
20. Luke 17:21
21. Matthew 25:34
22. Luke 23:43
23. Journal of Near-Death Studies, IANDS, Vol 10, PMH Atwater, 1992
24. Heading Toward Omega, Ring, Quill, Chap 3
25. Journal of Near-Death Studies, IANDS, Vol 10, Atwater, 1992
26. Matthew 25:46
27. Mark 3:29

Chapter Sixteen
Health, Healing and Medicine

1. Seattle Times, 11/1/92 - (Rochester Democratic and Chronicle Times)
2. San Diego Union, 3/25/94
3. Quantum Healing, Chopra, Bantam New Age
4. Good Medicine, PCRM, Spring 1994
5. The San Diego Union, 7/2/96
6. Reversing Heart Disease, Ornish, Ballantine Books, Reviews
7. Newsweek, April 27, 1998
8. PCRM News Release, 6/29/94
9. Family Circle, 6/28/94
10. Heading Toward Omega, Ring, Quill

11. Romans 8:31
12. The San Diego Union, March 20, 1998

Chapter Seventeen
Conclusion

1. Matthew 5:17,18
2. Matthew 6:10
3. Koran Surah 8:36-40
4. Isaiah 11:9
5. As A Man Thinketh, Allen, Running Press
6. Body Mind Spirit Magazine, June 1994
7. Isaiah 2:4
8. Newsweek, 7/18/94
9. II John 1:5,6

Order Form

Telephone Orders: Call **Toll Free** (888) 300-2001
Please have your AMEX, VISA or Master Card Ready.

Postal Orders: **Probe Press**, P.O. Box 68673
Oro Valley, AZ 85737-0003

Name: _____
Address: _____
City: _____ State: ____ Zip: _____
Telephone: (____) _____

Please send me ____ copies of **So You Want To Get To Heaven**. I understand that I may return any books for a full refund, for any reason, no questions asked.

$17.95 X number of copies ____ $ _____
Sales Tax if applicable $ _____
Total $ _____

Sales Tax (California residents only):
  Add 7.75% ($1.39) per book
Shipping:
  We pay shipping costs within USA and Canada.

Payment:
  __Cheque
  __Credit Card: AMEX, VISA, Master Card.
    Card number: _____
    Name on card: _____
    Expiration date: _____

Thank you for your order.